Managing Pupil Behaviour

Can anyone become good at classroom management?

Classroom management is a major element of the teaching and learning process, impacting on standards of achievement, pupil motivation and the quality of teachers' working lives. It has been cited as the single most prominent concern of trainee and newly qualified teachers, and is an important and problematic issue in most schools in the UK.

Managing Pupil Behaviour: key issues in teaching and learning provides routes through the classroom management maze and will help practising and aspiring teachers to manage behaviour effectively in their classrooms, so that pupils can learn, and teachers can enjoy their work. The book draws on the eloquent testimonies of teachers and pupils to develop insights into the whole range of factors impinging on teachers' ability to manage their classes, and explain why some teachers become better than others at getting pupils to want to learn and to behave well.

The book includes a 10-point scale that encourages teachers to think about the degree to which they are relaxed and in assured control of their classrooms and can enjoy their teaching. The scale is designed to get teachers to think about:

- the factors influencing the working atmosphere in the classroom
- the influence of the working atmosphere in classrooms on teaching and learning
- the equal opportunities issues surrounding the tension between inclusion and situations where some pupils may be spoiling the learning of others.

This book will be vital for teachers at all stages of their careers, assisting them to reflect on different ways forward in this important facet of their working lives.

Terry Haydn is currently Reader in Education at the University of East Anglia. He worked at a challenging inner city school in Manchester for 20 years and more recently has worked in initial teacher education in Manchester, London and East Anglia.

Managing Pupil Behaviour

Key issues in teaching and learning

Terry Haydn

Routledge
Taylor & Francis Group

LONDON AND NEW YORK

First published 2007
by Routledge
2 Park Square, Milton Park, Abingdon, Oxon OX14 4RN

Simultaneously published in the USA and Canada
by Routledge
270 Madison Ave, New York, NY 10016

Routledge is an imprint of the Taylor & Francis Group, an informa business

© 2007 Terry Haydn

Typeset in Goudy and Gill Sans by
Florence Production Ltd, Stoodleigh, Devon
Printed and bound by
TJ International Ltd, Padstow, Cornwall

British Library Cataloguing in Publication Data
A catalogue record for this book is available from the British Library

Library of Congress Cataloging in Publication Data
Haydn, Terry, 1951–
    Managing Pupil Behviour: key issues in teaching and learning/
    Terry Haydn
        p. cm.
    Includes bibliographical references.
    1. Classroom environment.   2. Behaviour modification.
    3. Students – Psychology.   I. Title.
    LB3013.H365 2007
    371.102′4–dc22   2006018085

ISBN10: 0–415–39467–8 (hbk)
ISBN10: 0–415–28782–0 (pbk)
ISBN10: 0–203–96711–9 (ebk)

ISBN13: 978–0–415–39467–3 (hbk)
ISBN13: 978–0–415–28782–1 (pbk)
ISBN13: 978–0–203–96711–9 (ebk)

Contents

Illustrations

Boxes

Acknowledgements

I would like to thank all the teachers and head teachers who were kind enough to give up their time to help me with my research. In so far as this book is dedicated to anybody, it is to all the teachers who do such a worthwhile and difficult job, and particularly those who have the comparatively thankless, or to be more precise, 'unthanked' and undervalued task of working in challenging schools.

I would also like to thank Joe Haydn for drawing the illustrations for the book.

1 The working atmosphere in the classroom and the right to learn

I would be surprised if there were any schools where pupil behaviour did not have *any* impact on pupil attainment.

(Head teacher)

Every timetabled lesson of every day there will be some lessons in the school where pupil behaviour will affect teaching and learning outcomes.

(Head teacher)

Introduction: what this book is about

This book focuses on a particular aspect of class management: the working atmosphere in the classroom. By this, I mean the extent to which teachers are in relaxed and assured control of their classrooms, the extent to which pupils' learning is not limited by the poor behaviour of other pupils, and the fact that teachers are having to plan lessons around 'control' factors rather than 'learning' factors. The working atmosphere in the classroom can be thought of as a continuum: between classrooms where the teacher feels completely in control of proceedings, and there are no pupil behaviour issues that might impede the learning of others, and classrooms where the teacher has no control over what goes on in the classroom and little or no learning can take place because of the poor behaviour of some pupils.

The book is based on my experiences of working in schools, conversations with heads, teachers and trainees in the course of my work, and, more recently, on surveys of over 300 trainee teachers in London and East Anglia, interviews with over 100 teachers and head teachers in the Eastern region, with 12 teacher educators, and a questionnaire survey of 708 pupils in Norfolk schools.

A sample of 118 interviews, with teachers and heads working in 80 different schools, mainly in the East of England, clearly cannot claim to present a comprehensive, authoritative and accurate picture of the levels of control prevalent in classrooms in the UK. Nearly all those interviewed were known to the author and/or had some form of working relationship with the author (many were former trainees or heads of department with whom the author currently works). This may have some effects on the data emerging from the interviews. The respondents are aware that I have an interest in deficits in the working atmosphere in the classroom. There might be 'insider' influences on testimony (Elliott, 1988). Against this, it is possible that the working relationship (and assurance of confidentiality) might induce a degree of frankness not possible in dialogue with, for instance, Ofsted inspectors. There was no reason to feel that heads and teachers were not being frank and measured in their responses. East Anglia, where over 85 per cent of the interviews were carried out, is not a particular 'black spot' in terms of containing an above average number of schools in challenging circumstances. I did not make a conscious effort to seek out large numbers of schools in difficult circumstances. Nine of the respondents worked, or had worked, in schools 'in special measures', but many worked in schools that were popular, oversubscribed, and had received various awards and distinctions. Seven of the respondents worked, or had worked, in the independent sector at some point. Overall, the teachers came from schools that were broadly representative of schools in the East Anglia region. The respondents' testimony indicated that *to some degree*, pupil behaviour and disengagement from learning are problems in nearly all schools, and the questions of how to motivate pupils to want to learn, and how to get a calm, purposeful and collaborative working atmosphere in all classrooms are relevant to large numbers of teachers in UK schools. The extracts from the interviews were selected on the grounds of being broadly representative of the thinking of a number of teachers, or because it was felt that they provided some insight into teachers' decision making processes when dealing with problematic pupil behaviour and trying to manage learning in the classroom.

The book is an attempt to develop understanding of the factors that influence the working atmosphere in the classroom by providing access to the voices of heads, teachers and pupils who are actually in schools at the moment, and who, between them, are working to manage the very difficult tensions that arise from attempting to educate all pupils without allowing some to hinder the learning of others. I hope that their perspectives, contributions and perceptions will provide alternative insights to those that might be derived from other sources, such as Ofsted inspection reports, policy reviews, politicians' pronouncements and behaviour management experts. I hope that somewhere in the book, there will be something that is of use to those who have the very difficult and important job of managing pupil learning in secondary schools in the UK.

The working atmosphere in the classroom: a continuum

One of the instruments used in the research that went into this book is a 10-point scale that attempts to describe this continuum. The scale (see Box 1.1) is an attempt to get teachers and trainee teachers to think about the levels on the scale that they encounter in the schools they work in, and to consider the factors that influence the levels that prevail in their classrooms, those of colleagues in their own school, and in other schools.

The scale was initially devised to encourage trainee teachers to think about the degree to which teachers are in relaxed and assured control of their classrooms and can enjoy their teaching, and also, the extent to which there is a 'right to learn' for pupils, free from the noise and disruption of others. It was not designed to be used to pass judgement on the class management skills of teachers, but to get trainee teachers (and teachers, departments and schools) to think about the factors influencing classroom climate, the influence of classroom climate on teaching and learning, and the equal opportunities issues surrounding the tension between the

Box 1.1 The working atmosphere in the classroom, a 10-point scale

Level 10

You feel completely relaxed and comfortable; able to undertake any form of lesson activity without concern. 'Class control' not really an issue – teacher and pupils working together, enjoying the experiences involved.

Level 9

You feel completely in control of the class and can undertake any sort of class-room activity, but you need to exercise some control/authority at times to maintain a calm and purposeful working atmosphere. This can be done in a friendly and relaxed manner and is no more than a gentle reminder.

Level 8

You can establish and maintain a relaxed and cooperative working atmosphere and undertake any form of classroom activity, but this requires a considerable amount of thought and effort on your part at times. Some forms of lesson activity may be less calm and under control than others.

Level 7

You can undertake any form of lesson activity, but the class may well be rather 'bubbly' and rowdy; there may be minor instances of a few pupils messing around on the fringes of the lesson but they desist when required to do so. No one goes out of their way to annoy you or challenges your authority. When you address the class, they listen in silence, straight away.

Level 6

You don't really look forward to teaching the class, it is often a major effort to establish and maintain a relaxed and calm atmosphere. Several pupils will not remain on task without persistent surveillance/exhortation/threats. At times you feel harassed, and at the end of the lesson you feel rather drained. There are times when you feel it is wisest not to attempt certain types of pupil activity, in order to try to keep things under control. It is sometimes difficult to get pupils to be quiet while you are talking, or stop them calling out, or talking to each other at will across the room but in spite of this, no one directly challenges your authority, and there is no refusal or major disruption.

Level 5

There are times in the lesson when you would feel awkward or embarrassed if the head/a governor/an inspector came into the room, because your control of the class is limited. The atmosphere is at times rather chaotic, with several pupils manifestly not listening to your instructions. Some of the pupils are, in effect, challenging your authority by their dilatory or desultory compliance with your instructions and requests. Lesson format is constrained by these factors; there are some sorts of lesson you would not attempt because you know they would be rowdy and chaotic, but in the last resort, there is no open refusal, no major atrocities, just a lack of purposefulness and calm. Pupils who wanted to work could get on with it, albeit in a rather noisy atmosphere.

Level 4
You have to accept that your control is limited. It takes time and effort to get the class to listen to your instructions. You try to get onto the worksheet/written part of the lesson fairly quickly in order to 'get their heads down'. Lesson preparation is influenced more by control and 'passing the time' factors than by educational ones. Pupils talk while you are talking, minor transgressions (no pen, no exercise book, distracting others by talking) go unpunished because too much is going on to pick everything up. You become reluctant to sort out the ringleaders as you feel this may well escalate problems. You try to 'keep the lid on things' and concentrate on those pupils who are trying to get on with their work.

Level 3
You dread the thought of the lesson. There will be major disruption; many pupils will pay little or no heed to your presence in the room. Even pupils who want to work will have difficulty doing so. Swearwords may go unchecked, pupils will walk round the room at will. You find yourself reluctant to deal with transgressions because you have lost confidence. When you write on the board, objects will be thrown around the room. You can't wait for the lesson to end and be out of the room.

Level 2
The pupils largely determine what will go on in the lesson. You take materials into the lesson as a matter of form, but once distributed they will be ignored, drawn on or made into paper aeroplanes. When you write on the board, objects will be thrown at you rather than round the room. You go into the room hoping that they will be in a good mood and will leave you alone and just chat to each other.

Level 1
Your entry into the classroom is greeted by jeers and abuse. There are so many transgressions of the rules and what constitutes reasonable behaviour that it is difficult to know where to start. You turn a blind eye to some atrocities because you feel that your intervention may well lead to confrontation, refusal or escalation of the problem. This is difficult because some pupils are deliberately committing atrocities under your nose, for amusement. You wish you had not gone into teaching.

Note: For further development of the use of the scale, see Haydn, 2002.

ideals of educational inclusion and the reality of situations where some pupils are impeding the learning of others.

The idea in phrasing the level descriptors was to attempt to evince a chord of recognition in practising teachers and trainee teachers, and to be sufficiently transparent and accessible as to be meaningful to others involved in the educational process – teachers, parents, governors and policy makers. The scale was originally used in work with trainee teachers, based on the idea that it would be helpful for them to have some ideas about where they stood in the continuum between relaxed control and anarchy, to think about levels to aspire to, about what factors influenced the working atmosphere in the classroom, and why there were differences both between and within schools, (some trainees reported seeing or experiencing level 1 to level 10 within the same school placement). Trainees who used the scale in the course of their teaching placement were also asked to consider what influence the scale had on their lesson planning and delivery, in terms of learning objectives and pedagogy. Implicit in the level descriptors is the suggestion that below a certain point on the scale, the atmosphere in the classroom will influence not just the outcomes of the learning process, but the inputs as well, in that below certain levels on the scale, planning may be directed to at least some extent towards the objective of control rather than learning.

The scale is, of course, an artificial construct and does not encompass the full range of disruptive behaviour in classrooms. I have seen classes that would fall below level 1 as described here and have witnessed all of the levels on the scale. It should be stressed that there are many schools where the lower levels never occur. But it is also worth noting that the outcomes of the surveys described in the chapters that follow suggest that there are few schools where there are no 'deficits' in the working atmosphere in classrooms; where all classrooms in the school are regularly functioning at levels 9 and 10.

The model is based on the belief that it can be helpful to have some idea, at least in rough terms, where one stands on the continuum, and of the levels to aspire to. The following quotes from some of the interviewees point to the dangers that might stem from teachers not being fully aware of the full breadth of atmospheres possible, and the advantages of becoming aware of the parameters that prevail even within the same institution:

> It is possible that there are staff here who have neither experienced or seen a level 10 lesson ... who think that the norm ... or an inevitable fact of life in teaching ... at least in this school ... is that pupils talk while they are talking ... that they move around and ignore the formal structure of the lesson at some points.
>
> (Assistant head)

> There are some trainees who get despondent, demoralised and on the verge of packing it in because they are struggling to get to the higher levels on the scale. But they're actually doing quite well, they're getting there. They've got to realise that in a school like this, it takes time to get to know the kids. One of the key things is whether things are going in the right direction ... are they getting better or worse as the placement goes on?
>
> (Assistant head)

It is helpful to think that there are lower levels on the scale than the ones I am working at. I have become aware of the massive differences even within this school . . . the time of day, the weather, the area of the school . . . some departments have it more sewn up than others.

(Experienced teacher)

I have worked with some teachers who seem perfectly happy with levels around 7 and 8; they don't seem that bothered about going the extra mile to get the kids really sorted out so that they can just go in there and relax.

(Head of year)

There's a stage at which, if you are at level 9 or 10 for a few lessons in a row . . . where they get used to it and it becomes 'the norm'. They expect the lesson to be ok. There's a lot of behaviourism in it. They can be conditioned to behave . . . Not in a fascist, control freak way but just getting them used to things . . . rituals and routines, being able to have a bit of a laugh and relax at some points in the lesson.

(Experienced teacher)

I worried that talking about, or even acknowledging the lower levels on the scale might increase the trainees' anxieties about class management. It's an area that a lot of them are wound up about when they are in the early stages of first place-ment. But it led to some light hearted discussion of levels which they had encountered when they were pupils and given that none of them were at level 1 with all their classes, they could see that things could be worse.

(Assistant head)

The scale was not designed to judge the class management skills of individual teachers and it is easy to see how its use might be unhelpful and corrosive of teacher morale and solidarity (see Chapter 6) if used as a managerial tool or in an inquisi-tional way, to make comparisons. The hope is that trainee and newly qualified teachers might think carefully about the levels they are working at, look outside their own classrooms, and share ideas and strategies for improving the climate in their classrooms. If professional dialogue about behaviour issues can avoid defensiveness, there is the possibility of collaborative action to explore ways of dealing with disrup-tive and disengaged pupils. It can lead to concerted action to support colleagues who are working with particularly difficult teaching groups (see Chapter 6).

If you are a teacher or a trainee teacher who works in a school where all the classes are under the relaxed control of their teachers, and the climate in all classes is such that pupil behaviour is not really an issue, then this book is perhaps not an essential read, although I hope it might still be of some interest. I wanted to write the book because I believe that the working atmosphere in the classroom is an important educational issue, and one that affects the quality of many teachers' working lives. I also believe that deficits in the working atmosphere in classrooms are one of the major causes of educational underachievement in the UK.

The prevalence of deficits in the working atmosphere in classrooms

The problem of 'deficits' in the working atmosphere in the classroom is not one that just affects a handful of inner-city schools. It is *to at least some degree*, an issue in a large number of schools. There are few secondary schools in the UK where the working atmosphere is consistently at levels 9 and 10 in all classrooms. It is an issue that has a bearing on the quality of most teachers' working lives.

My teaching background was at a northern inner-city comprehensive school. For many of the years I taught there it was unexceptional in terms of its intake and in terms of pupil behaviour. It was not by any means 'notorious', but pupil behaviour was certainly an issue for most teachers. Some teachers were better at establishing control in their classrooms than others, but most of us had to think about control issues when planning our lessons. You could not assume that you could just 'go in and teach'. But the school then went through 'a bad patch' and behaviour did become a major issue. Many of the pupils from middle-class backgrounds moved away from the school and as the school was not full, it was obliged to accept large numbers of pupils excluded from other schools (see Macdonald, 1989; Haydn, 1995b, 1997).

I left secondary teaching to go into teacher education in 1992 and have since worked in teacher education in the north-west of England, in London and in East Anglia. The nature of my work means that I go into large numbers of schools, mainly to observe trainee teachers on their teaching placements. As well as observing trainees in the classroom, I regularly talk to and work with teachers and head teachers in a wide range of schools. I also interview dozens of applicants for my PGCE (Post Graduate Certificate of Education) course, many of whom have worked as classroom assistants in order to gain classroom experience before applying for the PGCE.

Although it is reasonable to assume that trainee teachers may struggle more than experienced ones to control their classes, my interviews with a lot of experienced and successful teachers led me to believe that pupil behaviour and disengagement from learning were issues relevant to many schools (see Chapter 7).

The misleading and unhelpful nature of much of the public discourse on the management of pupil behaviour

There is some dispute over the degree to which pupil behaviour and classroom climate are issues in British schools. One recent Secretary of State for Education argued that poor pupil behaviour is a problem that affects 'a small number of pupils in a small number of schools' (Patten, 1994). In 2003, a DfES (Department for Education and Skills) official estimated that behaviour was a problem in one in 12 secondary schools and one in 100 primary schools (Clark, 2003). Although newspaper headlines have talked of 'Schools crisis over standards and discipline' (*The Times*, 3 February 2005), 'Anarchy rules in our schools' (*Daily Express*, 16 September 2005), and 'Classrooms are riots without police' (*Evening Standard*, 28 April 2005), Ofsted findings on behaviour in schools have consistently reported that behaviour is unsatisfactory in under 10 per cent of secondary schools (Ofsted, 2003, 2004, 2005). The question of the prevalence of deficits in the working atmosphere in classrooms is considered in more detail in Chapter 2.

Much of the commentary in newspapers and from politicians is profoundly unhelpful and misleading, and displays a lack of understanding of the challenges that teachers and schools face in the area of class management. There is often an assumption that the 'default' state of affairs in classrooms is level 10 on the scale: that any competent teacher in a well-run school will be operating at level 10 with all their classes, and that any 'deficit' from that level is due to bad teaching or poor school management. There must be someone to blame. Hence, the appearance of headlines such as 'Lax teachers need a short sharp lesson in discipline' (*Daily Express*, 7 November 1996), 'Teachers who fail to keep order face sack in a month' (*The Times*, 18 July 1997). State schools have been urged to 'take a tip from public schools' and bring in a house system (*The Guardian*, 18 May 2004), and emulate 'the ethos of good discipline' that private schools promulgate (*Today Programme*, Radio 4, 26 January 2006).

In launching the Steer Working Group on pupil behaviour and school discipline, the Secretary of State for Education espoused the hope that the group would recommend three or four programmes that are 'proven to work' on badly behaved pupils 'then we can say to schools, you should adopt one of these programmes and there is no excuse any more for poor behaviour in the classroom' (*Today Programme*, Radio 4, May 2006, quoted in *Times Educational Supplement*, 27 May 2006). No dumping of blame there then.

Such comments are redolent of First World War Generals operating some miles behind the front lines. The rules of engagement in schools, and critical commentary

Box 1.2 Press and television coverage of pupil behaviour has tended to sensationalise the issue of pupil behaviour

on class management and discipline in schools, are issued by politicians and policy-makers whose children do not generally attend challenging state secondary schools, and who literally do not have a clue about the scale of problems facing teachers who work 'at the sharp end'. For a graphic illustration of this point, see the testimony of an anonymous head to the Westminster Education Forum seminar on pupil behaviour and school discipline (Westminster Education Forum, 2006: 100–1). As the anonymous head points out:

> adults whose experience has only been of 'middle England' and do not work in a school in challenging circumstances are frequently not aware of the pressures that exist both inside the school and in the surroundings where the students live … there are children who are very difficult to help and their behaviour continually gets in the way of their learning.
>
> (ibid: 100)

Schostak (1991) and Elliott (1998) have argued that the 'deviance' model of pupil disaffection (that disaffection from schooling is a form of deviant behaviour) is misleading, and that for many pupils, the decision to disengage from education is a quite rational and sensible one. Doherty (2001) found that many pupils did not attend school primarily to learn, 'to get an education'; they came in for social and pecuniary reasons, 'to see their mates', 'to do business'. One of the most powerful formative experiences that our PGCE trainees undertake is to follow a group of pupils through a whole school day. The majority of them report that for many pupils, particularly the less able, the school day is not 'a bowl of cherries', full of joyful and life affirming experiences. It is important that both policymakers and those who go into teaching take account of these perspectives.

Some of the factors that influence the management of learning are beyond the control of individual schools and teachers, they are not 'free agents'. Mike Tomlinson (2005), putting the case for the revision of a curriculum which is unappealing and inappropriate for many pupils, claimed that 'most teachers know that the root problem with behaviour lies in the curriculum'. Rogers (2005) also argues that the issue of behaviour in schools is 'far more complex than most politicians and commentators have recently been suggesting. It is not an issue caused by schools, nor one which schools alone can solve'. Wragg (2005: 32) goes as far as to say that 'few people outside a school truly understand the problems and their possible solutions'. Watkins and Wagner (2000) argue the case for a three-level model for understanding behaviour in schools, citing the research of Gottfredson *et al.* (1993: 182):

> Research implies that misbehaviour in schools has determinants at three levels:
>
> a   some individuals are more likely than others to behave;
> b   some teachers are more likely than others to produce higher levels of misconduct in their classroom by their management and organisation practices; and
> c   some schools more often than others fail to control student behaviour.

Although this makes the issue of pupil behaviour and classroom climate complicated, in some ways this is 'good news' for beginning teachers. If there are deficits in pupil behaviour and classroom climate, much of it may not be your fault. In framing advice on behaviour for new teachers, Watkins (2000: 6) adds the important caveats: 'Not all of these suggestions will be appropriate for your situation, not all these suggestions will be appealing to you as a teacher, not all these suggestions will work – especially if we take that to mean producing obedience.'

As McPhillimy (1996) points out, even with pupils without problems, it would be rather surprising if large groups of pupils forced into classrooms, in many cases against their inclination, did not mess about and misbehave. Level 10 is not a natural state of affairs. It takes a great deal of skill to get to a position where the teacher is in completely relaxed and assured control of the classroom, able to undertake any form of activity, however complex, without having to even think about control issues.

One of the most important messages arising out of both my own experiences in schools and the research that I have conducted over the past 18 months is that there are many experienced, accomplished teachers who are adroit at managing classes and interacting with pupils (and in some cases, within their schools, are acknowledged to be 'as good as it gets' at dealing with pupil behaviour) who nonetheless struggle to get to level 10 with all their classes (see Chapter 7). Because much of the public discourse on managing behaviour in schools is misleading and ill-informed, there is a need to hear the voices of the people who actually do the job in schools, who have to cope with disaffected and disruptive pupils, and who have a realistic and 'grounded' view of the things that can sometimes make a difference to classroom climate and pupil behaviour. There is, of course, a substantial volume of literature in the area of managing classes and pupil behaviour, written by experts in the field. Many of these were mentioned by the teachers and trainee teachers I interviewed, and were found to be helpful in a range of ways. However, even here, there is a tendency for such works (understandably) to dwell predominantly on strategies for achieving success, for making things better. Less time is spent on counselling teachers and trainees about what to do when the suggested strategies fail, on damage limitation, on how to cope when in spite of following the advice proffered, you still haven't got reasonable control of the class, and are still floundering in the lower levels of the scale. In Chapter 4, teachers reflect on what they do when they are not in full control of a class. How do you survive, how do you get through the lesson, through the term, through the year, when you have classes over which your control is limited?

The impact of the working atmosphere in the classroom on the quality of teachers' working lives

There are very few things in professional life less edifying than being, in effect, locked in a room with 30 children not fully under your control. Perhaps surprisingly, some of the teachers interviewed spoke positively about the enjoyment and 'buzz' they derived from 'wrestling with' groups that were extremely difficult to manage, and where they were around levels 4–6 on the scale (see Chapter 4). There was less evidence of trainees and newly qualified teachers waxing lyrical about this challenge. But without exception, those teachers who had experience of working at levels 9 and 10 described it in very positive terms, as the following excerpts show:

> I cannot stress how wonderful it is to teach a well behaved class. It actually enables you to lower your guard and completely relax. Even though I was teaching them about a religious pilgrimage, I really enjoyed the lesson and the children did too . . . I could tell.
>
> (Trainee)

You just get to the stage with some classes where you can relax and you feel that you are not under pressure, not having to keep your guard up, sneak glances when you've got your back turned or are helping individuals or working with particular groups. You could just ask them to carry on with something if something crops up that you've got to deal with.

(Experienced teacher)

In a funny sort of way, it puts a bit of pressure on you when you've got a great class which you get on really well with ... you keep thinking what you are going to do to give them a great lesson ... to keep it up ... it keeps you on your toes. But the lessons are great. You come out feeling great. You know that you have their respect, they rate you, they think you are a good teacher.

(NQT (Newly Qualified Teacher))

Your teaching actually gets better when you are at levels 9 and 10 ... your exposition is more fluent, you can think of things off the top of your head ... you seem to be able to think of lots of good ideas because you're not thinking at the back of your mind about control and surveillance issues. You get a buzz out of it and you can let your hair down more, take a few more risks.

(Experienced teacher)

As you are walking round the classroom, or looking out of the window, you think to yourself, there aren't many people who have a job as fulfilling and enjoyable as this.

(Experienced teacher)

In terms of how much you enjoy your teaching, there's a massive difference between operating at levels 7 and 8 ... which are ok ... no big hassle ... and level 10, when it's just a fantastic job, pure pleasure ... you can get a real buzz out of the interaction with pupils. It's like the adverts for teaching on the TV but in real life.

(NQT)

The converse of this is that teaching is very difficult to enjoy if the working atmosphere with the majority of your classes is below, say, level 6 (and perhaps higher). Most of the trainees and NQTs interviewed acknowledged that they experienced a range of levels on the scale while on school placement and in their NQT year (see Chapter 7). Even experienced teachers who were well established in their school reported that they would not be working at levels 9 and 10 with all their teaching groups, and that the planning of lessons would take into account pupil behaviour and the need to stay in control of the lesson with some groups. One very experienced and successful head of department told me:

I'm senior member of staff, I'm very experienced and I am supposed to be good at managing pupils and classes – it's supposed to be one of my strengths. And yet I've got a year 7 class where I've got to plan the lesson around control ... get their heads down, get them writing, punish someone early in the lesson to send out a message. You can't enjoy teaching when it's like that.

It seemed to be particularly dispiriting when trainees or NQTs find that *all* their lessons are dominated by 'crowd control' rather than learning, although, fortunately, there seemed to be few instances where things were so unremittingly grim. Most of the trainees and NQTs interviewed reported that they had some classes where they could concentrate on their subject and enjoy their teaching. The numbers involved in interviews were not large enough to come to any authoritative judgements about the quality of teachers' lives in their first few years of teaching, but it seems reasonable to suggest that there may be a significant number of new teachers working in schools where behaviour and control issues have impacted on the degree to which they find teaching fulfilling and enjoyable. Of the 59 teachers who were in the first three years of teaching, it was perhaps a positive indicator that over three-quarters of them said that they were enjoying the job overall, although the degree to which this was because of, or in spite of, the working atmosphere prevailing in their classes is difficult to say.

Recent research on teacher retention confirms that difficulties with pupil behaviour are one of the main reasons for new teachers leaving the profession within three years (Hutchings *et al.*, 2002; Cockburn and Haydn, 2004). You don't necessarily get more money for creating a good working atmosphere with your classes, but it makes it much easier to enjoy teaching.

The impact of the working atmosphere in the classroom on pupil attainment

Recent research on teacher recruitment and retention also reveals that most people who go into teaching do so for generally idealistic and altruistic reasons (Cockburn *et al.*, 2000; NFER (National Foundation for Educational Research), 2000; Cockburn and Haydn, 2004). Prominent in this is the pleasure to be derived from helping young people to learn, something that emerged from all the above studies as a major factor in teacher job satisfaction. Perhaps not all teachers retain their idealism, perhaps not all teachers become expert at helping pupils to learn, but when they go into the profession, this is one of the things that is at the forefront of their motives for many teachers.

This came out strongly in many of the interviews:

> It is a nice feeling when you know that everyone in the class is learning and making progress . . . and they know they are making progress. And no one is stopping the learning. This doesn't happen with all my classes but it's nice when it does.
>
> (NQT)

> The best moment . . . a pupil who's very limited . . . not even on the N/C levels . . . he now takes an active part in the lessons, he puts his hand up and wants to join in, to answer questions, to contribute, to be part of things because there's a nice atmosphere in the room.
>
> (NQT)

> It is hard work, and I'm exhausted at times, but when parents tell you that their child likes history now . . . they didn't used to be interested . . . it does make you feel good. You feel you are doing something really worthwhile.
>
> (NQT)

Teaching has its ups and downs, it's that sort of job even when you've been doing it for a few years. But when a class does well, when you get the exam results and it's even better than you dared to hope.... There was nothing to match that in my previous job.

(Teacher who had moved from another profession)

I've got a year 10 GCSE class who are fantastic, a real pleasure to teach. I can often get level 8 and sometimes 9 and 10 ... that feeling that you can do anything. ... They respond brilliantly ... there's a good positive climate in the classroom. I think we all really enjoy the lessons.

(AST (Advanced Skills Teacher) working in a challenging school)

Conversely, teachers who talked about operating at the lower levels of the scale were not just disenchanted because it wasn't a very pleasant experience, but because it was frustrating when all the work that had gone into planning the lesson was wasted because of pupils messing around, 'not giving the lesson a chance':

I've got one class who are really difficult, and I bust a gut to think of a starter that will get them interested, that will at least get them to give the lesson a chance, give me chance to get going ... I scour the net and the newspapers for something that will grab them, just for a minute or two. And nothing has worked yet. You feel that you are wasting your time. It wouldn't make any difference if they just had a supply teacher who didn't give a toss. If all my classes were like this one, I don't think I could stand it.

(NQT)

I took a lot of time and trouble to do a card sort exercise for the start of the lesson so that we weren't just doing another worksheet or working from the text book. At my first placement school, this sort of activity had worked really well, I'd got a great response from the kids. Here, they just tore them up.

(Trainee)

Several respondents were angry and bitter about the unfairness of 'the system', when they worked in schools where it was difficult to stop some pupils spoiling the learning of others:

You are aware that even in your most difficult classes, there are some kids who just quietly get on with it, who would like to learn but who are quietly fed up ... or quietly resigned about the fact that the whole lesson will be pretty much a shambles because I haven't got the power to stop some of the pupils destroying the lesson. It's a horrible feeling, because obviously you blame yourself and think what more you could do ... and then you walk past the other classrooms and see it happening to teachers who've been at the school for years.

(Trainee)

It's difficult to do this job without thinking how unfair the system is. I've worked in several schools and it's so obviously not a fair contest. I used to work in an inner-city school with a lot of difficult kids. The staff were great, a lot of them were fantastic teachers. My exam results there weren't great … now I work at a much easier school and I get a lot of praise for my exam results. I'm the same teacher.

(Experienced head of department)

Many heads and teachers interviewed acknowledged that under the present system, pupils with problems are not distributed equally between schools and that some schools have to accept large numbers of difficult pupils. The working atmosphere in the classroom is an important issue, not just because it impacts on pupil attainment, but because there is a social justice issue at stake. One of the biggest inequalities of opportunity in the UK education system is whether pupils are in classrooms that are under the relaxed and assured control of their teachers or in classrooms where the lower levels on the scale prevail. It was interesting to hear one teacher who had worked in two comprehensive schools before moving into the private sector talking of pupil 'overachievement' where all the classes ran at levels 9 and 10 on the scale:

The kids here aren't that different from the kids at X and Y in terms of how bright they are. There's an amazing amount of overachievement really. When you look at their IQ Test scores, they're nothing special and yet in terms of results, they do really well. Nothing is allowed to get in the way of their learning, and there's none of the settling them down, getting them quiet stuff that wastes so much time. We have some kids here who are bone idle, who don't want to do well and have to be forced … but they are never allowed to spoil the learning of others.

(Experienced teacher)

MORI surveys have consistently pointed out the impact of 'good behaviour' on parental choice of secondary schools:

the reason for school choice altered little and the most important concern – as in 1989 – was good discipline, cited by 84% of parents. 80% were influenced by exam results – but only 15% of senior school parents identified league table positions as important indicators of school choice.

('Class divide deepens in poll', *Times Educational Supplement*, 11 February 1994)

The Hay McBer Report (2000) on effective teaching suggested that lack of disruption and classroom climate were two of the most significant influences on pupils' learning opportunities and progress. Commenting on a summary of research on effective teaching in the US, Wragg (1997: 44) concluded that 'class management seemed to bear most strongly on how well pupils achieved'.

Although there is no simple relationship between the working atmosphere in the classroom and pupil attainment, the overwhelming majority of teachers and head teachers believe that pupils learn best when there is a calm, purposeful and collaborative atmosphere in the classroom. Teachers don't want to be at level 10 in their classrooms because they want an easy number or because they are control freaks. They want to be in control of the classroom because that is one of the conditions that enables learning to take place, and that is teachers' 'core business', it's one of the key reasons they do the job. Teachers are keenly aware of the potential impact they have on pupils' life chances and don't feel too good about themselves when they are aware that they are not doing their best for their pupils.

The complexity of managing classrooms, pupil behaviour and learning

This is not an aspect of teaching that is straightforward or susceptible to simple solutions or quick fixes. Ruth Kelly's suggestion (*Times Educational Supplement*, 27 May 2006) that a working group could come up with three or four things 'that work', and that there would then be 'no excuse any more for poor behaviour in the classroom' is an ingenuous and unrealistic one. Given the complexity and intractability of the problem of pupil behaviour, it is unlikely that the solution will be 'shrink-wrapped'.

Schools do not exist in a vacuum; as Bernstein (1970: 387) pointed out, 'education cannot compensate for society'. Pupils who are not in the least awed by the police are not going to be cowed by detentions, the withdrawal room or exclusion. (A few years ago, a national newspaper reported the case of a primary school calling for assistance from the police. When the police were told the names of the pupils involved in the disturbance, they told the school they would have to wait for reinforcements before they came in.) For teachers with long memories, The Steer Report on school behaviour and discipline (2005a) is just the latest in a series of government convened committees to investigate the problem of behaviour in schools. As Lee (2005) notes: 'It is an issue which was supposed to have been dealt with comprehensively by the Elton Report (1989), a 12 month, 300 page examination of discipline problems in schools.' There were also the DfE (Department for Education) circulars on pupil behaviour and discipline issued in 1993, which suggested that schools might use merit marks and detentions to improve behaviour, and try to be less reliant on exclusions (DfE, 1993).

The reality is that schools and teachers will always have to work hard, and with considerable initiative and ingenuity, to minimise the problem of disruptive behaviour. The idea that it can be eradicated by a couple of good new policies is wishful thinking. Steer himself made it clear that he thought there was no 'magic bullet' that could bring order to every classroom ('Why the behaviour battle will never end', *Times Educational Supplement*, 27 May 2006).

An important part of creating a climate where professionals and policymakers can talk openly and constructively to each other about how to manage pupil behaviour and learning is to get away from the idea that if there are classrooms not fully under the control of teachers, it is *necessarily* someone's fault. It does not necessarily mean that the school management is not fully supporting the teaching staff; it does not mean that there is bad teaching going on. Good teachers working in good schools can go into a classroom with a well-planned lesson and have difficulty controlling the class. Several head teachers pointed out that the problems that have led to increased problems in society generally inevitably have an impact on schools. The following two examples are not unrepresentative of many other comments that were made:

> There are huge problems caused by the break up of stable families and the chaotic, sometimes appalling background that some pupils come from. We are picking up the pieces of some horrendous social situations.

Even in my time in teaching, there has been a massive increase in the number of pupils from dysfunctional families, pupils who don't get supervised in the evenings, with very little respect for parental or school control.

Given that nearly all those interviewed acknowledged that it was not a 'level playing field' in terms of the distribution of difficult pupils across schools, a 'level 6' lesson might be a minor triumph of management and pedagogy in adversity. Many schools designated as 'failing', 'in special measures', 'with serious weaknesses' contain teachers who are extremely talented and effective managers of pupil learning. As Phillip Beadle, former Secondary Teacher of the Year argued:

Let there be no doubt about this, if any of the (media) commentators visited the 'failing' schools they so deride, they would find pockets of astonishing success, astounding individuals, teachers and students – indefatigable spirit, creative brilliance. Teachers working in such schools are often the finest the profession has to offer.

(*Guardian Education*, 7 February 2006)

Developing an understanding of the factors that have a bearing on the working atmosphere in the classroom, and the behaviour of individual pupils is one of the ways in which teachers become accomplished at managing pupils' learning. An unsatisfactory classroom climate can be caused by a particularly toxic combination of difficult pupils within a group, poor planning, an inappropriate curriculum, lack of attention to differentiation – both in terms of access and challenge, poor school and colleague support systems, the time of day or term, unclear hierarchies of sanctions, what happened in the previous lesson or in the playground, a lousy teaching room, the re-entry of one pupil who is bent on destroying the lesson so that he can be suspended again, and, some would add, the weather (windy, hot – bad news), the phase of the moon. These factors interact in a complicated and often unpredictable way. Teaching is not like bricklaying, plumbing or playing a backhand drop shot on a squash court, where there is generally a technically 'correct' way of doing something, and all the other ways are wrong. There are no handy hints (or policies) that are guaranteed to work with all pupils, in all classrooms, all schools.

John Marks, education policy advisor to John Major, compared examination results from a number of comprehensive schools 'so as to compare like with like' (Marks, 1993: 1). The idea that all comprehensive schools are similar in terms of either intake, climate or culture is profoundly misleading. Most PGCE tutors are aware that they are sometimes sending some trainees to the equivalent of 'The Eastern Front' when they make allocations to schools, and that they are sending others to schools that are not at 'the sharp end'. The aim is to balance the degree of challenge involved over the two placements, but even within a two-placement model, it is often not possible to make trainees aware of the full spectrum of behaviour that occurs in schools. There are massive variations between schools in terms of the levels of control and behaviour that prevail. There are many schools where it would be unusual for the level of behaviour to slip below level 7 or 8, and even then, this might be only with weaker trainees or weak and inexperienced NQTs. Moreover, there are schools where even if incidents of disruption arose in particular corners of the school, the school system and the authority of the senior teachers could quickly be mobilised and the temporary 'blip' on the behaviour radar would soon be dealt with. There are still many schools where the pupils will fall silent and behave perfectly if a head or an established teacher passes by or drops in to a classroom.

However, there are schools where levels in classrooms will fall to some of the lower levels on the scale, and where even competent and experienced teachers struggle to get to the highest levels with some classes (see Chapter 7 for further development of this point). It's not just about differences in terms of levels of control or indiscipline, as Watkins (1995: 1) points out, 'schools differ in key characteristics, disciplinary climate, sense of community, and ways of explaining difficult behaviour'.

These differences have profound implications for the ways in which teachers manage learning in their classrooms. Strategies that work in some schools are ineffective in others.

One example of this is Cowley's advice (2001, 2003) about waiting for pupils to be quiet and attentive before starting the lesson. The case for attempting this strategy is cogently and compellingly explained (this emerged as a very commonly suggested course of action by experienced teachers and is a strategy that I wholeheartedly recommend to my trainees). However, there are some classrooms where it doesn't appear to work:

> I really tried hard to make it work ... I got to 23 minutes on one occasion but then gave up ... I was getting nowhere. ... the kids really weren't that bothered. With this group anyway, it just didn't work.
>
> (Trainee)

> One experienced member of staff told me that he had waited 40 minutes for them to be quiet. I just don't think that a new teacher would have the confidence to do that and I'm not sure that after a few minutes it's even the right thing to do.
>
> (Second year of teaching)

> We do have some classes now where even established teachers struggle to get them quiet throughout the lesson. Sometimes we have to teach to the pupils who want to learn, and try and ignore the ones who are messing around. Often if you do ignore the low level stuff ... if you don't take the bait, they will settle down and just slump or mutter to each other. I honestly feel that more learning gets done this way than if I were to try and get things perfect before starting. I know it's not ideal but it's my way of getting through the day with my worst classes.
>
> (Experienced teacher)

(Other variations in terms of teachers views on 'what works' are considered in Chapter 2.)

Another aspect of managing learning that can vary considerably between schools is related to the levels of tolerance or 'accommodation' of difficult pupils. Some schools espouse a 'zero tolerance' policy on behaviour, and teachers are not encouraged to condone, excuse or make allowances for breaches of the school codes of behaviour (*Times Educational Supplement*, 5 December 2003, 13 May 2005; *The Observer*, 10 July 2005). In some schools, swearing in lessons would be considered a fairly serious matter, in others, it is not something for which a pupil would necessarily incur serious 'consequences', and it may well not be dealt with by any sanction. In most schools, not handing in homework is considered a serious breach of school policy and trainees and NQTs would be expected to chase up and act on such derelictions assiduously. In some schools, homework has been taken out of the disciplinary system, it is set for pupils who might want to do it, and it is at least tacitly accepted that not doing it will not bring about reprisals. Even pupil culture can vary substantially between ostensibly similar schools and influence how incidents are dealt with:

> At my first school, fire alarms were set off on a fairly regular basis ... there was no chance of finding out who did it. It was us against them, the whole cohort. They would get together to stitch up some really innocuous kid who you knew hadn't done it, it was a sort of game. Sometimes the fire alarm goes off here but if it does, we usually get to the bottom of it. Whenever anything like that happens, we find out who did it because someone or other lets us know, and the pupil usually ends up being excluded until their parents come in to discuss the matter.
>
> (Head of department)

> Yes, we do sometimes get some pupils behaving in a way that gets in the way of other pupils' learning. It does happen, but again, there's a big difference in the climate and the social relations in classrooms. There isn't a pupils' 'trade union' here; they don't always stick together no matter what. If someone is messing around and clearly breaking the rules ... going beyond ... the other kids usually keep their distance and don't get involved. There is a critical mass of basically cooperative pupils ... the ones who try and mess about, play up, attention seek, disrupt or whatever, are isolated.
>
> (Head teacher)

These variations are just one of the strands of complexity relating to managing pupil learning which make life difficult for trainee teachers and NQTs working in their first post.

Most trainees felt that it was best to 'get your tough school in first', rather than the other way round. The radical differences in behaviour levels and 'what is expected', in different schools, can cause considerable stress.

> I had a very successful first placement and was told by both the teachers I worked with and my university tutor that class management appeared to be a particular strength. I did feel confident and was able to get a good working atmosphere with all my classes. Then I went to a similar school down the road and just could not get the control I was used to ... it was traumatic having been able to get control and then feeling impotent ... helpless. The staff were great and very supportive but I spent a lot of time in tears in the staffroom and nearly packed it in.
>
> (Head of department)

This might be a long way of stating the fairly obvious point that it is easier to manage pupil learning in some schools compared to others but it is a point that seems to have eluded some policymakers and politicians (there are other examples, but the idea that tough comprehensive schools have much to learn about class management from the independent sector is a particularly clueless suggestion).

It might be felt that trainees should not have to work in tough schools in the course of their training, but many of the interviewees saw the experience of working with teachers who were accomplished at managing learning with difficult pupils as the most valuable part of their training (see Chapter 7). Moreover, in giving people qualified teacher status, you are giving them a licence to teach at any school. I believe that you must feel at the very least that a trainee could cope at an 'average' comprehensive if they are going to be unleashed on generations of children. It does trainees no favours to work at two schools where discipline is not really a significant problem with any class. It is an invaluable experience for trainees to work with at least one class where they have to really work hard over a sustained period of time to get pupils 'sorted out' and under reasonable control.

To add to the complexity of the factors influencing judgement calls on how to handle pupil behaviour, several responses indicated that in some cases there were major differences in policy even *within* schools. What was considered an appropriate response to pupil transgressions would depend of which department or part of the school you were working with:

> Both the people in the department were in effect 'Black belts' at managing the kids; this meant that in our bit of the building, kids would be more quiet, better behaved, as they came into the block. You would see them putting their ties on, tucking their shirts in. So if I was teaching in this bit of the school, I would be more confident and would tend to ask X and Y for help to sort incidents out rather than use the formal remove system ... it would be quicker and more effective.
>
> (NQT in challenging school)

> The conventions for sending kids out of the room aren't even the same throughout the school, never mind the LEA [Local Education Authority] or the area. In our corridor we have several experienced teachers who are really good with the kids so we don't tend to send them to the exclusion room, we 'mind' kids for each other. But in other bits of the school, other departments, they use the central system. Trainees have got to adjust to different ways of working, there's no standard rule that you can apply to say 'when X happens, always do this ...'.
>
> (Head of department, fifth year of teaching)

Tensions between educational inclusion and protecting 'the right to learn' of other pupils

In 1996, David Hart, leader of the National Association of Head Teachers, outlined a dilemma confronting many of his members; the tension between the ideal of educational inclusion, that all children have a right to be educated; balanced against 'the right of others to learn and not be disrupted by a small minority of pupils' (Hart, 1996). There are few head teachers who do not at some point have to make difficult decisions about balancing the rights of difficult and disruptive pupils to an education against protecting 'the right to learn', in reasonable conditions, of pupils who want to learn. This is not a problem that just affects head teachers. Large numbers of teachers have to make difficult decisions about how to stop some pupils spoiling the learning of others. Many of the teachers interviewed talked about situations where one or two pupils in a class were patently interfering with the learning of others, and the thinking that underpinned decisions on how to deal with such situations (see Chapter 4). As in other aspects of custom and practice, schools have very different ideas about in what circumstances it is alright to send a pupil out of a normal classroom, either to stand outside for some or all of the lesson, or to go to some form of 'internal exclusion', or 'removal' room, where they are separated from normal classes for some or all lessons. Similar dilemmas apply to the circumstances in which pupils might be excluded from the school itself, either for a fixed term, or permanently. There are also interesting questions about what happens to pupils who have been permanently excluded from a school (see Chapter 7).

Chapters 4 and 7 give the views of practising teachers and head teachers on the thinking underpinning their decision making in these areas. An indication of the nature of these problematic situations is given in the following extract from an interview with a head of department at a challenging school, talking about handling a very disruptive pupil who had recently been excluded from another school:

> I'm doing my best to cut her a bit of slack ... to make some allowances for the fact that she's unsettled, she's just come from another school, she's got big problems ... at the same time you're trying hard to be consistent, to keep the ground rules you've tried to establish with the other pupils who you know better. You have incredibly hard decisions to make trying to balance these tensions ... making that judgement about when they have to go out. But if the other pupils can understand why you are cutting them some slack, why you are not being consistent, that you are trying to give them a chance ... you're bending over backwards to avoid just kicking them out ... that helps with the behaviour of the other pupils.
>
> (Head of department, fourth year of teaching)

The interviews revealed significant differences in teacher actions relating to the issue and practice of 'inclusion'. This is not to say that some teachers were against the principle of educational inclusion, but that there were different views about the stage at which pupil transgressions were serious enough to merit sending pupils out of the room to protect the learning of other pupils. In some schools, it was expected that teachers should try to keep pupils in the room if at all possible, even if things weren't perfect; at others, there was a much lower 'threshold' for sending pupils out. The factors influencing teacher judgements in this area are considered in Chapter 4.

The relationship between pupil behaviour and learning

The issue of managing pupil behaviour is sometimes considered (particularly in media reporting of education) as something entirely separate from the management of pupil learning. Some think-tank critiques make the assumption that all pupils come to school wanting to learn, and consider this as a 'given' in the classroom equation (see, for example, Lawlor, 1989). There is also a school of thought that suggests that sorting out behaviour in some way 'comes first' (weeks 1–3, establish control, weeks 4–12, commence pupil learning). Although many respondents acknowledged that there was an 'establishment' agenda when they first encountered new teaching groups, there was also an understanding that from the first minutes of the first lesson, getting as many pupils to want to learn as possible was an important part of managing pupil behaviour. It did not come after getting control, for most experienced teachers it was generally the primary consideration in planning the first encounters with new teaching groups (see Chapter 3).

Of course, trainees and newly qualified teachers do not have a massive 'archive' of brilliant ideas for engaging pupils in learning compared to experienced teachers. It takes time to build up pedagogical expertise in the classroom. Just as you can't speak a language fluently or be a maestro in the piano straight away, it takes time to become accomplished in terms of subject pedagogy; how to teach all aspects of your subject in a way that is effective, and in a way that elicits the commitment and enthusiasm of even reluctant and half-hearted scholars (and this is probably a matter of years, not months). For this reason, new teachers need 'coping' strategies to control pupils who are not engaged, until they become more accomplished at persuading pupils into learning. My own PGCE tutor didn't really like us doing 'reading round the class' (see Chapter 4), dictating notes or having pupils copying from the board, but he accepted that rather than having the lesson getting out of control, it might be necessary at times to employ 'settling' activities (MacLennan, 1987) as we were learning to teach.

Understanding and developing pupils' 'learning agendas' (Elliott *et al.*, 2001) was seen as a fundamental step towards getting to the top levels of the scale, and getting past the 'us versus them' mentality, where the pupils were seen as 'the enemy'. In the words of one head of department:

> In the long term, you have got to be able to get them to want to learn ... to at least have a go some of the time, to join in. There must be at least some bit of some lessons that they are interested in, or can enjoy, or can see the point of ... or just a good atmosphere in the room, so that at least things are pleasant and friendly, relaxed, secure. Without that, even if you're quite good at the control side of things, teaching will not be an enjoyable experience ... if you are just containing a surly and hostile crowd by force.

However, as another head of department pointed out, there are some schools where:

> A good, experienced teacher can go in there with a really well planned lesson, execute it skilfully, in a way that engages most of the pupils, and you will still get some kids who will mess about, who will try and aggravate the teacher, who will try and spoil the lesson.

A teaching assistant talked of there being 'a balance' between thinking about how to control the pupils and how to lure them into learning:

> There's a sort of balance ... before coming into the room they have thought about how to discourage some kids from messing around, but they have also thought about how to do something that the class just might get interested in ... there is some 'offering' that at least acknowledges that there is a need to get the pupils interested in the topic, that they are not all driven scholars with a passionate desire to do well in geography or whatever.

Box 1.3 Two agendas relating to the working atmosphere in the classroom

Control	*Engagement*
'We have to operate within a school framework of rules.'	'This is worthwhile and important.'
	'My job is to help you to do well.'
'I have high expectations of you.'	
	'I am interested in you as a human being, not just as a student of history/ maths or whatever.'
'It is my professional responsibility to establish a climate where you can all learn (I'm not just a fascist control freak).'	
	'If you give it a chance, this might be interesting and enjoyable.'
'You will have a more enjoyable time if you try to comply with my standards and expectations.'	'You can all learn, you can all get better.'
'We are here to work.'	(This area is partly about pedagogy and partly about social relations).

There are, therefore, two major agendas for teachers to manage pupil learning effectively and get a calm, controlled and purposeful working atmosphere in the classroom: they must try to get the pupils to want to learn, and they must be able to discourage pupils who don't want to learn from spoiling the lesson for other pupils (see Box 1.3).

SUMMARY

- Classroom climate, or the working atmosphere in the classroom is an important issue in education, in terms of pupil attainment, equality of educational opportunity and the quality of teachers' working lives.

- The working atmosphere in the classroom can be thought of in terms of a continuum, between classes where the teacher is in relaxed and assured control of the lesson, and classrooms where little learning can take place because some pupils are spoiling the learning of others.

- It can be helpful for teachers to reflect on the extent to which they are able to manage learning in the classroom in an effective way for all pupils.

- Classroom climate is an issue that is relevant to most teachers and most schools. It is not a problem that is limited to a small number of challenging inner-city schools.

- It can be helpful for new teachers to consider the views of experienced teachers and head teachers on the issue of classroom climate. Some media and political treatment of this issue is unhelpful and ill-informed.

- Classroom climate and pupil behaviour are complex and intractable issues and are not susceptible to simple solutions and 'quick fixes'.

- Most teachers and head teachers will face difficult decisions in reconciling ideals of educational inclusion with the rights of pupils to learn without interference from other pupils.

- There are two 'agendas' relating to classroom climate: one is concerned with trying to get pupils to want to learn, the other is concerned with discouraging pupils who do not want to learn from spoiling the learning of others.

2 Teachers' views about colleagues who are good at managing learning

> Like most heads, I have some teachers who are exceptionally accomplished at working with difficult and troubled pupils, they are incredibly resourceful, persevering . . . and clever. Some trainees and NQTs learn from them, others don't pick things up.
>
> (Head teacher)

Teachers make a difference

Reynolds (1999: 13) has argued that how teachers behave in their classrooms is the most important factor determining the educational standards of pupils:

> First, in statistical analyses it is clear that the teacher 'level' explains three to four times more in terms of pupil results than the school 'level'. Second, there is evidence of substantial variability in quality within our schools, in terms of departmental performance and in teachers' effectiveness. Indeed, the range of effectiveness within schools dwarfs the variation between them.

This is as true of the management of pupil behaviour as it is of standards of attainment. Although there are variations in levels of control between different schools there are also major variations *within* schools. In the early stages of their careers, teachers are likely to encounter a wide range of the levels on the 10-point scale (Haydn, 2002). Although levels 1–3 were uncommon, the majority of respondents felt that they had experienced or observed lessons in the territory of levels 4–7, and there were few whose early experiences of teaching and observing in schools were limited to levels 8 to 10. In terms of 'impact' learning, seeing a class behaving well with a teacher who was adept at managing pupil behaviour after having seen the same group of pupils behaving badly was a powerful learning experience for many trainees. In the words of two of the trainees:

> You couldn't do a placement at X school without realising what a fantastic difference the individual teacher makes. Groups that I had regarded as unteachable would behave like little angels, not just under control but relaxed, pleasant, helpful. They would just go quiet when he gave some small signal that he wanted to talk. At one level it was depressing because it made me realise how crap I was, but in another

way it was inspiring … it made you realise what a fantastic difference teachers can make.

You can't do a school placement without realising that the bottom line, in terms of the deal that the pupil gets, is which teacher they have.

Teaching assistants are in a good position to consider 'teacher effect', given that by the nature of their job, they have to work with a wide range of teachers:

As a TA [Teaching Assistant] you sometimes follow a group or a particular pupil around for the whole day or even for several lessons over a period of weeks. You would see the same group at level 10 with some teachers and down to level 2 or 3 with others. It made you realise what a massive difference the individual teacher makes. It made you really appreciate just how good some of them are, how wide the range of skills are that enable you to cope in difficult circumstances. You can also learn from bad practice … you can see what it is that some teachers do that puts their backs up … that sets them off, provokes them almost.

Most trainees go into classrooms some weeks after the teacher has taken over the class, when a lot of the 'sorting out', and establishing of rituals, routines and ground rules has been done. It is not always apparent to new trainees exactly why the pupils are behaving so well, why it all seems so effortless. Experienced teachers were quick to stress that it often took time and effort to get to a stage of being able to relax with a class, and that 'reputation' was an advantage that was not available to trainees and NQTs.

In terms of developing a sophisticated understanding of classroom climate, part of it is about comprehending the wide range of factors that can influence the working atmosphere in the classroom, part of it is realising that some things are not fully under the teacher's control and that it's about the art of the possible: you've just got to get on with it. However, it is also about grasping that in spite of these complexities, the most influential 'variable' is generally the teacher. There are few schools where things are so desperate that good teachers are unable to make a difference to the prevailing atmosphere in the classroom.

Why do some teachers become better than others at managing classrooms and getting pupils to want to learn? This chapter gives the views of practising teachers on this question.

How helpful are the 'Qualifying to teach' Standards for teaching and class management?

The Standards are helpful and important in clarifying exactly what it is that trainees have to be able to do to achieve Qualified Teacher Status (QTS) in the area of managing classrooms and pupil behaviour. The Standards are invaluable in getting beginning teachers to become aware of all the things that they have to think about, and become competent in, if they are to be able to manage classes effectively. They do not, however, provide any insight into the order in which these competences need to be acquired, and which areas might be more important or essential. For example, Standard 3.3.10 of the 02/02 Standards (DfES/TTA (Teacher Training Agency; now known as the TDA, Teacher Development Agency), 2002: 11) requires that trainees become competent at using ICT (information and communications

Box 2.1 What are the characteristics of teachers who are good at managing pupil behaviour?

technology) purposefully in their teaching and, indeed, being able to make effective use of new technology can be one of the ways of getting pupils to want to learn (see Chapter 3). However, many mentors responsible for the supervision of trainees on school placement felt that if trainees were struggling with class management issues, they should forget about ICT for the moment and focus on the more urgent issue of getting classes under a reasonable degree of control. In the words of one mentor:

> You do want the trainees to bear in mind the full breadth of the Standards over the course of the whole placement, but there are difficult decisions to be made about what to address first . . . what is most urgent as a stepping stone to progress. I don't want trainees messing about with PowerPoint or data handling if they can't get the kids to sit in their places. In the short and medium term, some things are essential and some are desirable. Getting classes under reasonable control is one of the fundamentals. You can't make progress in lots of other aspects of the Standards if you can't do that because the kids won't give the lesson a chance.

Nor is it easy to 'isolate' the competences relating to getting pupils to behave. Pupils' response to lessons will be influenced by trainees' strengths and weaknesses in other aspects of the Standards, such as professional values and practice, subject knowledge and planning.

The idea that success is dependent on proficiency in every strand of the Standards is misleading. The Hay McBer Report into teacher effectiveness (2000) identified 16 teacher attributes linked to effective teaching, but added that it was possible to be a successful teacher without necessarily being proficient in all 16 areas.

In his paper, 'Thinking about the technical and the personal in teaching', Lefstein outlines contrasting models of teacher development, which he describes as 'instrumental rationality' and 'experiential wisdom' respectively (Lefstein, 2005: 333). The Standards are a manifestation of the former of these models: an attempt to define teacher effectiveness through a set of discrete competence statements. These statements can be helpful in enabling those involved in teacher education to make objective judgements on whether trainees will be 'fit to teach'. Later chapters in the book consider some of the specific techniques and ideas that teachers use to manage classrooms and control the behaviour of pupils. This chapter focuses principally on teachers' views on the human qualities, or to use Lefstein's term, 'experiential wisdom', which impacts on the development of technical competence in teaching.

One assistant head warned of the dangers of a 'tick list' approach to the Standards:

> I know that we are supposed to look at each of the standards and judge them against each one but that isn't a realistic way of doing it. I know it's against 'the rules' and what they get told at the university but I say to my student teachers on first placement, 'if you have done your best to do your best for your classes, worked really hard preparing your lessons and been generally professional and conscientious, and show that you can learn from advice, observation and experience, I will recommend that you pass your placement.' If they've got those qualities, they will probably develop into a good teacher eventually.

A head of department made the point that teaching is not just a set of technical competences, and that teachers possessing particular general characteristics were more likely to make progress in meeting the Standards for QTS:

> What you are looking for as a mentor is not proficiency across all the competences . . . it's unusual to find student teachers who are good at everything . . . the standards are a bit artificial in that sense . . . lots of very good experienced teachers have some gaps in their 'competence' . . . it's more about how hard they are trying to get better and how good they are at learning and getting better . . . there are a core of key qualities such as trying really hard to do things well, being conscientious in trying to prepare good lessons, keeping trying when things aren't going well and not giving up or going through the motions.

This is not to be dismissive of the importance of the Standards. They are central to the process of acquiring a licence to teach, they are the rules of engagement. If trainees are not at least competent in all areas of the Standards, they should not be passed. Keeping in mind the full breadth of the Standards is essential to stop trainees 'plateauing' and to stop them thinking that they are a 'complete' teacher just because pupils are behaving and are 'on task'. However, there is a danger of 'not seeing the wood for the trees' if individual Standards are considered in isolation. This chapter focuses on broader professional attributes that experienced teachers believe help trainees to make progress in managing learning in the classroom. These qualities have a bearing on both how quickly trainees will become competent in this area of the Standards, and how far they will develop towards excellence in managing learning in classrooms.

How do teachers get better at managing pupil learning and behaviour?

Does the ability to manage classrooms derive from personality and character or training and experience? Former Chief Inspector of Schools Chris Woodhead and

---

Box 2.2 Trainees' views of what factors they felt had been most helpful in enabling them to improve their ability to manage learning in the classroom

Survey undertaken at the end of the first term of the course; factors given in order of the importance attached to them by trainees

1 **'Doing it'** – your own experience of teaching in the classroom.

2 **Observing** – watching experienced teachers in the classroom.

3 **Advice** – comments from and conversations with your subject mentor, link tutor, university tutor.

4 **Teaching sessions** – formal seminars/lectures or workshops, either at school or at the university.

5 **Reading** – either prescribed reading, reading for assignments or casual reading of the Times Educational Supplement, education articles in newspapers.

6 **Talking** – with fellow trainees, in school, at the university or socially.

Professor Alan Smithers have argued that university-based teacher training courses should be closed down, and that teachers should be trained entirely in schools, in an apprenticeship model (in Lawlor, 2004). Is class management best learned by working with grizzled combat veterans and learning 'on the job' (albeit in independent schools)? Do lectures, seminars and reading have nothing to offer the beginning teacher? Certainly, the views of a cohort of trainee teachers at the end of the first term of their course at the University of East Anglia (UEA) indicated that trainees felt that they learned significantly more from their own experiences in the classroom and from observing experienced teachers in action than from reading and university-based seminars. When asked to rank the factors outlined in Box 2.2 in terms of which had been most helpful in enabling them to improve their skills in managing classes, the order was as given above in Box 2.2, with learning from their own experience at the top, and talking about class management issues with fellow trainees at the bottom.

However, there are some potential problems with the apprenticeship model of managing classrooms. First, as Calderhead (1994) has pointed out, there is the danger that trainees may be socialised into a specific professional culture, a particular way of doing things, which may work in one school but not another. There is also a question of timing. It is not surprising that trainees feel that they learn most from their own experience in the classroom in their first few weeks of teaching, given the vividness of that experience and the complexity of it – there is almost too much for them to think about just analysing their own practice, without devouring the skips full of literature on behaviour management.

A third argument about the 'experience' model of teacher education is that there is no obvious correlation between how much experience teachers have had, and how good they are at managing classrooms. As one head teacher remarked:

I've got teachers here who have worked in this school for years who are still at level 3 with some of their classes, and I've got NQTs who are already very assured in dealing with pupil behaviour, who have virtually no problems with their classes after the first term. Some teachers are much better than others at this … it's not just a question of serving your time.

Getting better at managing classrooms is clearly not just an aggregative process, it's not like clocking up flying hours (the more lessons you teach, the better you will be). Head teachers and experienced teachers interviewed had clear views on the characteristics of teachers who were likely to become accomplished in this area, and there were some differences between their views and those of trainees and NQTs (see Chapter 6).

Can any teacher become good at managing classrooms?

Every year, thousands of people go into teaching. Do they all have an equal chance at becoming accomplished at this facet of teaching or are some entrants 'genetically' advantaged because they possess particular inherited characteristics (they are, by nature, for example, 'hard as nails', or 'charismatic'), or by virtue of previously acquired experience (a couple of years in the SAS, psychiatric social work)? It has been suggested that extroverts are likely to make better teachers than introverts (*Today Programme*, Radio 4, 17 March 1991), and that initial teacher training providers should invite stand-up comedians in to give advice on performance skills (Pike, 1994). If you are taciturn, quiet and undemonstrative, does this mean that you are likely to find this facet of teaching difficult? Head teachers, experienced teachers and teacher educators were asked whether they thought some teachers and trainees were severely disadvantaged in the area of managing pupil behaviour because of such personal characteristics. Very few of the responses mentioned size, voice, presence or 'extroversion' as significant factors. The most commonly mentioned barrier to success that was thought of as 'the kiss of death' was lack of self-awareness on the part of the teacher or trainee:

Can anyone become good at it? No. If they haven't got self-awareness there's no chance. They won't get better because they can't see it, they can't understand. It's as if they are pedagogically autistic. They can't take things on board, try things out, adjust and adapt in the light of experience and advice. They've made their minds up … they know how to do it. It's all the kids' fault, it's not me.

(Teacher educator)

Some of them overdo the self-flagellation bit in their evaluations, you can beat yourself up too much, but rather that than that they can't grasp that they are doing things wrong … stubborn, closed minded, rebutting rather than considering comments which mentors are making to try and help them. If fact most mentors are fairly gentle in terms of pointing things out and making tentative suggestions. But some of them just won't have it. They seem to be incapable of genuine reflection. They are not good learners. They either won't get through the course, or they will scrape through and be whipping boys for the kids for years.

(Teacher educator)

> If you are working with someone who has a reasonable degree of self-awareness, who is honest and open about the fact that they are having problems, you are in with a chance, you can work with them, you can try and work together. If they are in denial, if they can't admit that they are not coping well with a class . . . it's more a matter of managing the situation, damage limitation. This is 'heartsink' territory.
>
> (Head of year)

Other than this flaw, it was generally felt that most people who had satisfied the selection criteria to get on the course in the first place ('such as being professional in approach, intelligent, reasonable skills of communication, able to learn') could become at least competent in managing classes, 'as long as they are not then pitch-forked into situations way beyond their experience and ability to cope', but that personal characteristics might make it quicker for some to get there than others:

> Yes, but the length of time it could take might vary quite a lot, it might take some people up to five years to reach higher levels, others get there more quickly.
>
> (Teacher educator)

> I think it is easier or quicker for some of them than others. . . . I've got some that seem to have 'don't mess with me' written all over them. . . . It's slightly indefinable exactly what it is, why it's there. Some grab their attention the way they speak. . . . Perhaps it's in the eyes . . . a sort of quiet calm firmness of purpose. Nothing to do with size . . . I've got one trainee – very small, short . . . I suspect she may have been difficult to teach herself.
>
> (Teacher educator)

> I had one trainee who did have a bit of a weakness in this area . . . she was good in lots of other ways but class management wasn't her strength. I had to say 'don't worry it will come with time' and I saw her three years later and she came up to me and said, 'You were right, it did come with time . . . for the first two years the exercise books used to have graffiti on them . . . they don't this year. I don't know why, I don't know what I'm doing differently. It's just stopped.'
>
> (Teacher educator)

> Some teachers are better at this than others, some seem to sail through and others seem to be permanently mired in problems of class management. But having said this, even the ones who struggle can get there if they are determined and keep working at it.
>
> (Head teacher)

One teacher in her second year of teaching argued that not being 'a natural' had its advantages:

> I know this is little help to a struggling PGCE student, however, I think it's important to make the point that good class management is not something you are born with or without; it can be developed. Indeed, in some ways I think it's better for your teaching to find classroom management a struggle in the early days, because it forces you to plan your lessons very carefully.

In similar vein, a head teacher suggested that 'good learners' often overtook those with natural assets but less application:

> We see them developing over several years, not just in their training year. Some of the ones who are intelligent, good learners, end up being better . . . getting to higher levels . . . than those who have some natural assets and advantages but aren't as clever at learning from experience and colleagues.

This raises an important point about this facet of being a teacher; there are two questions here. One is about how quickly someone will reach a reasonable standard so that they are 'safe' to be given a licence to teach. The other is 'how good will they get'? Will they progress to excellence, or will they stay at the level of 'reasonable competence'? The second question is probably the more interesting and important one. No one goes into teaching wanting to be just 'competent'.

It was interesting to find that respondents talked of 'prosaic' or 'ordinary' qualities as being an underrated facet of teacher competence in managing pupil behaviour. Heads, heads of department, year heads and teacher educators talked of the virtues of being 'conscientious', 'a good learner', 'not giving up', as attributes that were likely to make teachers successful in this area. This would not appear to rule out substantial numbers of beginning teachers as having the potential to become accomplished at managing learning in classrooms and controlling pupil behaviour adroitly.

Teachers' views of the characteristics of colleagues who are good at managing classrooms

This section is an attempt to distil the responses from over a hundred interviews with heads, teachers and teacher educators about the general characteristics of teachers who they felt were good at controlling the behaviour of pupils. It attempts to identify areas where there was a degree of consensus about these qualities. The following five attributes emerged as those most frequently mentioned by experienced teachers in interview transcripts. There were significant differences from new trainees' views on effective disciplinarians, with far fewer references to 'performance' attributes such as physical presence, 'charisma' and voice. It was even suggested that 'performance skills' or 'egocentric approaches' might be unhelpful:

> Over the top approaches can be a bit overwhelming for some pupils, they get too excited, silly, and don't know the limits of what's appropriate. Performance, 'charisma' type approaches can get the pupils wound up.
>
> (Teacher educator)

> There's the danger that they think it's all about them, not about pupil learning. Of them thinking 'How was I?', rather than 'How was it for them?'
>
> (Head of department)

'A particular kind of confidence'

Confidence is generally thought to be 'a good thing' but just as there are 'the wrong sorts of leaves' that fall on railway lines, it would appear that there are 'the wrong kinds of confidence' among trainees. This is, perhaps, a difficult concept to define; but several respondents were at pains to emphasise that there were some 'forms' of confidence that were actually unhelpful:

> Some mature trainees feel that because they have experience of life after school and university, this a priori bestows on them some sort of superior wisdom which makes them superior beings to those who have gone straight from school to university. It actually makes them narrow minded and opinionated, reluctant to consider new ideas, and it pisses off mentors when they start in schools, proffering strong opinions on day 2 of teaching placement. This is not an argument against mature trainees, some of them are wise and a delight to work with.
>
> (Head of department)

> It's the gung-ho confidence that completely underestimates how difficult it is going to be that sets off alarm bells. 'No need to worry about me' ... If they are like that, if they don't acknowledge problems and difficulties, I know I will have problems working with them.
>
> (Mentor)

> How they deal with 'conscious incompetence' is an interesting area. What are they like when confronting an aspect of teaching that they are not that confident about ... it doesn't matter whether it is ICT or pupil behaviour ... but it tells you whether they are going to be ok or not. If they are honest and say 'I'm quite nervous about this bit ...' that's generally a good sign. If they have issues in the area of unconscious incompetence – where they think they are good at something and they are not, or they can't see that they are struggling with some bits ... most trainees struggle with some bits ... then that's a real danger sign.
>
> (Mentor)

One mentor reported that his new trainee had displayed 'an appropriate degree of fear and trepidation' after his first visits to his school placement and considered this 'a good sign'.

The form of confidence that was deemed to be an asset was of a more quiet, self-contained and sensitive variety. The following extracts attempt to give an indication of this:

> A deep internal confidence in themselves ... not aggressive, nothing like that. They could be very quiet but just quietly confident, with a self-belief that they are allowed to be in charge of the classroom, and that this will help the pupils and be in their interest, and that they are not harming pupils or being horrible to them ... by doing things to discourage or persuade them not to spoil the learning of others.

> They are quick to articulate the boundaries they are going to accept, they look at the system they are working in and are clear in themselves about what they will accept and manage to transmit that to the pupils, so pupils quickly learn what they will and will not put up with before using sanctions.
>
> (Teacher educator)

It's not necessarily an 'all-singing, all-dancing thing' ... many of the best students I've seen are fairly introvert, quite quiet ... they have a sort of intelligent serious thoughtfulness, they treat the topic they are doing as important and this serious-ness can get through to the pupils ... we're doing something important and worthwhile here.

(Teacher educator)

It's a particular form of confidence. A quiet confidence. Not getting flustered, not getting in a panic, staying calm, Being able to think on your feet yes ... but not rushing into precipitate and ill-considered action or, rather, over reaction, taking a few seconds to work out what is the best option to take, or even to just say, 'Don't worry about it now, just get on with your work ... see me about it later', to give yourself a bit of time, to give yourself some options. This sense of calm purpose-fulness gets across to the pupils, even the younger ones. I think you can train your-self to keep calm under pressure, not to flap, not to bluster. Even if you're not feeling completely relaxed inside, you can try and come across as quite relaxed.

(Teacher educator)

There are some people who've just got a sort of poise ... self-assurance ... inner strength, who are comfortable with themselves, who either have, or have cultivated a calm, quiet confidence.

(Teacher educator)

Perseverance

Time after time (in over 40 of the responses), 'perseverance', 'not giving up', 'being patient and determined', 'determination' and 'resilience' emerged as factors that experienced teachers mentioned as delineating between beginning teachers who became accomplished at managing their classes, and those who stayed on the lower levels of the 10-point scale. This did not just apply to trainees and NQTs: teachers who had moved on to teach in new schools as heads of department were at pains to stress that it took time, patience, effort and determination to get pupils to comply with the standards of behaviour that were desired:

It's good now, I'm enjoying it but the first half term was really difficult. We get a lot of kids who don't really know how to behave normally coming up from their middle schools in terms of putting their hands up, not moving round and so on. A lot of it is embedding basic codes of behaviour. You have to be really calm, firm and patient. It takes time, you can't change how they are overnight. It's towards the end of the second term now and I can more or less get them to do what I want and I am able to do whatever sort of lesson I want.

(Head of department, having moved to a more difficult school)

There was no easy answer that anyone could give me. For all that they were nice and supportive, there was nothing they could do to make it easy. In a school like this, you have to have a degree of determination to get through the first term. It's partly about being, or learning to be, resilient.

(NQT working in a challenging school)

> Being prepared to follow things through, to not give up and stop trying, both in individual instances and generally with more difficult classes.
>
> (Teacher educator)

> Remorselessness ... keep working at it ... keep trying to get the standards you want. Be patient. Persevere. Dispassionately try and discourage them from messing you about. It won't reform them but they will pick on someone else who can't be bothered to do the sorting out.
>
> (Teacher educator)

This last point is an important one. No one is claiming here that by following things up and working hard to inconvenience pupils who have attempted to 'ambush' lessons, pupils will be in some way reformed and seriously consider their moral position in jeopardising the education of others. It is, however, possible that they will keep their heads down and mess about in the lessons of someone who has not got the energy and determination to try to get the standards of behaviour that is in their best interest, and the interests of their pupils.

'Resilience' was often mentioned alongside perseverance; 'developing a thick skin', 'not taking things personally'. One mentor talked of a trainee who had been upset by a poor lesson and gone home for two days:

> She's got to realise that you've got to get back in there and have another disappointing lesson ... to understand that the world doesn't come to a stop when you have a bad lesson ... there's no court martial for it ... life goes on, get over it and get on with it.

A head teacher also mentioned the development of resilience, an ability to shrug shoulders and carry on, as being helpful:

> I suppose there's an inner toughness in there as well with the ones who are really strong in this area. Because you could love the kids, be really fanatical about your subject, but not have that toughness to withstand the odd phrase or comment that can upset. Perhaps this comes more naturally to some than others but it's a disposition which can be developed ... I've seen quite diffident souls become much more determined ... mentally much less brittle ... without losing their inner nice-guy persona.

Some teachers felt that although there were groups where some form of 'breakthrough' could be achieved, after which things became much easier, they also talked of groups where progress could be slow and erratic, groups could 'relapse' and the slow, patient campaign to get the standards of behaviour required had to be continued. Sometimes it was a case of gradual progress, of things at least going in the right direction:

> I rarely have to chuck kids out now. I do have to occasionally stop things and read the riot act but now I can get them back if I try, lessons aren't out of control all the way through. Some groups are slow to settle so you've got to work to settle them down, then they'll be ok for 20 minutes, then you will have to settle them again, especially younger kids. They just forget the ground rules.
>
> (Second year of teaching)

'Keeping going', 'not giving up', 'working hard at it' may sound like pedestrian virtues, but simple perseverance was one of the most frequently mentioned qualities that mentors referred to when asked about the key differences between successful trainees and less successful ones.

'Reputation'

This point is connected with the previous one. It is easy for beginning teachers to underestimate the role of 'reputation' in influencing the working atmosphere in class-rooms. It is a factor where trainees and NQTs are at a huge disadvantage compared to teachers who are 'established' in a school, but this does not mean that they should not try to establish a reputation for being firm, consistent, fair and generally on top of things. Several mentors felt that in a short placement, trainees might not reap the full benefits of beginning to get a reputation, but that they would get a 'feel' for whether they were the sort of teacher who would become strong in the area of class management. In the words of one mentor 'a key question I ask of trainees is, "Are things going in the right direction ... is the behaviour of classes getting better or worse over time?".'

Acquiring the right sort of reputation is an investment. It is not something that can be acquired in a few days by a few acts of random severity. In the words of one head of department: 'It's not about being a hard man, ideally, it's that your lessons are good and that you are quite strict ... if you are a pupil, you are ok as long as you don't mess about.' This can take weeks, or even months and during this period it takes time and energy, following things up, keeping pupils behind at break, dinner-time and after school where possible, writing up incidents, talking to form teachers and year heads, contacting parents. But after a sustained period of being well organised, administratively efficient, planning sound lessons, and being consistent and firm in dealings with pupils, it was felt that in most schools, things would start to become easier as the pupil 'grapevine' did its work and as pupils got used to a teacher's ways of working and the standards of behaviour they expected. In the following extracts, three teachers in their NQT year or second year of teaching talk about the gradual benefits brought about by 'reputation':

> One of my mentors told me to just hammer on with a few basic ground rules ... particularly trying to get them quiet. To just go on and on trying to ram home a few key rules and do everything in your power to make them stick, even when it seems hopeless. He said that although teaching placement was often too short to reap the benefits, if you take this approach it lays the foundations for working with all your classes in your NQT year. The pupils do talk to each other and word gets round about what you are like and what your rules are. And it has happened just like that ... in my second term, it's starting to get quite a bit better ... and this is a tough school.
>
> (NQT)

> Perhaps some teachers are a bit lazy ... they can't quite be bothered to keep kids in or take time to sort things out ... they want to go to the staff room for a cup of tea ... they just want to get away from the classroom. I soon realised how important reputation was. Some teachers seemed to not even have to think about

class management techniques because the kids just behaved for them. Word gets round about what you are like. There is a very efficient pupil grapevine ... within your first year in a school there is a view about whether you are easy prey or 'take care'. That's not quite true ... if you have to cover classes who don't know who you are they often get frisky and you have to do the sorting out bit but now I'm in my second year, most kids behave without me having to do much if I make sure I'm really clear and firm in the first few lessons.

(Second year of teaching)

The other thing I've learned is consistency and following things up. The kids can sense when teachers issue threats that are hollow, which teachers follow things through and which can't be bothered. You can't follow everything up, it's the art of the possible, but the more effort you put in to sorting things out, the more word gets around.

(NQT)

The need to acquire a reputation is not limited to NQTs; experienced teachers who had moved to new schools also spoke of the need to go through all the 'spade-work' needed to get established:

If you go to a new school it's like starting as an NQT again ... you're taken aback because you thought you'd got all that sorted out and you're thinking whoah! What on earth's going on here, why are you doing this to me? It did make you remember what a big thing reputation is ... it's a big advantage if you are seen as part of the furniture ... if word has got round that you are quite strict and run a tight class-room.

(Head of department)

Open-mindedness

Several experienced teachers mentioned the word 'humility' as being a helpful quality for beginning teachers to possess, not in terms of being timid or nervous, but in terms of 'not having made their minds up already', 'not entrenched in their views about what goes on and what works in classrooms'. Mentors reported that some trainees were prepared to try things out, to be flexible, where others might be reluctant to try things that went against their preconceptions and 'fixed' beliefs, unwilling to consider that some things in the area of pupil behaviour might be counter-intuitive:

The good ones [trainees] are willing to find out and explore what the school and departmental policies are and what teachers tend to do in particular situations, and not think they know best straight away, not to let their preconceptions about how things work and what things work close their minds at an early stage ... being open minded.

(Mentor)

Trying out behaviour management strategies and techniques and ideas where there is some evidence that they work, and genuinely trying to make them work, persevering with them. One example: using ten times more praise than blame, even when it doesn't seem warranted . . . and not saying or thinking 'why should I praise them for being quiet?'

(Teacher educator)

This approach ties in with Stenhouse's idea (1975) of teachers testing ideas out against their own experience, seeing what works and what doesn't and refining their teaching approaches accordingly. Trainees and NQTs often reported that ideas which had been suggested had not worked, but had been worth experimenting with, either because they led to greater understanding of situations, or that they had 'partially' worked, as in the following example:

I've just tried lots of the things which have been suggested to see if and when they work. Lining pupils up outside the classroom and getting them quiet before they are allowed in . . . great in some bits of the school but in noisy corridors . . . probably not.

(NQT)

Mentors felt that some trainees were more open to trying out different ideas and approaches, and that this generally helped them to make progress, as long as it was combined with intelligent reflection (see below) when weighing up the outcomes of such experiments, and was sensible and realistic, free from 'kamikaze' and 'Charge of the Light Brigade' excesses.

'A particular sort of intelligence'

Unsurprisingly, many of the heads, heads of department and teacher educators felt that one of the attributes that marked out their strongest trainees or teachers was that they were highly intelligent. As with confidence, however, it was a particular type of intelligence. It was what one head of department termed 'applied' intelligence:

You have to apply your intellect as much to sorting kids out as to learning to teach your subject. It's a sort of practical or 'applied' intelligence and some people who are obviously very clever haven't got it. It's about being quick to learn, change, adapt and it's about having good self-awareness . . . and good interpersonal skills.

This was echoed by another experienced teacher:

It's a particular type of intelligence. I had a very bright trainee in the department, academically outstanding, fantastic subject knowledge. But just seemed completely unable to learn when it came to dealing with the kids. In multiple intelligence terms, it's having the intrapersonal skills, knowing and understanding yourself.

(Mentor)

The idea of 'the reflective practitioner' has been influential in teacher education and development in recent years (see, for example, Schon, 1983; Elliott, 1993;

Loughran, 1996; Moore, 2004). The idea that teachers who were able to learn from reflecting on their experience were likely to develop higher levels than non-reflective practitioners was a prevalent strand in many responses, with frequent reference to qualities such as self-awareness and the ability to learn from mistakes. An example of such testimony is given in this extract from a teacher educator:

> The word that trainees most use at interview when asked about which teachers are good at getting a relaxed and calm working atmosphere in the classroom is 'respect' but they are sometimes a bit vague about exactly what it is that gets teachers that respect. This is where genuine 'reflective practice' can help them ... if they really wrestle with their experiences and observations to think what gives some teachers more 'respect' than others.

With its emphasis on teachers' own evaluation of their teaching, reflective practice offers the seductive idea that teaching can be improved by thinking about things. But as Boler (1999: 196–8) points out, 'self-reflection in and of itself may result in no measurable change or good, to others or oneself'. The other facet of intelligence that was thought to be helpful by experienced teachers was that some sort of action would be triggered by reflection:

> Just being honest, open and sincere can make up for lots of weaknesses in particular strands of the Standards as long as they go on to try and do something positive as a response to a problem. Sometimes the evaluation of the lesson says something like 'must try to be firmer with this group next time' but it's just words, nothing changes.
>
> (Head of department)

> Sometimes, they nod sagely, as if they have taken the point you are trying to make on board, they are agreeing with you, but they don't seem capable of making changes to the way they do things ... They can see the idea, the theory, but they can't put it into practice, they can't change the way they are.
>
> (Mentor)

This brings us back to the issue of how people cope with 'conscious incompetence'. It is one thing for beginning teachers to sense that there is a weakness in their teaching persona. Probably most teachers know, at some level, that there are bits of the job that they are not good at. It is another matter to be able to address those weaknesses by changing yourself as a person, to change how you deal with problems. Labbett (1996) cites Stenhouse's idea of 'principles of procedure' as a construct for helping teachers to change their approach to dealing with problems. Rather than approaching something in a way that has become 'ingrained', a conscious effort is made to pursue an alternative course of action. An example of a principle of procedure is given in Box 2.3. Often such principles of procedure address an area of acknowledged personal weakness: 'Can I change this, am I capable of working on this weakness and doing something about it?' Although such processes are often very difficult and can cause a degree of angst, they are also potentially powerful learning experiences – the idea that people can work on their weaknesses and change how they handle challenges in the area of managing classrooms is a potentially liberating

---

Box 2.3 A 'principle of procedure' relating to class management

'After a lesson where one or more pupils have tried to disrupt the lesson, rather than forgetting about it and doing nothing beyond hoping that the lesson will go better next time, I will explore what I might be able to do in the interim period which might discourage pupils from misbehaving in the next lesson.'

---

one. Klemp (1977) argues that such achievements, labelled 'cognitive initiative' can change professionals' perceptions of the degree to which they have control over their working lives, or whether they see themselves as helpless victims of events (for a summary of Klemp's ideas in this area, see also Elliott, 1991: 128–30).

There was a degree of tension here between the idea that people can develop themselves as teachers, and work to address weaknesses, and the idea that teachers must in the last resort 'be themselves' and not attempt to model themselves on other teachers who have fundamentally different abilities and ways of working. Although the ability to learn from experienced colleagues was deemed to be a positive attribute, several respondents mentioned the danger of inexperienced teachers attempting to model themselves on 'heroic' or idiosyncratic colleagues when they did not have the attributes to carry this off successfully:

> When I started I tried to be like X in my class management style but it didn't work, I couldn't be like her ... she's just got a funny sort of way with them ... I just can't do it like that. I felt that my class management was actually getting worse and I started to lose the confidence I had built up in my PGCE year. Then after a couple of years I stopped trying to be like her and doing things her way and I now feel much better and I've got methods that work for me ... I can't quell them at a glance but I can get them under control and I now really enjoy my teaching and I enjoy working here.
>
> (Seven years in teaching, member of Senior Management Team [SMT])

> Our kids hate pretension, and last year they saw through my attempts to be a disciplinarian/Bill Rogers disciple/Mary Poppins and punished me for them. My attempts to copy the techniques of one of our school's experienced veterans backfired completely: 'You're trying to be Miss X and you can't do it,' they told me.
>
> (Second year of teaching)

Common mistakes

In the same way that teachers had clear views about the characteristics of trainees and NQTs who were likely to be successful in establishing good working relations with pupils and managing their classrooms skilfully, there was a degree of consensus about the most common mistakes made by some trainees and NQTs. Box 2.4 gives a list of the mistakes that were mentioned by a number of interviewees, with an accompanying example of teacher testimony.

Box 2.4 Common mistakes

Talking over the pupils
'Some of them don't even seem to make the effort to get them quiet before they start talking, even when it is quite an easy group.'

Not using school and departmental systems
'They don't use the agreed systems which the school has . . . you would think that anyone new to the school, or a student teacher would be extra keen to stick to the rules and do something reasonable which would fall within the parameters of what other members of staff would do . . . the norms, but it doesn't seem to work like that.'

Repeated telling off without action
'Just going on and on at them in a narky, negative and aggressive way, just moaning at them without actually doing anything about it . . . worst of both worlds. It can actually wind up passive kids who were just slumped quietly over their desks.'

Not following things up
'The kids soon work out which trainees just make empty threats . . . "I'm going to tell so and so", "You will do a detention" or whatever, but nothing ever happens.'

Not reading signals from the pupils
'A sort of autism . . . it's as if they are not receiving and decoding the signals coming in from the pupils. Things just aren't registering. They are doing things but with no sense of what the effects are . . . they don't seem to see that what they are doing is making things worse . . . or is even causing the problem.'

Leaving action too late
'Waiting far too long before taking reasonable and appropriate action. By this stage the lesson is often in chaos, there are lots of kids messing around and belated action comes across to them as arbitrary and unfair.'

Just blaming the pupils
'Not considering that it might be you . . . the task you set . . . not doing the right things to set up the work . . . it might have been a poorly planned lesson. They don't stop to think that the same class behaves really well for other teachers and think what it might be what other teachers are doing that makes a difference.'

Using disproportionate sanctions
'Going straight for the thermo-nuclear option without using a yellow caution card or going through the full range of low key options.'

Displaying dislike of pupils
'Some of our pupils are not particularly likeable but they mustn't be treated any differently. You've got to be polite and treat them the same as the other pupils even if they are being really exasperating. You mustn't let your dislike of them show.'

Getting angry, losing composure
'You can learn to stay calm even when things get quite torrid. It just doesn't usually help to shout, get angry or agitated. For some of our pupils, that might be the most enjoyable bit of their day.'

There are different ways of being good at managing classrooms and pupils

Moore (2004) makes the important point that there are different ways of being a good teacher. He elaborates three models in some detail (the competent craftsperson, the reflective practitioner and the charismatic teacher), but there are probably many more than this (perusal of the various 'My best teacher' columns suggests that there are dozens of different ways of being an inspirational and effective teacher).

Teaching assistants are in a particularly good position to appreciate this:

> One of the things about being a TA is that you see such a wide range of teachers dealing with behaviour issues. . . . There are so many different ways of approaching it. There's one teacher . . . I'd love to be able to do it like her. They really like her and she is very softly spoken and nice with them . . . If someone does something wrong she very quietly and discreetly goes up to them and has a quiet word in their ear and they go quiet . . . I have seen more than one pupil burst into tears because they are upset that she is disappointed with them and they do seem to genuinely regret what they have done. I don't really know how she does it and I'm fairly sure I couldn't do it that way, much as I would like to. Another of the teachers uses the school system to the letter, every time. First offence, name on board, just a warning, second incident, name underlined, which means that they miss their break, third time, they have to do after school detention. The kids are not daft . . . after their name goes up, the vast majority of them keep their heads down because they know what will happen. Every time, the same procedure. They know where they stand.

Heads, teachers and teacher educators were all resistant to the idea of a template for effective classroom managers. Mention of particular attributes and characteristics was generally hedged with a range of caveats:

> Difficult . . . there are so many different ways they can be effective at managing pupils and classes, there's no formula.
>
> (Head teacher)

> It's about lots of qualities, it's complex and sometimes surprising. There are Clark Kent and Superman moments sometimes. I've got someone who's quiet and seems slightly timid and lacking in confidence in taught sessions, and then when they are with the kids it's as if they are different people, they are in their element. They find relating to kids easier than relating to adults.
>
> (Teacher educator)

> I look round the staff room at the people who are good at it and there are all sorts . . . there's no template . . . there are lots of teachers with very different temperaments and personalities who have developed a wide repertoire of techniques, routines, scripts, strategies for getting the kids to go along with things. Perhaps one thing that they have in common is that they haven't just carried on doing things that don't work . . . they learn from their mistakes.
>
> (Head of department)

What part can 'theory' play in helping teachers to get better at managing classrooms?

In their first days of planning and teaching lessons, trainees are unlikely to make a beeline for the library to browse through tomes on educational theory at the end of the day. When teachers have only taught a handful of lessons, there is a lot to learn from each classroom encounter. When they have taught scores of lessons, there can be a degree of 'sameness' and repetition to their experiences; lesson evaluations can become a tedious chore rather than a fascinating and insightful analysis of the events of the day. As the course progresses, and as they progress into their NQT year, many trainees realise that there may be limits to what they can learn from their own experience and working with a small group of teachers in a particular school. Reading and talking about managing classrooms outside the school they are working in can provide exposure to ideas that they have not come across. Is there nothing that has been written in the history of education that might not be of some use and relevance in developing expertise in this area?

Some trainees can be dismissive of education 'theory', particularly in the early stages of the course. In a sense 'theory' just means 'ideas' about things that might work and that have been tried. There is something arrogant and closed-minded about trainees thinking that there is nothing that they can learn from the experience and wisdom of others. It can be just as harmful for trainees (or politicians) to go to the other extreme and look for simple solutions and 'what works' precepts from the literature and research on managing classrooms. Calderhead (1994: 63) points out that 'teachers' knowledge is not held in the form of action recipes for typical situations – "this is what you do in X type situation"'.

Stenhouse (1975) saw the purpose of educational research as for teachers to test out ideas against their own experience. He saw it as important that teachers were open-minded, prepared to experiment, to reflect on what worked and what didn't and to refine teaching approaches accordingly – to do their own research. Much of the testimony of head teachers and experienced teachers suggested that 'open-mindedness' and a willingness to keep learning and take new ideas on board was one of the characteristics of teachers who were good at managing classrooms (see below). Teaching is a practical activity and beginning teachers may well learn most from their own experience, but getting better at managing classrooms is an incremental process, and engaging with ideas from outside their own experience, from reading, from the internet, from seminars, from Teachers' TV, from in-service courses can complement wisdom gained from direct experience. Many of the trainees interviewed could recall particular instances of such ideas from reading, seminars or lectures, which they had found helpful, and which they considered to have had an impact on their practice. It is interesting to note that many of the ideas which had been thought to have a positive impact were about learning rather than strategies for control:

> The guy who said ... was it Bruner? I can't remember ... that the best way to get good behaviour was to get the pupils interested. It might seem obvious but that had a big influence on the way I thought about class management.
>
> (NQT)

> Models of learning are important. I don't mean that you have to read the whole of Piaget but there are now some books about learning and things on the internet

which give you helpful ideas about how to structure tasks and order activities. Belle Wallace's TASC [Thinking in an Active Social Context] stuff (Wallace *et al.*, 2004) is fantastic, I'm really trying lots of the ideas out and it's working really well. The quality of the kids' work ... the outcomes ... is transformed ... they can tell that ... so they are enthusiastic about trying things out.

(Advanced skills teacher)

A book about thinking skills (Fisher, 2000) ... it transformed my approach to planning. It makes them think and provides a challenge for them but one which is accessible, which they can have a go at and it doesn't matter if they get it wrong. It's improved their work and their behaviour and I've got a clearer idea about what I'm trying to achieve now, and about how to get less able pupils working and involved and making progress.

(Advanced skills teacher)

At first I was a bit sniffy about all this learning styles stuff. It was 'the latest thing', the fashion ... and then I started trying out kinaesthetic stuff in my classroom and found the kids loved it ... they remembered things much better when we did things in a more active way. For 20-odd years I'd not really thought to use the classroom, to let them move about a bit, to do human continuum exercises, to go to different bits of the room according to their opinion about things. I suspect some teachers don't try it because it's one of those things that's counter-intuitive. They are better behaved if they can stretch their legs now and then and move around ... do something ... especially the boys. Plus it gives you the weapon that if they do start messing around we'll go back to the text book, the written work.

(29 years in teaching)

Several teachers mentioned the work of Bill Rogers (see, for example, Rogers, 1990, 1997, 2002), which seems to have been particularly influential on teachers' thinking about managing pupil behaviour:

I remember the Bill Rogers thing about dealing with the things you can control, not the things that you can't control. I try really hard to keep calm, even when provoked, I try hard not to let it get to me. You can make a mental effort not to get angry or upset or exasperated and that has helped me.

(NQT)

One of the main things I learned from Bill Rogers ... when to let something go ... with swearing ... whether it was directed at me and other kids heard or whether it was just pupils talking in the vernacular. His idea about 'secondary behaviour' ... I now realise that I didn't need to make a big scene about some things, I should have let them go and got on with the lesson. It's not just about how strict you are, there are judgement calls. You can be pedantic and make things worse.

(NQT)

I wish I'd known about Bill Rogers when I started teaching. The things he says just ring true and make a huge amount of sense. For instance, the 'act as if ...' aura ... say something as if you just assume it's going to happen. I sometimes see trainees at the other end of the spectrum, whose whole body language is screaming at kids

'Even as I say this I don't believe you're going to comply with what I say' ... it's all bluster.

(Teacher educator)

Although reading and 'theory' may not have the same impact on practice as powerful learning experiences in classrooms, particularly in the early stages of teaching, as with the trainees, many of the teachers interviewed could remember something that they had come across in their reading, or in seminars and lecture halls, which had influenced their practice in managing their classrooms. Reading is one of the ways in which teachers can improve their practice, but this is only likely to happen if it is linked to reflection and action.

'You must tell them ... It gets better ... it gets easier'

It was apparent from research conducted in 2002 (Haydn, 2002), and a follow-up survey in 2004 that in their early experiences in classrooms, the majority of trainees encounter a wide range of levels on the 10-point scale (see Chapter 7). The interviews conducted for this book corroborated these findings and suggested that nearly all trainees and NQTs have to work with at least some teaching groups that are not fully under their control. Many of them were, however, keen to stress that even within their first year of teaching, things improved substantially. This was described partly in terms of not experiencing the lower levels on the scale:

In my training year I would sometimes be at levels 3 and 4 of the scale, this year things probably haven't gone lower than level 6 in the classroom. It's in the corridors where you get the real hassle.

(NQT)

Certainly in my first year I had lots of classes which were frequently in the level 5–6 category, but it is so much easier in your second year. The balance of your easy and difficult classes changes. Now I've just got a couple of groups that I've got to be on the ball with. With all the others I feel quite relaxed and in control now and it's a great feeling when you just go in and teach and almost don't have to think about control issues. I love the job now, I am just so glad I went into it.

(Second year of teaching)

I had several classes in my first year that I dreaded teaching so much. This year, in the classroom things are pretty much ok, the kids are mostly on task, discipline is sorted. This year the trouble has been on the corridors and doing cover lessons with kids you don't know.

(Second year of teaching)

Others described classes that were improving but not 'trouble free', and talked about how they had learned to cope more successfully with challenging groups:

Everyone told me that it would get better with time and I didn't really believe them, but it has, things are out of all recognition better this term. You've just got to hang on in there and keep trying, and after a distressingly long time lag, it starts to get better.

(NQT in challenging school)

It's much better than at the start of the year. The early weeks were really difficult, it's a much harder school than the ones I did my teaching placement at and lots of people advised me not to take the job. Things still aren't perfect ... it's absolutely exhausting, you never have a quiet day, it's a struggle to get the kids to do the work and behave but things are getting much better now and I'm starting to really enjoy it.

(NQT in challenging school)

I've got a tough year 10 group but they just get used to you after a while and almost leave you alone. These kids would have destroyed me last year when I was on teaching placement. Just things like knowing their names helps.

(NQT in challenging school)

I had three kids burst into my room the other day, trying to drag a kid out with them. One of them swore at me viciously for about 5 minutes, in front of the class ... a really nice year 8 class. It was quite difficult to keep calm. I don't think I would have managed it in my first year, but I did this time.

(Second year of teaching in a challenging school)

You've got to tell them how much easier it is in your second year ... it's miles better when you know the kids, when you've started afresh with some new classes and you realise how much better you've got. It's still a constant struggle at this school but I've only had one incident this year when I've just wanted to run out.

(Second year of teaching in a challenging school)

Learning to manage pupil behaviour is a complex and challenging skill. It is unlikely to be acquired in a matter of weeks or as a result of receiving a few 'handy hints'. Nor is the implementation of a few sharp new policies likely to render this an unproblematic area. It is important that experienced teachers working with trainees and NQTs emphasise that it takes time and patience to become accomplished in this facet of teaching; that if you persevere and are open to learning, things get better, and that it is very rewarding when you do become good at getting pupils to behave well.

'Can they learn?'

Becoming accomplished at classroom management was seen to be less about performance skills, presence, sense of humour and personality than application, perseverance and intelligence, in the sense of being 'a good learner', 'quick to pick things up from others', 'learns from mistakes'. It is not about how much experience teachers have had, or how much they have read about managing classrooms, it is about the degree to which they are able to draw on their experience and their reading to 'test' elements of both in developing their practice. It is partly about developing their 'situational understanding' of what is going on in the classroom (Klemp, 1977), and partly about their ability to take intelligent action on the basis of their enhanced understanding (Elliott, 1991). In the language of the 02/02 Standards for QTS (DfES/TTA, 2002), the most pertinent Standard relating to class management was not to be found in the section on class management but in the section on professional values and practice:

1.7 They are able to improve their own teaching, by evaluating it, learning from the effective practice of others and from evidence. They are motivated and able to take an increasing responsibility for their own professional development.

(DfES/TTA, 2002: 6)

SUMMARY

- Although some schools have more difficult pupils than others, teachers and head teachers believe that the class management and teaching skills of individual teachers are important factors in determining classroom climate.

- Teachers and head teachers believe that there are a range of factors that influence teachers' ability to manage learning and pupil behaviour effectively.

- There are different ways of becoming good at managing learning and pupil behaviour: there is no simple model or 'template' for being good at managing pupil behaviour. Experienced teachers and head teachers believed that teachers with a wide range of attributes, dispositions and temperaments were capable of becoming accomplished in this area.

- Experienced teachers were able to identify a range of common mistakes made by inexperienced teachers.

- Exposure to 'ideas' about managing pupil behaviour, through reading, seminars, lectures and discussion with peers can complement gains made through direct teaching experience and observation of experienced teachers.

- Being open-minded and a 'good learner' were thought to be important attributes in getting better at managing pupil behaviour.

3 Planning for learning

> The biggest and most damaging mistakes are those that stem from inappropriate planning. Either there is no plan or the lesson is under prepared and the trainee hasn't put enough work and thought into it.
>
> (Teacher educator)
>
> I'm an experienced teacher and I'm not bad at getting kids to behave by controlling them. But the best way of getting them under control is to get them interested and engaged ... to show them something that they would like to be able to do or to learn and then give them the chance to do it with a reasonable chance of success.
>
> (Experienced teacher)

The primacy of planning

When asked what had most helped them to improve their management of classrooms, the majority of respondents cited things that related to steps that they had taken before going into the lesson, rather than 'tips' and techniques for controlling pupils within the lesson. As Wragg (1997: 44) noted, 'the trouble with the "bag of tricks" approach to discipline is that it addresses symptoms rather than causes': sometimes, poor pupil behaviour is a response to the quality of the learning experience that is being provided in the lesson. Differentiation is often thought of as something that teachers do, but pupils also differentiate, and one manifestation of this is poor behaviour when the purposes, structure, resources and activities in a lesson are weak, inappropriate or badly thought through. The majority of pupils behave better when the teacher comes into the lesson equipped with a well-prepared lesson. As one teacher educator remarked:

> You can't do this job without realising that there is a definite correlation between the quality of the planning for the lesson and what will happen in it in terms of the pupils' attitude and behaviour. In most schools, I can usually tell by looking at the lesson plan how well things will go. . . . Skilful interaction with pupils can help, a sense of humour can be useful, a cheerful, lively approach, yes ... but all of these things are just palliatives if lesson after lesson, the basic product, the lesson that has been put together by the teacher is basically poor.

A teacher who had previously taught at a difficult school 'in special measures' and moved to a top independent school talked about the discipline problems in the latter when planning had been neglected:

> Even at our place, pupils will mess teachers around if they are unprepared or aren't on top of their subject. Clever pupils can be disruptive in subtle ways and can be very accomplished in the way they do it. It helps if you have good subject knowledge of what you are teaching, and you have a clear plan for the lesson, even if that plan is just in your head. If you are not prepared, if you haven't got a plan or if you are having a real off day, our pupils will play up and can be quite difficult.

The importance of planning is emphasised in much of the literature on behaviour management that goes beyond the 'handy hints' approach. Blandford (1998: 76) makes the point that the curriculum which teachers present to pupils should be 'challenging, rewarding and appropriate to pupils' age, ability and intellectual development'. Given that many classes are of mixed ability, this is a formidable requirement, and it clearly takes time before teachers are able to consistently achieve these aims. There will be very few teachers who have reached expert levels in their planning for pupil learning in all aspects of their subject by the end of their first year in teaching.

There is also the importance of medium- and long-term planning (Burden, 2003). For understandable reasons, in their first few weeks of teaching, trainees tend to plan for one lesson at a time. If they do not move beyond that, there is a danger that pupils will get a routine and limited 'diet' of learning activities, and the trainee may well find that they fail to develop a wide range of pedagogical approaches, which can be the key to surviving and prospering in the longer term.

The importance of subject knowledge

Recent research into effective teaching has stressed the importance of teachers possessing sound subject knowledge. If teachers do not have greater knowledge and understanding of a topic than that which can be gleaned from the text book, pupils will quickly lose confidence in them. In a survey of 708 pupils in Norfolk secondary schools, 'knows their subject really well' emerged as the teacher characteristic that most pupils regarded as being 'very important' in having a positive influence on their attitude to learning (see http://www.uea.ac.uk/~m242/nasc/cross/cman/overallchar. htm).

Subject knowledge is sometimes thought of as being solely or primarily about teachers 'knowing their stuff', in terms of substantive subject content knowledge (knows all about Henry VIII, quadratic equations, volcanoes or whatever). However, as the 02/02 Standards made clear, substantive subject content knowledge is only one component of teachers' subject knowledge (DfES/TTA, 2002: 7–8). Another important facet of subject knowledge is what Shulman and others have termed 'pedagogic subject knowledge' (see, for example, Shulman, 1987; McNamara, 1991; Bennett, 1993). Such research suggests that there is a close relationship between teachers' pedagogic subject knowledge and the quality of pupils' learning experiences. This is a broader concept than simply having a sound grasp of the topic being taught and includes such things as being able to teach the topic in a way that makes sense to pupils, to think of worthwhile and appropriate tasks, to be able to answer pupils' questions in a helpful way, and to have an understanding of pupils' misconceptions and difficulties with the topic or concept.

Another important aspect of subject knowledge is that the teacher has a clear grasp of why their subject is helpful to young people. An assistant head talked of a likeable and conscientious trainee who was struggling with class management:

> He's a nice guy ... sincere, likeable, gets on well with the kids on a one-to-one basis but his lessons just don't interest them ... he doesn't seem to know why he is teaching this subject to classes, either overall, or with reference to particular topics. It makes you realise how important subject knowledge is. If the teacher isn't clear about why he is teaching something ...

This problem was also evident in the refreshingly honest but worrying extract from an evaluation which a trainee had written in her teaching file: 'I have no idea why I am teaching this.' If the grown-ups aren't clear about why they are teaching something, what hope is there that the pupils will commit to learning it? Pupils do not routinely ask why they are doing a particular topic or piece of work, but it can be good discipline in terms of planning for the teacher to have considered this question before putting together their lesson.

It is also obviously important that teachers can convey an enthusiasm for their subject; they must 'believe in their product'. In interviews for places on my PGCE course, when asked about their memories of the best teachers from their own school experience, 'enthusiasm for their subject' was perhaps the most common response. Pupils' attitudes to subjects are often conditioned by the teachers they have for the subject (Elliott *et al.*, 2001; Zamorski and Haydn, 2002; QCA, 2006). How the subject is planned and delivered by individual teachers will have a major impact on pupils' attitudes to learning in that subject.

But it is not just about teachers knowing why they are teaching a subject and being enthusiastic about it. Pedagogic subject knowledge is also being able to teach a subject in a way that 'makes sense' to pupils.

Lawlor (1989) is critical of teachers pandering to the idea of 'relevance' in their teaching, and yet pupil testimony suggests that pupil attitudes to learning are improved when they have some idea of why they are studying something (see Box 3.1).

This is particularly important for those who teach subjects which have no direct vocational relevance to pupils. Research by Adey and Biddulph revealed that of over 1,400 year 9 pupils, only a handful appeared to be able to give 'mature' and valid reasons for the value of studying history and geography, and that for the vast majority of pupils, 'their understanding of the relative usefulness of both history and geography in their future lives is limited to direct and naïve reference to forms of employment' (Adey and Biddulph, 2001: 439). The problem of pupils not having a clue why they are learning particular subjects is not limited to history and geography. Box 3.1 gives some examples of pupil responses to a question that asked them to identify the subject in which they made least effort to learn and why (see http://www.uea.ac.uk/~m242/nasc/cross/cman/leasteffort.htm for full details of pupil responses).

Many pupils in secondary schools in the UK are not driven scholars, passionate to learn, do well, 'come top'. They will not run sobbing to the toilets if told that

---

Box 3.1 'In what subject do you make the least effort to learn and why?'

'I don't really enjoy R.E., I don't want to be a priest or anything.' (Year 10)

'R.E. Because I do not believe in any religion and I don't want to know what other people believe in.' (Year 9)

'German, I shall never go to Germany, so there's no point in learning it!' (Year 9)

'I make least effort in P.E. because you don't have to do a GCSE in it so I don't really think it's that important. (Year 10)

'Art, because anything can be art.' (Year 9)

'Art, I can't see much point in this subject unless you want to be a artist.' (Year 9)

'English, it is not interesting and we talk about old geezers i.e. Mac Beth.' (*sic*) (Year 10)

'Science, It won't help me later in life.' (Year 8)

'History, I don't feel knowing about the past is important it's just boring we should be looking into the future.' (Year 9)

(See http://www.uea.ac.uk/~m242/nasc/cross/cman/quest.htm for full details of the survey).

---

they will not do well in their exams. But a lot of them are 'biddable' to the idea of learning if it is presented to them in a skilful and accomplished way, and good subject knowledge, in its broadest sense, is an important prerequisite for this. One head of department made the point that given that many pupils didn't really want to be in the classroom, learning a foreign language, a lot of them were surprisingly well behaved, or at least, passively and discreetly disengaged from learning:

> Given that most pupils have no real interest in learning a language, they are remarkably docile and compliant. They don't often ask what the point of learning French is, they don't storm out or argue or refuse point blank to do any work. They are just resigned, bored . . . perhaps a bit sullen . . . and some of them just do the basic minimum to get by without getting into trouble.

This is not a phenomenon limited to foreign languages. An important part of medium-term planning is working on pupils' attitude to learning.

In their lesson evaluations, trainees often use the phrase 'on task' to describe pupil behaviour, but this is a very general term which gives very little indication of the extent to which pupils are engaged in learning. In terms of understanding classroom climate, there is a much broader range of possibilities than 'on task' or 'not on task'. Desultory compliance is a not uncommon state of affairs in classrooms. There are things more troubling than desultory compliance, but just because pupils are quiet and 'on task' doesn't mean that the situation is satisfactory, there are higher levels to aspire to. It can be salutary for teachers to consider what proportion of the pupils in a class are genuinely trying their best to learn what they are trying to teach.

One of the characteristics of teachers who are accomplished at managing learning in their classrooms is that they have a clear grasp of the full breadth of benefits that their subject can bestow on their pupils, *and* an ability to transmit an appreciation of those benefits to their pupils. It is a way of avoiding the 'So what?' and 'What has this got to do with my life?' questions that are often in pupils' minds when they sit in classrooms, and it can have a transformative impact on pupils' attitudes towards learning a school subject. It has become fashionable to write aims and objectives on the board at the start of lessons, but this is not quite the same thing as persuading pupils that the general enterprise of learning French, history or whatever, is going to be a worthwhile and stimulating project that will be of use to them in a range of ways in their lives after school. The research of Adey and Biddulph (2001) suggests that teachers should give more time and thought to getting across to pupils *why* they are doing a particular school subject. When asked why he thought the government thought that pupils should learn history at school, one pupil responded, 'They don't let you know' (for further details of the survey, see http://www.qca.org.uk/15923.html).

Box 3.2 'Not all pupils are driven scholars'

Box 3.3 'Many pupils have an "instrumental" view of education'

Making it interesting?

To what lengths should teachers go to try to make their lessons interesting and *in what ways* should they try to make lessons interesting? These might seem ingenuous questions. Surely, teachers are always striving to make their lessons interesting, they are not worried that lessons might be *too* interesting, or that pupils have found the past few lessons *too* enjoyable.

Yet for many experienced teachers, there is a tension between planning rigorous, purposeful learning experiences into lessons, and planning into the lesson some components where the primary aim is to engage the interest of pupils, to grab their attention, to have some activity or interlude that is enjoyable, 'a bit of fun', which might impact positively on pupils' attitude to the subject, and to being in the classroom. The importance of paying some heed to the need to engage pupils in learning and get them to commit to the aims and objectives of the lesson have been acknowledged in recent DfES Key Stage 3 Strategy resources, in particular the use of 'starters', designed to 'develop early levels of engagement and motivation . . . help to get all pupils quickly on task and to inject a sense of pace and challenge . . . create an expectation that pupils will think and participate in the lesson' (DfES, 2004: 7.3). Ofsted (Office for Standards in Education) recommendations on managing pupil behaviour also acknowledge the importance of 'using curriculum flexibility to capture pupils' interests' and note that when the curriculum is limited and differentiation lacking 'there is a high level of poor behaviour, and pupils' interest, motivation and involvement decline' (Ofsted, 2005b: 13). Some recent research has suggested that in schools where students are motivated by an intrinsic desire to learn and achieve, formal systems of rewards and penalties may be redundant (Shreeve and Boddington, 2002). Elliott (1998: 25) goes as far as to suggest that 'all meaningful learning in relation to content involves students coming to see the content as intrinsically interesting'.

The desirability of engaging pupils in learning seems a relatively uncontentious proposal, but, in practice, it creates difficult tensions for teachers. Is engagement achieved at the expense of 'dumbing down', eschewing the challenge of 'real' learning, wasting pupils' time on meretricious and facile activities that have no intrinsic educational value . . . colouring in exercises, 'draw a picture of . . .', 'copy this diagram . . .' 'do this word search'?

Lawlor (1989: 68) argues the case against these forms of 'appeasement' in the struggle to get pupils to learn:

> Teaching should not be a form of salesmanship; and pupils will not necessarily learn through games and puzzles, or without hard work and conscious effort. Very many things in life – at school and in later life – including the acquisition of knowledge, require effort and concentration. Unless pupils are trained to concentrate and make the effort necessary to master knowledge, they will suffer in two ways: They will not necessarily master the required information and they will not become trained to cope with the demands of adult life.

Although it might be argued that Lawlor works at some distance from the realities of life in secondary classrooms, might there not be a degree of truth in her argument? In the course of giving talks about class management to trainees, I have asked if any of them can remember being given tasks to do as pupils which were pointless and which were fairly obviously designed to 'pass the time', or to 'get their heads down', 'keep them quiet'. On each occasion, almost every hand went up. (Although it was 41 years ago, I still remember being asked to draw a Roman vase in a history lesson and thinking that it was a fairly pointless thing to do.)

Secondary pupils have a degree of discernment about the value of the tasks that they are given, particularly as they make their way though the school. They will have encountered a number of 'settling' activities designed to quieten them down, and 'this will pass the time' activities where teachers have not been able to think of high-quality learning experiences. They do generally enjoy lessons that contain some elements of fun and enjoyment – light hearted video extracts, recap 'games' such as 'Blockbusters' or 'Who wants to be a 20p-aire?' (QCA (Qualifications and Curriculum Authority), 2006) but if it is overdone, if it becomes apparent that the teacher is just desperately looking for things for pupils to do until the bell goes, the law of diminishing returns will apply. Some teachers are able to gain the respect of their pupils largely through the quality of their pedagogic subject knowledge, and do not need to 'blend in' low-value components to sustain pupil engagement. One NQT talked admiringly of an experienced teacher who was able to do this, while acknowledging that not all teachers were able to achieve control in this way:

> He has fantastic control in the classroom. He doesn't believe in doing light-hearted, fun things, he doesn't go to any effort to make it relevant, topical. He makes it absolutely clear that they are here to learn. Although this seems an austere message, the pupils really like being in his classes. They like the fact that he is very strict

and in control. No one ever gets punished in his lesson because no one would dream of misbehaving. Also no time is wasted by kids messing about, there are no chaotic or messy bits to the lesson, the kids can see that he is a really good, effective teacher, that they are learning and that they will do well in the subject. Another member of the department is good but in a completely different way ... he is a fantastic planner, he has hundreds of great ideas for pupil activities and for structuring lessons effectively and there are lots of 'fun' bits in the lesson. You learn from experienced colleagues even if you can't replicate exactly what it is that they do, even if you can't do it like them.

The teachers who were interviewed had differing views about the ways in which teachers might try to engage pupils in learning but, overwhelmingly, they believed that planning needed to consider how to persuade the pupils to engage in learning:

> There are sometimes quite small things that you can do that will make a difference to their general attitude to being in your classroom. Just making them feel welcome as they come in, having something that might interest them or at least make them feel that you are doing your best ... that you are aware that it can be dull for them, that you care about what it's like for them.
>
> (Head of department)

> Anyone who just plans around control is on to a loser. Really thinking hard about making at least some bit of the lesson ... preferably at the start of the lesson ... interesting ... Making the kids feel they are achieving, persuading them that what you are doing together is worthwhile ... then you are in with a fighting chance. Doesn't mean that you won't get some kids trying to spoil the lesson and you'll have to use your control skills as well. If there's nothing for them to do or think about then more of them will start messing about.
>
> (Teacher educator)

> These days you have just got to try and make it interesting for them, to get some sliver of entertainment into the lesson no matter what subject you teach. They expect it and some teachers are good at it. You are up against it if there are never any bits of your lessons where you can have a bit of a laugh with them, or show them something interesting. If you try and do it through just cowing them, being severe, threatening them ... they might be quiet but it will be a surly, resentful quiet, there won't be a nice climate in the room. Better than getting slaughtered but not what you want in the longer term.
>
> (Head of department)

In her teaching file, one trainee formulated what might be termed a 'principle of procedure' (see Chapter 2) relating to her planning of lessons:

> I must make a conscious effort in every lesson to provide a good opener in the form of a hook to try and capture their interest. This will hopefully get at least some of the class interested and wanting to give the lesson a chance. I have found that when I adopt this approach to lessons, I nearly always have a successful lesson. I would therefore like to make this an integral part of all the lessons I plan.

It would be misleading to think that such an approach guarantees success. There are some teaching groups which have substantial numbers of pupils with problems, who may not give the lesson a chance however good the starter activity. However, it seems reasonable to suggest that this 'principle of procedure' might make a difference with some teaching groups. It might be stating the obvious to suggest that teachers should try to make at least some elements of their lessons interesting to pupils, but several heads of department felt that this was not apparent in the planning of some NQTs and trainees, and that some were much quicker than others to grasp the idea that when preparing a lesson, it would be helpful to give some thought to the nature and disposition of the 'audience'.

It was not felt to be necessarily about injecting 'fun' components into the lesson. One experienced teacher educator felt that some trainees were better than others at conveying to pupils the importance of what they would be doing in the lesson:

> They have a sort of intelligent serious thoughtfulness, they treat the topic they are doing as important and this seriousness can get through to the pupils ... we're doing something important and worthwhile here.

Teachers had different views about how to get their pupils to want to learn, but given the nature of the pupils they taught, they nearly all felt that it was an important consideration in planning. In the words of one teacher: 'Even with exam classes, you must not assume that they are all keen to learn and do well, to work to the best of their ability. Part of your job is to get them to want to do that.' In a lecture on differentiation, Professor Susan Hallam (1996) made the point that whereas differentiation is sometimes seen as a technical matter, of formulating tasks that provide the appropriate level of access and challenge for all pupils, what made the biggest difference in terms of how well pupils of all abilities performed was whether they were motivated to learn; whether they were interested. In her words: 'They must want to learn. If you lose that, you lose just about everything.'

A possible principle of procedure relating to planning?
Every lesson should have something ... just one bit of it ... which is interesting or enjoyable

(Head teacher)

The use of 'high-value' and 'low-value' activities

Heafford (1990) makes a useful distinction between high- and low-value activities in the classroom. In terms of language teaching, examples of 'low-value' activities would be word searches, copying from the board, reading round the class and light hearted games and quizzes. Dialogue in the target language, reading silently, vocabulary acquisition and 'doing written work of an error-avoiding nature' were cited as activities with high learning value. Teachers of other subjects would not find it difficult to find parallels for their own subject. (There is, of course, a distinction between 'low-value', and 'pointless'.)

This raises the question of why teachers don't always use high-value activities, the ones where 'the real learning' takes place. It is important to stress that there are many high-value activities that motivate and engage pupils, and low-value activities that bore pupils. High-challenge/'low-stakes' activities are often seen as being helpful in this respect, where pupils are asked to do something quite difficult, but assessment of their efforts is relaxed and informal; it's not a 'big deal' if mistakes are made. But most teachers sometimes use low-value activities at some point in their teaching.

First, teachers need to take account of their pupils. They need to have a sense of 'audience'. Not all learners can take unremitting, sustained high-value activities that require intense concentration (not even at undergraduate level, never mind disaffected year 9s). In the words of one head of department:

> They are not learning machines. Some of them don't really want to be in your classroom and haven't got any great desire to do well in your subject. But a lot of them can be lured into learning. There is almost like a 'credit' system . . . so that if they've had a bit of fun, a bit of a laugh, something interesting, then they will accept doing something that is hard work, that is not low-level stuff.

Another head of department talked of a good trainee who had not taken this on board:

> We had one trainee who was excellent . . . very bright, conscientious, good ideas. I'm sure he will have become a really good teacher. . . . But every single minute of every lesson was focused on things to get them through the exam. This might sound great . . . just what parents want. But the kids hated him and were resentful . . . reluctant to work for him . . . the homeworks went off, they would work under protest. Even sixth formers need a bit of thought to be devoted to interest and engagement, never mind year 10s.

A key skill in planning is the skilful interplay of high- and low-value activities so that pupil motivation and enthusiasm is maintained, while still ensuring that a large proportion of the lesson is focused on genuine gains in learning. Experienced teachers are often able to use low-value activities adroitly, in a way that quickly leads into high-value activity.

A second reason for using low-value activities is that it takes time to develop wide ranging, expert levels of pedagogic subject knowledge, to be able to teach every aspect of one's subject in a powerful and effective way. It can take years to amass a comprehensive archive of knowledge, ideas and activities that results in a formidable armoury of high-value 'scripts' and activities for every domain of a subject. While these archives are being developed, teachers need to develop 'coping' strategies, where lower-value activities are 'blended in' until more sophisticated, powerful learning experiences are available.

A third reason for teachers using low-value activities is that there are some that are 'low value', in terms of the learning gains made by pupils, but which in terms of 'task design' are helpful in terms of 'settling' pupils (MacLennan, 1987). Hence, trainees on first placement are likely to resort to low-value activities more than experienced teachers. I have come across history trainees who have been tempted to use questionably long extracts from 'Blackadder' to get through the lesson, together with copying paragraphs from the board, reading round the class and a range of 'fill in the missing word' exercises. This is understandable for trainees in the early stages of their first school placement. Much of first placement is about trainees becoming comfortable in the classroom, being able to teach from the front of the class, developing their skills of exposition and questioning, learning how to interact skilfully with pupils, how to plan and deliver a basic lesson, how to survive in the classroom. If they were able to be honest in their stated aims and objectives for their first lessons, 'to survive until the bell without anything bad happening' might feature prominently. Although the need for recourse to low-value activities is particularly acute for trainees and NQTs, there are also many classes where even experienced and effective teachers have to factor such strategies into their planning (see Chapter 7).

The use of word searches is an interesting example of such tasks and seems to divide teacher opinion – some regarding it as a legitimate and worthwhile activity, others regarding it as of questionable value ('Would you want *your* kid doing word searches?', in the words of one respondent). Reading round the class is another teaching approach that polarises opinion, with some teachers regarding it as a perfectly respectable activity, and others having a fairly low opinion of it as a teaching strategy. In terms of pupils' views about reading round the class, in one recent survey, the majority of Key Stage 3 pupils regarded reading round the class as neither useful nor enjoyable (QCA, 2006). Copying work was regarded by many teachers as a necessary evil or last resort, but one that could be helpful for novices in the classroom, until they found more appropriate strategies for settling classes. It is interesting to note that MacLennan (1987: 195) identified copying work as a strategy which, while superficially 'settling' pupils in the sense of giving them something to do, actually generates restlessness on the part of pupils as it is boring, unpopular and does not engage pupils' minds.

There is also a danger that trainees might construe differentiation as being primarily about providing access to learning. Failure to provide an appropriate degree of challenge for pupils was felt to be another weakness in some trainees' planning:

> Our pupils are quite streetwise ... they are aware when they are being given child-minding stuff. They resent it and feel patronised when an activity is patently designed to just pass the time until the bell goes.
>
> (Head of department)

Skill in terms of 'task design' was felt to be helpful in engaging pupils. Particularly where trainees could think up activities that were challenging *and* enjoyable (as a pupil once said 'We had a lot of fun but it was hard fun': quoted in Walker, 2001).

Several teachers stressed the importance of what they termed 'active' learning as a means of engaging pupils, with 'active' being interpreted at a mental rather than physical level:

> If you just transmit information, and the pupils are passive for large bits of the lesson, either just listening to the teacher or copying things out, you will have more problems with class management than if they are doing active learning, if you have

given them a real task that has a clear purpose that they can understand ... the sort of task a grown up might do ... Once they get into trying to solve or do whatever it is ... they stop thinking about messing about.

(Experienced head of department)

Planning should also ensure that there is some mechanism for making it clear to all pupils that they *have* learned something from being in the lesson. One department used a model for planning which suggested that all lessons should have at least three components: a starter to engage pupils, some form of active learning where pupils explore a particular question, and some form of 'construction of meaning', where an attempt is made to draw out what has been learned. The Key Stage 3 Strategy also stresses the importance of making learning outcomes explicit through the effective use of plenaries at the end of lessons (DfES, 2002a). Several trainees and NQTs said that they had found Battersby's (1997) idea of 'The Golden Nugget' helpful for giving a sense of purpose to lessons.[1]

The danger is that trainees and NQTs who are experiencing difficulty controlling their classes might be tempted to resort to activities which are 'low-value' in terms of learning outcomes, *and* which pupils regard as tedious and pointless:

At the start of the placement, I tell them that getting the pupils to copy a paragraph from the board can be a way of settling them down, but my heart sinks when I see them doing this lesson after lesson. There are lots of ways of settling pupils down and getting them started ... getting them into the learning.

(Head of department)

With all of this, the ones who think and use teaching strategies ... who are aware of and who use behaviour management strategies in order to get pupils to learn, not to behave ... so not just doing things that are deadly boring and which cut off opportunities to get the pupils into some worthwhile form of learning at some level.

(Teacher educator)

The 'pure' path to pupil engagement comes from making subject matter challenging, getting pupils to think, to engage with difficulty, to focus on achievement and 'real' learning. Ideally, it is for pupils to experience the profound pleasure that can come from learning, from getting better at something, and being able to do something that they couldn't do before (Csikszentmihalyi, 1997; Desforges, 2004). But if the teacher's pedagogic skills are unable to render the topic intellectually fascinating to pupils, it may be the lesser evil to try to keep the interest of pupils by less elevated means, than to 'lose them' by refusing to compromise on high-value approaches.

For understandable reasons, there will be a temptation for teachers' thinking about planning to be dominated by control issues when they are having a torrid time with a particular class, but teachers who keep trying to come up with something that might get pupils to want to learn are more likely to find a way forward. Hopefully, teachers will move towards using a higher proportion of high-value activities as their teaching skills and assurance with classes develops, but progress is partly about developing a wide range of both high- and low-value ideas and activities for pupil learning.

Box 3.4 **Factors influencing teacher control of the classroom**

Dozens of factors influence the degree to which pupils will commit to learning in a particular lesson. In one study, it was found that use of the exclusion room after morning break increased for pupils who had travelled long distances to school (see Elliott *et al.*, 2001).

The impact of control concerns on teachers' planning

After their first few lessons with a class, teachers usually have a reasonable idea of the parameters of behaviour that will occur with that class. Although the climate might vary according to the time of day, previous lesson, incidents in the playground and so on, they can generally predict whether behaviour will be likely to be a significant problem in the lesson.

How do teachers change their planning approaches when they have concerns about how pupils will behave? A survey of trainee teachers (Haydn, 2002) showed that there were different philosophies about this. Approximately two-thirds of the trainees reported that they would go for a 'safety first' approach, and rely more on 'settling' type activities (Maclennan, 1987). Box 3.5 gives some examples of their responses.

A smaller number of trainees said that they tried to do something a bit different, to break away from 'safety first' text book/worksheet approaches and take a few risks (see Box 3.6).

In terms of which approach was most successful, there was no clear relationship between 'taking a chance', and better behaviour. In some cases trainees reported that

---

Box 3.5 Adjustments to planning because of concerns about pupil behaviour: 'settling' activities

'I look for video extracts that they will watch quietly or slump over the desk and doss quietly. Generally, this avoids the potential for confrontations and refusals.'

'I give them a passage to summarise, they have to read it then get a summary into their exercise books. It gets me through a bit of the lesson.'

'Reading round the class. It's not ideal but it doesn't cause trouble.'

'I think up or find diagrams that they have to draw. A lot of them think this is ok compared to written work. At least some of them will get on with it quietly and they can all do it. There is no excuse for not working.'

'Lots of written work.'

'Get their heads down, give them things to do, answering questions from the text book, structured worksheets.'

'Project work. Some of them will get on with it and chat quietly, some will hardly do anything and chat with their mates but it's easier than talking to the whole class and trying to do question and answer when you can't stop them talking.'

'Keep away from discussion type activities.'

'Do not use drama, roleplay etc.'

'Group work impossible.'

'Copying a paragraph from the board, copying work or fill in the missing word comprehension exercises.'

---

it had worked well, in others it had made things worse, or had to be abandoned. Obviously, success is determined partly by the skill with which more expansive approaches are executed, but context – the nature of the group, the culture of the school – also has a bearing on outcomes.

Some of the experienced teachers interviewed talked about the same dilemma, between trying to do something that would get pupils interested and be a bit of a change, and less adventurous 'keep their heads down' approaches. In some cases, adventurousness and risk-taking did lead to real improvements in relations with teaching groups. One NQT talked of his decision to get his year 10 group to make a revision DVD:

> I'd not done it before . . . it was a bit of a risk, can I carry this off? At first quite a lot of the kids were not that bothered, a bit cynical. Gradually they did come on board, a few were really keen and got into it. Now they're all into it. The lessons have obviously been less boring than text book and worksheet, filling in the missing word exercises. The kids who aren't much good at written work were particularly keen. One pupil who finds written work really hard and has never really tried in

---

Box 3.6 Adjustments to planning because of concerns about pupil behaviour: 'stirring' activities

'I tried working with the video camera, getting them to do TV broadcasts.'

'I tried going to the ICT room to do stuff on the computers.'

'I attempted some roleplays with them.'

'I made a conscious attempt to get away from text book and worksheet type lessons.'

'I tried to do more oral work with them, more group work, debates about things.'

'I tried to go through the whole of Friday afternoon without doing any written work with them.'

'I experimented a bit with using the classroom more, getting them to move around into different groups according to what they felt about things . . . continuum exercises.'

---

my subject now comes up to me and asks me to ask him anything that's in the DVD. It has transformed their attitude to the subject. Kids from other groups ask if they can contribute. I've got writing teams, props teams, production teams. It's not the product, it's the process. I have tried really hard to find things that might interest the pupils but this is the best thing I have done. Class management is no longer an issue, every lesson is level 10, it's not me versus them or some of them, we're all working towards the same thing.

(NQT)

An experienced head of department working at a school in 'special measures' talked of eventual improvements in pupils' attitudes to learning after moving towards less 'containment' based activities:

In a way, you might as well take risks and try something a bit different like a role-play or something because they couldn't behave any worse anyway so there's nothing much to lose. The first few weeks were really difficult but they are much better now and I feel that I can do most things with them.

However, it would be misleading to suggest that more expansive and adventurous teaching approaches 'solved' the problem of pupil behaviour. As with the trainees, teachers had differing views about the degree to which it was possible to adopt more expansive teaching approaches with groups where control was limited:

I tried doing some active, slightly risky stuff with them but it didn't work, they wouldn't or couldn't stop themselves, give it a chance, so I had to resort to text book, written work, video extracts, get them writing, give them tasks, steer clear of exposition and questioning. With my other classes I really try hard to do interesting, enjoyable things with them, but I just couldn't make it work with these two groups . . . Just hope that some would just get on with it quietly and try and contain the rest. It's not ideal I know, but it's about the art of the possible. What is the best I can do for all the pupils in this class given that I am not in complete control?

(NQT)

It depends on the class. I've got two GCSE classes and with one I've constantly got to watch them, I'm a bit on edge, I've got to be careful and not take too many risks, or if I do, stop things promptly if they start to go awry . . . it's a pity because they sometimes miss out on things that might actually make it enjoyable for them if they gave it a chance, but you've to be pragmatic. With the other class I'll go for things and do some roleplay and debating . . . you get to a stage with a class where you can start to relax in a good way and there's just a good feel to the atmosphere.

(Second year of teaching)

'What works' in terms of planning to cope with difficult pupil behaviour emerges (like most things in teaching) as context-dependent. Variables include the teacher's skill in planning and executing more adventurous teaching approaches, the degree of difficulty of the teaching group and the effectiveness of departmental and whole-school arrangements for dealing with difficult pupil behaviour. There were, however, some areas of consensus about planning for working with difficult groups. One was that teachers should at least explore the possibilities of extending their teaching repertoire to include more expansive approaches, to test the boundaries of what might be possible with particular groups of pupils:

I do understand if they [trainees] try something and it doesn't work and they retreat, at least for the moment . . . with that particular class, to something a bit safer. But if they are not prepared to at least experiment . . . to go beyond the comfort zone, even with their easier classes . . . that sets alarm bells ringing.

(Mentor)

They [trainees] should at least be prepared to 'have a go'. When did kids last come out of a lesson saying 'Those questions on page 27 of the text book were great'?
(Teacher educator)

Experienced teachers were more likely to consider having a 'Plan A' and a 'Plan B' to allow for contingencies of pupil behaviour. This often involved having an initial intention of trying to allow for pupil talk, group working, drama and roleplay, pupil presentations and pupil movement within the classroom in the form of 'kinaesthetic' learning approaches, but having the 'fallback' position of more structured work if the class did not respond appropriately:

Some trainees stick to the lesson plan with grim determination even when it's clear that something isn't working . . . you've lost them, a component of the lesson isn't working . . . you need a Plan B . . . do something else.

(Experienced teacher)

We do try to almost strike a deal with them ... you'll have a good time in the lesson and enjoy it if you work, you'll get to do stuff, we can have a bit of fun if you know how far you can go ... when to stop. But you've got to be prepared to follow this up if Plan A isn't working, and you have to have something reasonable to do for Plan B ... preferably not just copying out the text book.

(Second year of teaching)

You hope that when you warn the pupils that if they don't calm down, the fun work will stop, the good kids in the class will exhort the ones who are messing about to stop. We know that they don't like worksheets and written work. Sometimes the threat works, sometimes it doesn't, but you must carry it out and you must have something planned for them to do as an alternative.

(Head of department)

Most kids, even in this school, are rational human beings. If you offer them something that is a bit different, or 'back to working from the text book' they will choose the pleasanter option. Having said that, we have some teaching groups who are exceptionally difficult and who will not give things a chance so you sometimes have to resort to crowd control type work, just trying to keep the lid on things.

(Head of department in a challenging school)

Experienced teachers had also had much more time to develop a range of 'intermediate' levels of activity which fell some way between the ambitious and the mundane. They were at pains to emphasise that it was not necessarily a question of ambitious 'all singing, all dancing' spectaculars, but of judicious use of activities that went beyond defensive and over-used teaching approaches. Pair work was mentioned by several teachers as an under-used technique, as in the following instance:

I learned that pair work was easier and less risky than larger group work ... they don't generally need to move about but it gives you the chance to give them something to do that is a bit more active, a bit different, a change from just more text book stuff, another worksheet. Also ... smaller groups are easier than bigger groups, and I learned to structure the work more so that they had a chart or table to fill in, note decisions and so on.

(Third year in teaching)

Experienced teachers pointed out that the teaching approach that was most revealing of a teacher's lack of control over a class was whole-class teaching from the front of the class, based on exposition and questioning. Group work and project work sometimes enabled trainees with limited control to at least work with some of the pupils in the class, and to strike tacit bargains with disaffected pupils by agreeing a basic minimum of work that would be deemed acceptable. But they also believed that this was at best, a temporary 'coping' strategy, and that at some point, trainees had to take on the challenge of teaching from the front of the class.

Initiative in developing a range of teaching approaches

By some way the most common 'planning' factor that teachers mentioned to differentiate between trainees who struggled to cope and those who tended to do well was initiative in developing a range of different ideas for things to do in lessons. One of the most difficult aspects of starting to teach is that generally, trainees have only a limited idea of the range of teaching approaches and activities that can be used in teaching. This predicament was described by an NQT, who also outlines the move towards realising the breadth of ideas that are publicly available to teachers:

> When you start, you haven't got many ideas about what you can do in terms of 'things to do in a classroom'.... You can use the text book, have reading round the class, worksheets ... showing them a video, talk to them, give them writing tasks, do a newspaper front page. It's fairly basic and dull repertoire and the kids probably have quite a bit if this stuff in other lessons. It wasn't until later in the course that I realised that there are hundreds of different activities you can do in a classroom, using the space in the room, pair work, dozens of different things with group work, continuum exercises, participation stuff with whiteboards, card sorts, getting the pupils doing things for themselves in terms of presentations, composition, competitions, quizzes, stuff from the net. The net in particular is a fantastic resource for teachers ... there are lots of websites where teachers share good ideas about how to vary what you do in the classroom.

Experienced teachers stressed the importance of planning a range of different learning experiences for pupils:

> a bit of variety, a bit of active learning, not sinking into the cul de sac of worksheets, writing from the text book ... anything that gets them out of doing things that they are probably doing far too much of in other people's lessons.
>
> (Head of department)

> There are hundreds of ideas for 'starters' out there and the good ones [trainees] have a degree of initiative and imagination about finding out about them and trying them out. It's partly about resourcefulness. You don't have to be brilliantly creative yourself and keep coming up with good ideas of your own. You can just be proactive in getting hold of other people's good ideas, by reading, taking things in, using the net intelligently.
>
> (Head of department)

> Above all, do things differently, build up as big a range of activities and bits and pieces, props, pictures as you can so that they wonder what they will be doing today. Some things won't work out, will flop, but anything is better than boring them to death.
>
> (Teacher educator)

> The ones that are good at it often do something eye catching or interesting at the start of a lesson which gets at least some of the pupils interested. They seem to be able to consistently come up with something that the pupils will engage with.
>
> (Teacher educator)

> Just doing something different at or near the start of the lesson, read a poem, show them part of a picture and ask them to guess what it is, blow a table tennis ball

round with a hair dryer ... ask them what happens when you freeze cotton wool, show them and talk about a newspaper article, ask about something that was on TV the previous night, use something from the net. Whisper something to them. Don't make every lesson a three-part lesson. Sometimes start with an activity not an introduction, don't lapse into a dull and safe routine.

(Teacher educator)

Key Stage 3 Strategy materials were regarded as a good source of ideas for developing the foundations of a reasonable range of teaching approaches, but teacher educators in particular were concerned that trainees should not limit themselves to strategy-based approaches:

Some of them are paralysed by QCA schemes of work which are rarely exciting or inspiring for pupils. They are locked into setting formulaic and dull objectives and scared of letting the children experiment a bit, play around with ideas, see what happens.

They've got trapped into strategy approaches. It's not that there aren't some good ideas in the strategies but teachers shouldn't be tyrannised by them. Sometimes you don't have a plenary at the end. Sometimes you don't assess the learning outcomes, or at least not formally. Assessment can often get in the way of learning if it's not done in the right way. Sometimes the children get turned off learning because of the teacher's obsession with having to assess things.

The idea that you always do anything in teaching is a real turn off for kids, whether it is writing the objectives on the board at the start of the lesson, having a plenary at the end, having a three-part lesson ... just doing something new or different can make a difference to how the pupils respond to your lessons.

In their final weeks of training, when there is a tendency towards 'plateauing' in performance, trainees might think about the extent to which they have developed a wide range of teaching approaches. Are you going to complete the course as a teacher who is well-equipped to cope with the NQT year, or one who has only a limited repertoire? (see Box 3.7).

Initiative with resources

Some trainees and NQTs were thought to be more proactive than others in looking out for resources that might help to make at least part of some lessons interesting. Although it was generally accepted that in the early stages of placement, trainees would be, to some extent, dependent on departmental resources, this went alongside the view that as soon as possible, trainees should start developing their own ideas for lessons, and should be always on the look out for materials to augment departmental resources. This might be in the form of artefacts, posters, quotations, pictures, cartoons, video extracts or newspaper articles, but some form of initiative and 'drive' in this area was thought to be desirable. Trainees, themselves, stressed how much easier it was to 'get through' lessons when you had built up a stock of materials and activities that helped to make a topic interesting to pupils, a process that Walsh

Box 3.7 The importance of developing a range of teaching approaches

'Are you going to complete the course as a teacher who is well-equipped to cope with the NQT year, or one who has only a limited repertoire?'

(2003) describes as 'building up learning packages'. Several trainees and NQTs pointed to the internet as a key source for building up collections of resources designed to engage pupils in learning:

> A lot of it is about being proactive with resources, not just relying on what is in the stock cupboard. The internet has more than quadrupled my stock of ideas for what activities I can do in my lessons.
>
> (NQT)

> It's hard when you start because you haven't got a vast stack of ideas about what sort of tasks to give them. This is where the internet is fantastic ... it's got hundreds of ideas for things to do ... they don't all work but at least it gets you trying out different things. I now know quite a few sites where there are a high percentage of activities that work, and which they enjoy. Some of them are just a quick bit of fun, idiosyncratic, not particularly relevant to the key concept you are trying to get across, but at least it gets across to the kids that you have made an effort to think about them.
>
> (Second year of teaching)

> You've also got to look at the sort of work pupils are getting ... you look at what's going on in terms of differentiation ... what sort of activities they are being asked

to do. Perhaps we're overdoing source work and they need more active, joining in stuff. Learning styles has become one of the new buzzwords and some staff are a bit cynical but we've found it does make a difference. I have been surprised how much doing some kinaesthetic stuff changes the behaviour of the boys.

(Head of department in difficult school)

Several recent studies have revealed that pupils often do not enjoy working from text books and worksheets (see for instance, Adey and Biddulph, 2001; QCA, 2006). Initiative with resources, and, in particular, skilful use of the internet, can provide access to materials that have a powerful impact on learners, and which help teachers to put across learning objectives in a vivid, memorable and effective way (for further development of the idea of 'impact' learning, see http://educationforum.ipbhost.com/index.php?showtopic=3355). Such initiative also provides a way of escaping from overdependence on text books and worksheets.

The effective use of new technology

Whereas a decade ago, many teachers were quite sceptical about the ability of new technology to improve teaching and learning in classrooms (NCET (National Council for Educational Technology), 1994; Summers and Easdown, 1996; DfEE, 1998a), in recent years, increasing numbers of teachers have become more positive about the potential of new technology for engaging pupils in learning (see, for example, DfES, 2002b). This was reflected in the comments of many of the teachers interviewed. A selection of comments which give an indication of some of the ways in which new technology might make it easier for teachers to manage classrooms is given in Box 3.8.

The use of ICT is not unproblematic, nor does it guarantee pupil engagement in learning. Even ICT enthusiasts acknowledged that there was an investment of time needed to use ICT effectively, which had to be balanced against competing priorities. In one school, pupils had drawn up a petition to the head, protesting about teachers' use of PowerPoint (is there anyone reading this who has not at some point been bored rigid by a PowerPoint presentation?). What several respondents emphasised was the importance of planning how to use ICT in a way that made learning more attractive to pupils:

I had a difficult year 8 group, low ability, lots of disaffected kids ... and then we moved into a new room with data projector and whiteboard. The attitude of the kids changed as soon as we walked into the room but it was only sustained because I worked out lots of ways to use whole-class projection facilities and net access to get them interested. Some teachers just use PowerPoint as an OHP [overhead projector] ... you can hear the kids sigh as teachers start the presentation ... loads of text, shoving information down kids' throats ... pupils entirely passive.

(Six years in teaching)

Pupils have complained about PowerPoint. New technology isn't a magic bullet. Teachers still have to think how to use it to get kids to think, to be active, to join in, to answer questions, to discuss things with each other. It's now a big dividing line in the school ... whether teachers can use ICT to engage pupils and get them involved ... or not.

(Head of department)

Box 3.8 Using new technology to engage pupils in learning

NQT in a challenging school

'The projector has made it so much easier to integrate bits and pieces, clips, interesting things from the net. Even if you've just got one or two things like this for a lesson, and they only last a few minutes, it helps break things up into manageable bits, it sees you on through towards the bell, towards the finishing line.'

NQT

'The whiteboard has been really useful; apart from the range of extra ideas for activities and things that you can get the kids to do, just in terms of having something to focus on when they come in to the lesson – a picture for them to look at, a cartoon, a scanned in newspaper headline from the Sunday Sport . . . it helps you to get the lesson started straight away.'

Experienced teacher

'Things like doing a roleplay . . . when there's a camera there, they take it more seriously . . . they care about how it looks, it brings the performer out in lots of cases . . . plus, they have to be a bit careful what they do if there is a camera about.'

Five years in teaching

'We've used a wide range of different applications, from bits of fun at the start and end of lessons – millionaire, blockbusters, to webquests, Quandary, Hot Potatoes, Captivate, Flash. It has transformed pupil attitudes to our subject, take up and results have improved, there is much less disruption in lessons in this department now.'

Five years in teaching

'We launched a revision website with a lot of publicity within the school; posters, t shirts, music. We built games into bits of the site to entice them onto it . . . loads of the kids use it.'

Head of department

'We've developed a wide range of things using ICT which have either helped to sharpen up the learning and make it more effective or just to engage and motivate the pupils. If you don't use ICT nowadays, you are missing out on something which has massive potential to change kids' attitudes to school.'

Experienced teacher

'I did some basic digital video editing with a not particularly well motivated group. Once I had modelled what it was they would be working on . . . showed them the film . . . showed them how to put their own titles, commentary and soundtrack on it . . . they enjoyed working out how to do it. Some of them came up with good ideas . . . most of them worked out how to do the basics by asking the others. By the end of the lesson, most of them had made their own film of the event in question. The main discipline problem I had was how to get them out of the room at the end of the lesson because a lot of them wanted to carry on with what they were doing.'

Planning for poor pupil behaviour

For all the emphasis in this chapter on the importance of trying to engage pupils in learning, it must be remembered that there are two agendas relating to classroom climate: engagement and control. In most schools, planning needs to take account of both these agendas. The extent to which pupils find at least some part of the lessons interesting, enjoyable, important or relevant is an important factor influencing pupil behaviour. But teachers can walk into the classroom with the best lesson in the world and there may still be some pupils who will try to mess about and spoil it. Some teachers appear to be better than others at keeping in mind both agendas. When asked what were the characteristics of trainees who were good at planning for learning, an experienced mentor replied:

> There's a sort of balance ... before coming into the room they have thought about how to discourage some kids from messing around, but they have also thought about having something that the class just might get interested in ... there is some 'offering' that at least acknowledges that there is a need to get the pupils interested in the topic.

As noted earlier in this chapter, after teaching a class for a few weeks, poor pupil behaviour rarely comes as a complete surprise. Teachers generally have an inkling of when learning may be jeopardised by disruption, and their planning needs to take account of this. Although they should not betray these negative feelings when starting a lesson, there are pragmatic steps which they can take 'just in case' it is a bad day with 9Z on a Friday afternoon. This can vary between simply getting to the classroom early and getting all the resources ready for a quick, efficient start, to asking where a senior colleague will be if a pupil is so disruptive that they have to be removed from the class. Box 3.9 gives some examples of teachers' 'contingency planning' for poor pupil behaviour. Some of the suggestions may seem to be stating the obvious, but mentors and heads of department suggested that not all trainees made sensible preparations for the possibility of poor pupil behaviour.

Box 3.9 Contingency planning for poor behaviour

NQT

'I've got a class last thing in the afternoon and early in the morning and I've realised that I have to have a different approach to these two lessons. I can't just plan as if time of day makes no difference to what can be done in the lesson. I build in more activities for them to do and rely less on my exposition and questioning if it's the afternoon lesson.'

NQT in a challenging school

'First and foremost, planning ... making sure I've got something for the more able ones and something for the pupils who can hardly read. With my most difficult class, I have to be one step ahead, I always try to get to the class first, and have things on the board or ready to give out, or on their desks as they come in. The planning is more structured, I've probably got several activities planned so I've got some options.'

Experienced teacher
'Always try and plan something into the lesson that everyone in the class can do
... so that there is no excuse for them not getting on with it ... drawing up a
simple table which is to be filled in, or doing some colour coding according to
what they think about something.'

Head of department
'You adjust your planning. As well as asking where people will be if you want to
send someone out to them, and trying to be well prepared, in the room before
them, equipment all ready, you think about how you just might get at least some
of the pupils interested by having a good 'starter' activity, and some activity for
pupils that is accessible, that they can all have a go at, but that is not just copying
or something that is transparently designed to just keep them occupied.'

Teacher educator
'Trying to build a few phases or activities into the lesson so that there is some
'pace' to the lesson ... they are not asked to do something for 25 minutes when
it is obvious that after 10 minutes, some of them will be going off task and have
had enough of it. Having one or two 'extra' activities planned so that you have
something in reserve just in case they get through everything quicker than you
thought.'

Head of year
They don't all think ahead ... with some classes, they might well have a hunch
about possible trouble and might have planned ahead about what steps to take.
Like, 'I'm having trouble with X, would it be ok to send him out if he is really
spoiling the lesson for others and I can't stop him without sending him out, where
will you be if I have to send X out ... where should I send him?'

Teacher educator
'Constructive anticipation ... as against just dreading the forthcoming lesson but
not doing anything to plan for contingencies. Some trainees have mentally worked
out what resources they have at their disposal if there are potential problems
from a class or a particular pupil or group of pupils ... in terms of carefully
ordered steps to take before using sanctions, using the school or departmental
system, using colleagues in the department ... and what to do if it's not possible
or convenient to send pupils out ... they think through how they will cope when
they are not in complete control ... how they will just keep going and focus on
the kids who might want to learn as far as possible.'

Second year of teaching in a difficult school
'I had several classes in my first year that I dreaded teaching so much. I planned
lots of different activities, lots of short tasks so if one bombed or didn't
work ... or if kids said they'd finished after 30 seconds ... I had a plan B and a
plan C. I also planned 'backup' for what I would do if any of the usual suspects
started.'

The quality of teachers' planning has a big impact on the learning climate in classrooms. Planning for learning when many pupils are not keen to learn is obviously a very complex and difficult skill to develop, and it probably takes years rather than months to attain the highest levels of expertise in this facet of teaching, but experienced teachers were clear that some teachers managed to get to higher levels much more quickly than others. Mentors believed that some trainees experienced problems in the early stages of their placement because they had underestimated the amount of time and thought that needed to go into lesson planning. A key step to making progress is to realise what a big difference effective planning can make to pupil behaviour.

SUMMARY

- It was felt that trainees and NQTs had a tendency to underestimate the part that the quality of planning for learning before the start of the lesson had on classroom climate and pupil behaviour.

- Experienced teachers and pupils reported that teachers' subject knowledge and ability to transmit to pupils the value of studying particular school subjects were factors which influenced pupils' response to being in classrooms, learning school subjects.

- Pupils' attitude to learning was felt to have an important influence on behaviour and classroom climate.

- There are difficult tensions to manage in terms of the ways in which and the lengths to which teachers should go in trying to make lessons interesting and enjoyable for pupils.

- It is helpful for new teachers to develop an understanding of the interplay of 'high-value' and 'low-value' activities in the classroom and of the ways in which the deployment of a range of 'stirring' and 'settling' activities can help to promote positive pupil behaviour.

- It is important to understand the effect that concerns about pupil behaviour can have on planning for learning and to acknowledge the possible tensions between planning for control and planning for learning.

- It is helpful for new teachers to develop a wide range of teaching approaches to avoid over-reliance on defensive control strategies which, if over-used, impact negatively on pupil motivation.

- Initiative with resources and in exploring the potential of new technology to enhance teaching and learning were felt to be helpful medium-term strategies for improving classroom climate and pupils' attitude towards learning.

Note

1 Battersby's idea of the 'Golden Nugget' is that in every lesson, the teacher tries to identify one particular thing that all the class will learn in the course of the lesson that they did not know before the lesson, they make this objective explicit to pupils in the course of the lesson, and check at the end of the lesson how many pupils can remember what the 'Golden Nugget' was for the lesson, and how many of them have learned it.

4 Managing learning in classrooms

> A punishment should never come as a surprise to a pupil. It should be apparent to them and to everyone in the room that it is coming. They shouldn't be able to say, 'Well, that came out of the blue, I'd no idea the teacher was going to do that.'
>
> (Teacher educator)

What is control for?

It might be helpful to clarify exactly what we are looking for in terms of the working atmosphere in the classroom. The statements of politicians in this area suggest that control *in itself* is 'a good thing' (see Box 4.1 for some examples).

There is already a considerable amount of disaffection and disengagement from learning in British schools (Elliott *et al.*, 2001; Elliott and Zamorski, 2002; Ofsted, 2005b); the idea of turning schools into boot camps to improve things is a fanciful one. The complete elimination of disruption is not a realistic aim unless the 'rules of engagement' are changed in a way that goes substantially beyond what has been suggested in recent legislation.

Teachers' views on control were more instrumental, rather than regarding control as an end in itself. They wanted to have enough control to teach in whatever way they wanted, and for pupils to be able to learn without some spoiling the learning of others. It should not be necessary to get pupils working silently in rows of desks in order to maintain control of the classroom; ideally, teachers can work in much more expansive and flexible ways and *still* be in control of proceedings. The word 'relaxed' however, occurred in many teachers' descriptions of what they wanted in terms of control in the classroom, as in these responses:

> Unless you are in control of your classes, you can't enjoy teaching. You want enough control to be able to relax, to feel that you can pretty much do what you want in terms of lesson format, and that you can get them quiet when you want, and they won't talk while you are talking.
>
> (NQT)

> Your teaching actually improves when you are at level 10 because you are at ease and you can think on your feet more clearly, you can come up with better ideas,

---

Box 4.1 Politicians' statements about discipline in schools

'Children sitting quietly in lines of desks' (Party Leader, 'Old style discipline urged for schools', *The Guardian*, 1 January 1994).

'"Oh my God, you'd have them all sitting quietly wouldn't you?", "Well, what's wrong with that?", I say' (MP, Westminster Education Forum, 2006: 7).

'Secondary moderns can be excellent. I visited one where children stand up when an adult walks in' (Party Spokesperson on Education, *The Guardian*, 14 March 2006).

'We will not allow a single child to disrupt the education of children who want to learn' (Party Leader, *Daily Telegraph*, 20 January 2000).

'The ethos of private schools ... good discipline, high standards' (Education Minister, BBC News, 23 October 2005).

---

better exposition and questioning because you've only got one track to think about, not two.

(Second year of teaching)

There were some interesting parallels here with pupils' views on the working atmosphere in the classroom. In what might appear a paradox, pupils expressed a dislike of teachers who were 'strict', but had a clear preference for teachers who were able to keep control of the classroom and stop pupils from spoiling the lesson (see Chapter 5 for further development of this point).

From the teachers' perspective, control is necessary so that they can teach (and enjoy their teaching) and so that pupils can learn, in whatever lesson format the teacher chooses.

How much control do you want?

If you want to be at point (a) on the scale in Box 4.2, you may have gone into the wrong profession (perhaps the armed services ... the prison sector?). There was a consensus among the teachers who were interviewed that it was no longer possible to physically frighten pupils into behaving well by using aggressive behaviour or by threats:

Certainly, shouting doesn't help at all. Kids aren't scared of teachers anymore. When I was at school we were scared of some of our teachers. Now they know that there's nothing you can do to physically intimidate them. You can't do it by anger, force, noise.

(Second year of teaching)

We don't have any sanctions that are available to us that would scare kids into compliance apart from perhaps reporting their behaviour to their parents in some cases.

(Assistant head)

Box 4.2 How much control do you want?

a   Palpable air of fear when you walk into the classroom.

b   When the occasion demands, you can conjure up 'a whiff of fear'.

c   You can get the class completely quiet and attentive by a simple word or gesture.

d   Pupils will not talk while you are talking.

e   You can get the class quiet with a bit of time and effort.

f   The class is 'bubbly' and a bit rowdy, some muttering when you talk but there is no real challenge to your authority.

g   Some pupils will not always immediately do as they are instructed, you have to work hard to get basic compliance with instructions.

h   Some pupils do not comply with your requests, you have to turn a blind eye to some things that are going on in order for the lesson to continue for pupils who might want to learn.

They know their rights, they know that teachers are not allowed to hit them and aggressive, threatening behaviour is generally counter-productive.

(Year head)

For pupils not to talk while the teacher was talking (point D on the scale) was felt to be a key level to aspire to (point C was considered by many teachers to be desirable, but more difficult to achieve):

This is the biggie. Unless you can get them quiet, even if just for five minutes at the beginning to explain the task, your lesson is sunk, you can never really relax and feel that you have reasonable control of the lesson.

(Second year of teaching)

I regard it as a sort of litmus test as to whether things are satisfactory with a class or not. It's a key stage of getting a class to be as you want them in terms of their behaviour.

(NQT)

You need to be at level 9 or 10 to have a satisfactory question and answer interlude with pupils, and that is a very common form of lesson activity. If kids are talking through this, it's not going to work well, you're not really in control of things.

(Head of department)

Whole-class discussion is really hard when you start teaching. It takes time to establish your ground rules and procedures, and some trainees don't work patiently enough to get the pupils accustomed to these over a period of several lessons. But when you can have a relaxed and ordered, under-control discussion with a group, it really opens up a lot of possibilities.

(Teacher educator)

Another facet of 'control' that emerged as important to teachers was that they felt able to undertake a wide range of teaching approaches with a class, and were not limited by considerations of pupil behaviour. There was often an awareness that keeping control was being achieved at the expense of 'real' learning for pupils but some saw this as a necessary compromise or 'lesser evil'.

I just know with one class that I would not take them out of the classroom into any public place because I don't feel confident that I would be fully in control of all members of the group. You know that this is not ideal, and that it is limiting the educational opportunities of some children, but you've got to be pragmatic, you can't risk having disasters.

(Second year of teaching)

You become aware that you start designing lessons around pupils' behaviour. I started giving them things to write down, get in their books. You don't like doing it because you know they're not learning anything, they're not doing anything worthwhile.

(NQT)

> For instance, with some groups, I found that I couldn't turn round and write things on the board. If you turned your back on them for two minutes, they were off ... calling out to each other and messing around. So I stopped using the blackboard.
>
> (Trainee)

> If you were walking round, from outside you might get the impression that perhaps as high a proportion as 70/80 per cent of classes were at levels 9 and 10, perhaps the average would be around 7, 8, 9 ... but inside the rooms you are sometimes aware that these levels are partly achieved by control strategies which limit how much worthwhile learning is going on ... teachers structure lessons so as to 'keep their heads down', and keep them busy. There are perhaps half a dozen teachers who will be struggling at around levels 3 and 4.
>
> (Advanced skills teacher)

Teachers varied in their views about the level at which it was still possible to enjoy one's teaching, and the level at which they felt that the learning of pupils would be adversely affected by lack of control. Less-experienced teachers were more inclined to think that levels 6 and 7 on the 10-point scale were 'ok' from both points of view. Experienced teachers tended to feel that lessons ought to be at levels 8 to 10 from the point of view of both teacher enjoyment and pupil learning, but there were exceptions:

> I think I'm probably different to a lot of my colleagues, I've got very high tolerance levels, perhaps the highest of anyone in the school ... I have very noisy classes ... I think I could be at level 5 and perhaps still be able to enjoy it but I don't think I'm typical. But pupil learning, that's a different matter ... probably around level 7 or perhaps even above that.
>
> (Advanced skills teacher)

Although there were variations in teachers' perceptions of the levels at which pupil learning and teacher job satisfaction were affected, it was possible to identify three important criteria about the degree of control that was felt to be desirable in the classroom (see Box 4.3).

Interview responses indicated that although the overall levels of challenge in the area of pupil behaviour varied significantly between schools, trainees and NQTs would generally encounter many of the same problems whatever school they were working in, in terms of 'day-to-day', low-level disruption of lessons. The most commonly encountered difficulties are presented in Box 4.4.

Although several recent inquiries have stressed that much of the disruption in schools is 'low-level' and is of the sort described in Box 4.4, it would be misleading to suggest that disruption is limited to such minor transgressions in all schools. There were several schools where more serious forms of disruption such as refusal, swearing and aggressive behaviour were not uncommon (see Chapter 7 for further development of this point), but the types of behaviour noted in Box 4.4 were likely to be encountered by the majority of trainees and NQTs. The list is not radically different from those emerging from other studies in this area over the past 20 years (see, for instance, Wragg, 1984; Elton, 1989; *The Teaching Student*, 1994).

Box 4.3 Teachers' ideas about the degree of control desirable in the classroom

- The pupils will generally listen in silence when the teacher is talking.

- The teacher does not feel constrained in terms of what forms of classroom activity he/she can undertake because of class management considerations.

- The amount of learning that takes place in the lesson will not be limited because some pupils are impeding the learning of others.

Although new teachers will generally encounter similar forms of low-level disruption whichever school they are teaching at, the means of dealing successfully with such problems will differ. This is psychologically difficult for teachers in their early experiences of working in classrooms. For understandable reasons they are looking for 'a rule', a standard procedure, 'tell me what to do when X happens'. However attractive this might seem, it is not a realistic way forward, given the complexity of

Box 4.4 The most commonly encountered problems of low-level disruption

• Not being quiet when the teacher is talking.

• Talking or 'messing about' with another pupil or pupils.

• Arriving late to the lesson.

• Not bringing equipment.

• Calling out/shouting across the room.

• Not getting down to work when asked to do so.

• Inappropriate/offensive remarks.

• Not completing homeworks.

schools, classrooms and pupils. One NQT made this point in relation to the system of writing pupils' names up on the board:

> At one of my teaching placement schools the kids would just laugh because they knew there was no system that would back it up at the end of the day, but here it works well in most cases.

As noted in Chapter 2, the 'craft' knowledge of experienced teachers is rarely held in the form of universally applicable prescriptions and most teachers are reluctant to stipulate a specific punishment for particular transgressions, although they are generally happy to suggest 'parameters' for appropriate action, and many of them believe in the patient application of pressure to get pupils into the habit of accepting and complying with particular 'ground rules' (see Box 4.5).

Occasionally, there are gurus of class management who have sufficient confidence to advise specific courses of action and provide exemplar 'scripts' for particular classroom problems, but a glance at Box 4.5 suggests that such prescriptive advice may not be effective in all school contexts. There are classrooms where 'raising an eyebrow' or 'the look' may quell latent disruption, but there is obviously no 'formula' that is guaranteed to work in every instance.

Of what use are precepts, suggestions, general advice and guidance for courses of action in classrooms? 'Don't smile before Christmas', 'Never use sarcasm on children', 'Always avoid confrontations', 'Never let pupils off', and so on. One of the problems here is that there is often conflicting advice; some suggest that teachers should smile and be friendly to pupils from day one (Rutter *et al.*, 1979; Rogers, 1990; Unitt, 1994). Some teachers appear to be able to disregard the precepts and yet it somehow works for them – they often let pupils off, or they are skilfully sarcastic with pupils. Sometimes trainees get conflicting advice from university tutors and the teachers they work with in school. Many teachers said that they found Rogers' (1990) advice on 'tactical ignoring' helpful, with regard to problems such as pupils swearing in class, but were at pains to add that it depended on the circumstances:

Box 4.5 How helpful are prescribed courses of action?

Action	What you should say to the pupil
Arrival late Put pupil's name in a book. On subsequent occasions, parents should be contacted, and possibly the Education Welfare Officer.	'Everyone is allowed one late arrival. You've just had yours. See – your name is in the book.'
Cheek The child has to be taken aside and told plainly that this behaviour is unacceptable.	'Get this straight. In no circumstances are you to be rude or to take the mickey out of adults. If you have a grievance, go to your form tutor. Report back here at 10.30 please.'
Comic behaviour It is as well to make a pre-emptive strike as soon as misplaced humour rears its head	'Tomkins, yes, you. Quite an amusing approach which we will discuss further at break. Meanwhile, back to our beloved decimals.'
Fidgeting Much fidgeting arises from children playing idly, and with bad posture. Start the pen and ruler drill on day one and stick to it.	'Yes, you Shufflebottom. Pen in ledge, ruler behind it, exercise book closed. Now, both the ups – sit up and shut up.'

(Peach, 1988: 18–19)

It's ok to ignore swearing if it is quite possible that the pupils think that you haven't heard it, but if everyone knows that you have, you are in a difficult position when the next kid swears loudly. It's often a judgement call, and you just hope that your percentages get better with experience.

(Third year of teaching)

Whether it is 'focusing on primary behaviours', or 'tactical ignoring' (Rogers, 1990), such advice should be regarded as possible 'principles of procedure' (see Chapter 2), to be tested out against experience. The teachers' advice for dealing with classroom incidents given later in the chapter was often accompanied by caveats, and phrases such as 'this doesn't always work but . . .', or 'with most classes . . .'. In many cases, it was felt to be about teachers finding the right point on a continuum, rather than adopting a particular course of action (see Box 4.6).

The next sections of the chapter address some of the areas that many teachers found difficult in the early stages of their teaching, and explore some of the complexities of the principles of procedure that were sometimes suggested in these areas.

Getting the class quiet

This was one of the most commonly mentioned problems for trainee teachers in particular, and the most common piece of advice from mentors was not to talk over the class, and to wait for the class to be silent and attentive before starting to talk, as with a conductor about to start a piece of music with an orchestra.

Cowley (2002: 22) eloquently makes a case for the power of this approach:

My first discussion with a new class is always about my requirement for silence whenever I address them. I make it clear that I will achieve this no matter what . . . If you work with challenging children, or in a school where behaviour is a big issue, this is not easy. The temptation is to give up at the first hurdle, to talk over them in your desperation to get some work done. But consider the signals you are giving if you talk while they are not listening. The unspoken message is that . . . you don't expect to be listened to.

Cowley goes on to suggest a range of strategies for following up this aim, including waiting for them to be quiet: 'If you have the nerve, call your students' bluff by waiting for them to fall silent. If you are willing to hold out, eventually many classes will become quiet without any further input from you.'

This is, perhaps, a good example of a principle of procedure, to be tested to see if it works or not. One of the standard questions I asked in the interviews with teachers was how they tried to get their classes to be quiet in order to start the lesson. Many of them mentioned the strategy of not starting the lesson until they were quiet. In two cases, teachers reported that it didn't work (after waiting 23 and 40 minutes). In several other cases, teachers questioned whether the time and effort spent waiting could be justified in terms of the teaching time lost:

With my most difficult groups in afternoon periods I still sometimes end up teaching over some talking, I still haven't got the power to get them all quiet for any length of time and the lesson would be too stop-start. . . . I'd waste too much time.

(NQT)

Box 4.6 Teaching styles, some continuums

Discursive or businesslike?
Some pupils like it when the teacher is willing to go off the subject and talk about 'other things', others find it indulgent and irritating. Some research evidence suggests that pupils prefer teachers who are purposeful and focused, where they learn nearly all the time, other research suggests that pupils like teachers where they can have 'a bit of fun' at least some of the time. Much depends of course on how much teachers go off-track, and how skilfully it is done.

Flexible or consistent?
Some teachers can be creatively flexible about how they handle incidents and might even change from lesson to lesson, and be idiosyncratic about using sanctions in a way that pupils like. Others make a virtue of trying to be absolutely consistent over time so that the pupils know absolutely where they stand.

Pedantic or casual?
Some teachers like to line pupils up in twos before they come in to the room, and have them stood behind their desks, with strict rituals about the start and end of lessons – and yet they can somehow make it fun and the pupils enjoy the rituals. Others like to keep rules to a minimum, as long as they can start when they want to, they are not bothered if the pupils chat as they come in. Similarly with registers, some like silence during the register, others are much more relaxed about this.

Friendly or formal?
Some teachers just have a much more informal and friendly style than others. Some pupils like this, others don't like teachers to be too 'chummy'. This can vary between schools and across age ranges.

One mentor suggested that trainee teachers, for understandable reasons, sometimes lacked the confidence to persevere with this strategy long enough for it to work:

> I see some trainees give up just too soon ... they start when the class is still not really quiet and paying attention ... they are nearly there ... if they just said 'We still don't quite have silence ... Gary? Alan ...?' Another minute and they could have had them just so but they just didn't quite have the confidence.
>
> (Third year of teaching)

Several teachers reported that sticking doggedly to not talking until pupils were quiet did work for them, although in several cases this took a considerable amount of time to achieve:

> More than anything, it was just stubbornness and perseverance. Until Christmas, I was continually pointing out that they mustn't talk while I am talking. We have a 5 steps system ... 5 times when your name is on the board for transgressions and

they have to go out. I had to constantly use that system, marking it on the board when kids talked out of turn. It didn't seem to be working and then after Christmas, it started to take effect ... it started to work.

(NQT in a challenging school)

I had one year 8 class, I just couldn't get them quiet. On occasions, the deputy head had to come in to get them to be quiet. After a term of flogging the same rule, lesson after lesson, it has started to work. Even kids coming back into the class from the behaviour unit fall in with it ... they do what the other kids have got used to doing. I'm not saying that they are quiet all the time, or that things are easy, but compared to the first term, it's a transformation.

(NQT)

With a new class I make a conscious effort in the first lesson, the first week, to spend a lot of time and effort very reasonably but firmly and clearly getting across a few key ground rules ... Only two or three, and the biggest one is not talking while I talk. I make it clear that if they talk over me, I will pick that up, that is not ok and there will be a smallish, reasonable sanction applied. The second anyone breaks it, I pick it up. If you can just get this accepted and applied so everyone knows the score from week one ... that it's the norm that you don't talk while I'm talking ... it makes it so much easier and at our place this is achievable with most of the classes if you work really hard at it. It won't work if you have a rules overload ... if there are ten of them (rules) to remember and apply ... you're chewing ... your coat's not off, no turning round, no tapping, if you are going on at them about everything, being mercilessly and gratingly negative ... it won't work. First things first. If you can get them to be quiet while you are talking, that is a really important move.

(Fourth year of teaching)

It's a series of small steps ... I'll wait for quiet. If some are still talking I'll raise my eyebrow and make eye contact, just to give them a signal. Some of them will cotton on and stop talking at that point. I'll thank the ones who are quiet, 'Thank you 7R for being so helpful'. I'll ask one who is still talking, by name, to please stop talking. If they don't stop, I'll point out to them that if they don't stop talking, they'll have to stay behind at the end to see me about it. They know that I will do something at the end of the lesson to inconvenience them in some way. I try and give them every chance to comply. It takes a few moments and a bit of patience but at my school, with most classes and most kids, it works, partly because they're used to this ritual, this way of doing things. I'm aware that it might not work everywhere, or if you didn't know the kids. It takes time to get your routines and rituals established.'

(NQT)

There are a few lucky people with such natural presence and charisma that it only takes them one glare and the students are reduced to silence. Not being one of them, the only thing I've found that works is sheer persistence – stopping every time you're interrupted and making an example of a couple of people early in the year – phone calls to parents and detentions etc.

(Second year of teaching)

With the year 9s it's harder, they haven't internalised it yet so I can't just glance or warn ... I have to stop, praise and thank the ones who are quiet, restate the rules ... send out a yellow caution card message – if it doesn't stop I will have to take some specified action to discourage them.

(Second year of teaching)

You make progress gradually and at different rates with different groups. You need to adjust how you handle things according to how good or bad things are. With some groups, I'm confident enough to stop the lesson if there is someone talking. Pick out a few kids and ask them to be quiet please, politely but confidently, firmly ... ask them by name.

(NQT)

Another teacher talked of the importance of not forcing pupils to be quiet when it wasn't necessary:

'Silence is precious – don't waste it'. A cheesy motto perhaps, but remembering this has really improved my classroom management. Some teachers ask students to line up outside the classroom in silence; I think this is misguided – it penalises the good kids who arrive early. It's also a waste of good silence; why should children be silent if there's nothing interesting to keep quiet for? I make a big fuss about the parts of the lesson where silence is needed – I say something like, 'Now this is the part of the lesson where you are going to have to be quiet for five minutes while I explain what we are going to be doing'. This is particularly important with lower ability groups and groups with lots of ADHD [Attention Deficit Hyperactivity Disorder] kids; they have half a chance of containing their talking if they know how long they have to hold out for. With really tricky groups, I even get one of them to time me – and to add on an extra two minutes when somebody talks.

(Third year of teaching)

One last piece of feedback in this area; a teaching assistant, giving his opinion of how often the strategy of waiting for quiet appeared to work:

What surprised me was how often it worked.... Over 90 per cent of the time ... sometimes more quickly than others ... but not every time.

What conclusions might be drawn from such testimony? That just waiting for pupils to be quiet doesn't always work? That sometimes it doesn't justify the time it wastes? That sometimes teachers don't persevere with it for long enough? That it has to be used in conjunction with other methods to make it work – for example, picking up on pupils who are reluctant to be quiet and punishing them? That the chances of success depend on the school you are working in?

Several teacher educators suggested that one of the differences between trainees who develop towards excellence in this facet of teaching and those who make less progress is partly a question of 'open-mindedness'. Has reading the extracts above made any difference to your views of waiting for silence; will your practice be in any way different as a result of reading the extracts, or will you carry on pretty much as before?

Moving pupils

Another issue that was prominent in discussions about managing classrooms was whether or not moving pupils within the classroom was a useful strategy for limiting interference with pupils' learning, and whether seating plans were a good idea for assisting the teacher's control of the lesson.

As with waiting for pupils to be quiet, there was no clear consensus of opinion over the effectiveness of moving pupils within the class. Even within the same school, it was felt to work better with some classes than others:

> With some classes it works really well . . . brilliant, a really good safety valve. With others they will just shout across the room to each other, it won't make any difference.
>
> (NQT)

> In this school, moving kids generally works. They will generally comply. I've only had refusal to move once. But they don't always behave perfectly once moved . . . often you have to take consequences a step further by sending them out or keeping them behind or putting them in a detention.
>
> (Third year of teaching)

> Sometimes it does work, and it's definitely one of the strategies that trainees should experiment with. Sometimes I would plan where pupils sat so I could have some pupils as 'barriers' between others who they might combust with, but it doesn't work all the time . . . with some groups you will just get the pupils you have separated shouting at each other across the room rather than being able to just talk quietly to their mate in a less disruptive manner.
>
> (Teacher educator who had worked at a school 'in special measures')

At some schools, moving pupils was thought to be of limited value; perhaps a step that had to be gone through on the route to removing someone from the classroom altogether, but a gambit likely to provoke hostility, argument, and possibly refusal:

> It's a hassle to do it . . . you have to at least try it sometimes as one of the steps that might come before sending them out altogether but our kids know their rights and can be quick to get stroppy. The problem is that they often protest against being asked to move and that stretches things out . . . it can take up lesson time as you get dragged into persuading them . . . threatening them.
>
> (NQT)

> Yes, it's one of the sensible stages you go through. It will sometimes stop a group of two or three from getting each other into trouble . . . sometimes they can't stop themselves. Sometimes it works. Sometimes they complain and resist . . . 'move someone else, it's not fair' etc. . . . and it escalates. You've got to be polite, patient and firm . . . not make big deal out of it . . . steer them towards low-level choice . . . give them a way out . . . choice A . . . not big deal, choice B . . . you get in bigger trouble . . . think about it . . . you know it makes sense. Try and keep it light

hearted and low key but once you've asked them to move, do everything you can to get them to do it even if in the last resort you do have to take serious measures at a later stage for the refusal.

(Experienced teacher)

One answer to the problem of wrangles over which pupil should be moved was to move both pupils:

A common problem with moving kids is that the one you move says 'Not fair . . . why me, why not him . . .?', so I move both of them to separate corners of the room. It just speeds things up sometimes, cuts down the potential for bickering and dragging things out. Of course, sometimes you just get both of them complaining. The main thing is that you don't want to get in a protracted argument that stops the lesson from continuing so you've got to sort it quickly whatever you do. You don't want an eight-minute stand-off with other kids observing with interest and some kids who would quite like to get on with learning getting cheesed off. So if you get refusal to move, give them a quick option, this or something more serious . . . consequences, and if they keep it up, impose the detention or whatever it is.

(Experienced teacher)

One tentative hypothesis that might be advanced is that moving pupils would be more likely to work in an unproblematic way in schools with very strong systems for managing pupil behaviour and strong 'consequences' for pupils who might go beyond being moved to being ejected from the room, or who might get in much more trouble for not complying with the request to move immediately (see Chapter 6). The teacher responses chimed with Rogers' (1990) advice about ignoring 'secondary behaviour' (in this case, the moans and whinges about having to move), as long as the primary goal of separating two troublesome individuals was met. The biggest danger appeared to be that if the negotiations over the move were protracted, learning for the whole class would be put on hold, and all the other pupils in the class would have nothing to do other than observe the show, get on with their work quietly, or decide to mess about themselves. There is sometimes a tension between sorting out a problem and maintaining the learning momentum of the lesson. Also, in some cases, insisting on a move led to escalation in the form of refusal to move.

Different tensions arose in the area of seating plans. Several teachers spoke positively of the use of seating plans:

It made a massive difference at the start of my second year. It sent a message . . . you are not in the playground now . . . it's not the messing about chatting to your mates zone, it's the learning zone, we are here to learn and I'm responsible for making this happen on behalf of the group.

(Third year of teaching)

At our place, I've found that seating plans work really well. It's nearly always worked . . . I'm always amazed at how much better it makes things and wonder why I didn't try it before.

(NQT)

> Prevention is better than cure – it's all in the seating plan. If a kid is sitting next to two people that he doesn't like enough to talk to, but doesn't hate enough to wind up, the most interesting thing around should be your lesson.
>
> (Second year of teaching)

However, this was felt to be a strategy that was much easier for established teachers to use, from the start of the year. It was felt to be much harder for trainees who were coming into the class at some point during the year, when it was likely to lead to 'we were here first' resentment, or for NQTs who decided to move towards the use of seating plans half way through the year. In the words of two respondents:

> It's always best when you start straight away with it rather than bringing it in later, then they can get resentful about it rather than just accepting it.
>
> (NQT)

> Seating plans from day one – much easier than bringing it in later as a response to problems.
>
> (Experienced teacher)

There is also the issue of how the seating plan is presented to pupils. Brighouse (2001) makes the case for 'non-provocative' ways of initiating seating plans, planned to coincide with new learning experiences rather than being explicitly imposed to assert control.

Some teachers felt uncomfortable about seating plans for other reasons, which related more to what sort of teacher they wanted to be. As noted earlier in this chapter, there are some continuums in terms of teaching 'style' and one of them is between being controlling and relaxed in approach. The following extracts are examples of teachers explaining why they didn't use seating plans:

> Teachers have different styles and you've got to choose the one you're comfortable with. I usually let them sit in friendship groups and then move them if they mess around ... I let them move back with their mates next lesson, I don't keep them apart ... Sometimes being easy going and relaxed works as long as you do take action appropriately if they do start to go too far ... Our kids respond well to this on the whole.
>
> (Experienced teacher)

> I feel uncomfortable making them sit to a plan. It feels mean and punitive, as if it assumes the worst of pupils, it sends negative messages. Perhaps it's more efficient in a horrible sort of Victorian way but a lot of pupils have little enough fun in school and being able to sit next to your friends as long as you behave doesn't seem a lot to ask. I prefer to have a default position that you can sit where you want as long as you don't mess about.
>
> (Experienced teacher)

Pupils' views on seating plans were unequivocally negative (see Chapter 5): one of the biggest causes of resentment against school and against being in classrooms was not being able to sit with friends.

There is a possible tension here between classrooms as 'democratic spaces', which respect pupil friendships and autonomy, and teachers exercising 'leadership' in the classroom 'for the pupils' own good', and so that they will find it easier to control the lessons. As in so many areas, there is a judgement call to be made here by new teachers, which will depend on school culture (to what extent are pupils used to being told where to sit?), the custom and practice of the preceding teacher in the subject, the personality and educational philosophy of the teacher concerned, the nature of the individual class, and the time of year when the seating plan is imposed. Suggestions for consideration here are that new teachers contemplating imposing a seating plan might ask for advice from teachers who have been *in situ*, and that they might at some point explore both methods of working and see which works best for them.

Sending pupils out

One of the most common dilemmas facing the teachers interviewed (and this applied not just to trainees and NQTs), was what to do when they were not able to prevent one or more pupils from spoiling the working atmosphere in the classroom. In some cases the behaviour involved was extreme (see Chapter 7), and in a sense this made decision making easier, but more often there were difficult decisions to be made about whether a pupil had forfeited the right to stay in the classroom. These decisions were complicated by the fact that schools (and sometimes departments) had different policies for dealing with such difficulties, different 'tolerance levels' for pupil disruption. The nature of the class and the 'pupil culture' within the school (see Chapter 6) can also influence the effectiveness of taking such action against pupils. In some schools, a group of pupils may tacitly or overtly support the pupil being sent out. In other circumstances, pupils may well be on the side of the teacher doing the sending out:

> We are lucky here because generally the kids are glad to get rid of them ... 'Nice one, he's out of the room', I can tell that they are pleased about it, that you've sorted it out, done something.
>
> (NQT)

This was not the only example of other pupils' attitudes influencing decision making about whether to send pupils out. In the following instance, the fact that other pupils were 'onside', and not colluding with a difficult pupil led to a teacher deciding *not* to send the pupil out:

> I couldn't claim that his behaviour had no effect on the quality of the lesson for the other pupils ... but the lesson kept going, the pupils learned something, it wasn't perfect but nearly all the pupils were 'onside', they could see that I was doing my best, trying to be reasonable. They were tacitly on my side even if they couldn't do much to help.
>
> (Four years in teaching, working in a difficult school)

Although to some extent it was often down to the individual teacher's judgement as to whether and in what circumstances to send pupils out, decision making was influenced by school and departmental policy and practice. In some schools, there was an understanding that if a pupil could not be prevented from interfering with the learning of others, even at quite a low level, they should not be allowed to stay in the classroom. In others, teachers were encouraged to regard sending out as a last resort, and even then, to try to get pupils back into the classroom as quickly as possible, after a few minutes 'cooling off' time and a warning about their behaviour.

In some cases, teachers' decisions were influenced by how efficiently school systems worked:

> We're not supposed to put kids out on the corridor. The system is to send them to the 'Remove' room if they are misbehaving to the extent that they are spoiling the learning of others. Someone is supposed to come and get them and take them down. This sounds great but it can take 20 minutes for someone to arrive, and in the meantime you've got to just put up with the kid spoiling your lesson. Sometimes there's no one there or no one comes because whoever is on the Remove room is off or has forgotten. It's made me realise that I just have to get on with it myself. Perhaps it's good because it's made me really think hard about what I can do, how to react, it's made me more self-reliant, but I am jealous of fellow NQTs who've really got a close support network of people in the department.
>
> (NQT)

(One NQT talked wistfully of being on placement at a school where two burly non-teaching staff came at almost instant notice and led troublemakers away to an exclusion room, but this level of service did not appear to be widely available.)

It would be helpful for new teachers if there was a clear set of criteria for when to send pupils out, such as the principle outlined by one head of department:

> If they are disrupting the learning of others ... stopping pupils who would like to learn from doing so, and they don't stop after requests and warnings ... they should go out.

However, while this might be eminently practicable in some schools, in others it was not felt to be feasible:

> There was a timeout room but it was for extreme behaviour ... less extreme things you were supposed to just send them out for a few minutes to calm down, have a quiet word with them just outside so they weren't acting up in front of their friends. Everybody knew that if you sent out every kid who was messing about, the system would be overwhelmed. It was not ideal but you just had to manage things as best you could, in terms of damage limitation. What is the best I can do here given that the situation is dire?
>
> (Second in department in a school in special measures)

These examples underline the importance of teachers having to be flexible, resilient and self-reliant. Part of learning to teach is about how to handle things when the situation is *not* perfect. Given the range of people and factors influencing the quality of life of the trainee or NQT, it would be surprising if all colleagues and all facets of a school were perfect. Several experienced mentors suggested that a degree of 'adaptability', 'quickness to adjust, pick things up' was a helpful quality for new teachers as opposed to those who were 'waiting for the answer lady to come round' (Teacher educator). In the words of another teacher educator:

> It's about their intelligence in ascertaining what the boundaries of acceptable 'normal' behaviour are. It's not just about your values and standards, but the school's, and these vary enormously. In some schools they run a very tight ship and you are expected to send kids out if there is the slightest interference with learning, in others you are expected to cope with quite a lot and keep them in (the class-room). It's the speed with which some trainees tune in to the norms and conventions which operate in particular school contexts. It's about how quick they are to pick things up, to learn and adapt.

In addition to 'health and safety' issues, and violent, aggressive or threatening behaviour, one of the criteria for sending out that was mentioned by many experienced teachers was persistent and 'targeted' disruption, in the sense of behaviour that had the deliberate intention of wrecking the lesson:

> If it's calculated ... if they are quite deliberately trying to sabotage the whole lesson and it's a sustained attack designed to stop learning taking place. Then you have to send them out. ... You can put up with some incidents if it's spontaneous – some of our pupils are very volatile but they are just children, they do have emotions, some of them are genuinely very troubled and they do get upset some-times. We're the adults, we should be able to understand that and if it's just a moment of silliness or lack of control and then they stop and settle down, that's usually ok.
>
> (Fourth year of teaching in a difficult school)

> Is it a one-off incident where you can say 'never mind, see me at the end about it', or a sustained attack on the lesson, a deliberate challenge to your authority which is going to carry on until you do something about it? If it is the latter, you do perhaps move to thinking about getting them out of the lesson if you have tried warning, moving and so on.
>
> (Experienced head of department)

> We have some kids here who find normal classroom behaviour very difficult. They do not have self-discipline, self-control, basic manners. But that is just how they are, they are not cynically trying to spoil your lesson in a premeditated way. You have to try and finesse them into being ok, settling them down, learning to get on with them, cajoling them into getting on with the work. Skilful handling can keep kids in the classroom. Some teachers kick out a lot more than others. Sometimes it's the right thing to do to send a kid out, but you can't just send dozens of kids out on a regular basis. Some corridors are almost like a refugee community during lessons because so many pupils have been sent out.
>
> (Head of year in a difficult school)

> Sometimes it is necessary, it's the right thing to do, not a sign of failure on your part, but unless it's a major atrocity which is ongoing, just for a few minutes, to calm things down, have a quiet word and try and get them back in and settled.
>
> (Head of department in a difficult school)

> It's like raising your voice, you get diminishing returns if you do it too much ... plus if you've already sent one kid out, it doesn't work as well, they're beginning to get strength in numbers – they've got a friend to play with, talk to, discuss how to wind you up some more ... you're building up a little insurgency out there.
>
> (Teacher educator)

Almost without exception, the teachers and heads interviewed felt that there were times when sending pupils out was an appropriate course of action; as a safety valve, to allow for 'cooling off', to assert the teacher's right to teach and to protect the rights of pupils who wanted to learn.

Experienced teachers also had views about *how* to send pupils out. A commonly expressed view was that some trainees and NQTs were too indecisive, 'dithered', warned but did not then act, and often left it too long to send pupils out:

> I had to be on the ball in terms of being clear about picking up the first one to go too far after a clear warning, then a particular person could be dealt with by the department, and the others would quieten down. If you don't pick things up early, and leave it until a few of them have gone beyond what's acceptable, it's much harder because you don't know where to start, it's too widespread, you are being arbitrary and unfair, you've lost it. I've learned to act earlier and more decisively, I don't let it get out of control before taking action.
>
> (NQT)

> I've become more decisive about sending pupils out, I'm more clear in my own mind about when it's necessary, when it's the right thing to do. You tend to be a bit uncertain in your PGCE year. Give them a clear warning or warnings and then go ahead and do it and don't wait too long.
>
> (NQT)

> What kids hate is when there's a lack of consistency, when punishments are arbitrary, when 'it's not fair' and other pupils can see it's not fair.
>
> (Head teacher)

> Some are too timid to intervene. I sometimes ask, 'why didn't you send him out of the classroom?' and they say, 'because you were here'. They see it as losing face, a sign of weakness. They let things slide until lots of kids are messing about and then panic and send someone out without a warning, just pick on someone at random because they have become flustered under pressure.
>
> (Teacher educator)

The majority of respondents advocated a 'low-key', understated tone and manner for asking pupils to go out of the room, rather than angry and declamatory words and gestures:

Don't do it as if it's a big deal ... 'Just wait outside for a minute and I'll come out in a minute when I've just set this task ...'. When they are out, mention the options ... go back in, just get on with things quietly ... that's it, all over, forgotten ... just get on with it quietly.

(Head of department in a difficult school)

I try and do it in a low-key way, not show down at the OK Corral ... 'Can you just wait outside for a minute and I'll pop out and have a word with you in a minute'. Perhaps open the door and then carry on giving some instructions to the rest of the class. And then quietly go up to them if they haven't already gone out and remind them that they've got to go out, I haven't forgotten.

(Third year of teaching)

Another common problem with sending out pupils is that they often seek attention from outside the room; jumping up and down outside the window, pulling faces, tapping on the window, asking if they can come back in yet. 'Tactical ignoring' was the most commonly recommended response to this:

Just send them out for five or ten minutes, so they get bored and want to come back in. And if they are messing about outside, just ignore them, get on with teaching the class, they generally just subside after a few minutes and slump quietly.

(NQT)

Some trainees send them out for too long, forget they are out there and then kids go wandering off. You've got to keep a bit of an eye out if you send them out but not let them know that. Try and be relaxed and calm with the rest of the class and then pop out nonchalantly to have a word with them.

(Head of department)

Whether sending out pupils 'works', whether pupils behave when they are allowed back in, whether they agree to go out or refuse depends on what further steps are available to the teacher, the 'tightness' of the school system for following things up, the degree to which the teacher is prepared to follow up incidents of disruption, and the extent to which parents will be supportive of the school. One interesting question is what happens to a pupil who has had to be sent out of a lesson and then continues to misbehave? Nothing? 'Is that it?', or will 'consequences' follow? And who will take the time and trouble to sort out the consequences; the teacher who has sent the pupil out, or 'the system'? Heads and heads of department both suggested that the teacher who had done the sending out should try to take at least some responsibility for following things up:

Sending pupils out is a possible next step, if moving them within the classroom hasn't worked. Ideally, in a good school or departmental system, there will also be the option of further steps, like sending them to the time out room, or to sit in someone else's classroom. If bad behaviour is repeated in the next lesson, and the one after, something more serious needs to be done, and this may involve parents, year head and so on. But teachers need to be prepared to put in time and effort to following things up, keeping kids in, contacting parents and so on. They shouldn't just pass it on to someone else. It's what happens after the lesson that usually determines whether pupils' behaviour is sorted out.

(Teacher educator)

When you talk to them outside the class, when they are not in front of their friends, explain to them that this is getting serious, it is significant. They can either come back in and keep their head down until the end of the lesson, and that will be the end of it, or there will be serious consequences and their behaviour will be the subject of more serious deliberation ... this could be form teacher, year head, contacting parents. Explain the options to them clearly.

(Head of department)

What refinements might teachers consider making to their practice in the light of these comments? This might depend on the nature of their current practice in this area. They may already tend to send pupils out, if anything, too precipitately, so the suggestion that some teachers wait too long before sending pupils out does not apply to them. But teachers can reflect about how their practice compares to that of other teachers within the same school, and whether they make any of the misjudgements mentioned above. They can experiment to see if adjustments to their usual way of doing things makes a difference, and they can ask other teachers (especially those whose levels on the 10-point scale tend to be high) how they handle the issue of sending pupils out.

Refusal

Sending pupils out was acknowledged to be one of the teacher actions (together with asking pupils to move within the classroom) that might lead to pupil refusal to comply with a teacher's request. The prevalence of pupil refusal obviously varies from school to school. In some schools it rarely occurred, in others it was 'very common'. There was a general consensus among teachers that refusal should be taken very seriously, and was not something that could be just forgotten about or glossed over:

Something must happen to send a message to all the pupils that this is not acceptable. Ideally, it would be that the child is sent home until the parents come in to discuss the matter, or the child is taken out of circulation for a period so that other pupils understand the seriousness of refusal. There is a safety issue here. Who would want to send their kids to a school where the kids routinely don't do as the teachers say?

(Experienced teacher)

Refusal is one of the few things I call for help on; it is suicide to let a class see somebody refusing and getting away with it.

(Second year of teaching)

You can't run a school where the kids can pick and choose whether they do what the teacher says. It's important that something happens if a pupil refuses, that it is seen as very serious and unacceptable. Even if the sanction doesn't 'cure' the problem, doesn't deter the pupil from refusing again at some point, it must be clear

Figure 4.7 Sending pupils out

'It's what happens *after* the lesson that usually determines whether pupils' behaviour is sorted out.'

to the others that there will be serious consequences if they do not do as the teacher tells them.

(Head of department)

One teacher used refusal to take off coats at the start of the lesson (a school policy), to remove uncooperative pupils from the lesson at an early stage:

At the beginning of every lesson, I insist that children take their coats off and put MP3 players away. Some teachers don't bother with this at my school, but for me it's the litmus test of a child's willingness to accept my authority. The chances are that if they won't take their coat off, they won't do anything else I ask either.

> The coat test gives me the excuse I need (after the requisite three warnings) to send any complete refusers to the withdrawal room.
>
> (Second year of teaching)

Although there was a consensus that refusal was very serious, and that some form of serious 'consequences' should unfailingly apply to pupils who refused, teachers did not feel that it was politic to 'use such force as is reasonable' (DfEE (Department for Education and Employment), 1998b: 4) to remove the pupils from the room, especially in the case of a trainee or NQT.

The act allows teachers to 'use such force as is reasonable' if a pupil is committing a criminal offence, injuring themselves or others, or causing damage to property. More pertinent to teachers' day-to-day lives, the act also sanctions teachers to use reasonable force if pupils are 'engaging in any behaviour prejudicial to maintaining good order and discipline at the school or among any of its pupils, whether that behaviour occurs in a classroom during a teaching session or elsewhere' (DfEE, 1998b: 4).

Almost without exception, teachers felt that 'reasonable force' should only be used against pupils in extreme situations, such as if a pupil was endangering the health and safety of others. An intelligent precaution in this area is for teachers to be aware of the school's Health and Safety Policy, and ensure that they act within the parameters of this policy. Most respondents did not feel that force should be used in the case of pupil refusal, and generally felt that teachers should always try to keep 'an appropriate professional distance' between themselves and pupils. Simply reminding the pupil of the seriousness of refusal and trying to point them towards less serious courses of behaviour, and then sending a pupil to a senior member of staff or following the refusal up later if the pupil remained obdurate, were more commonly suggested ways forward:

> Certainly I would never march or frogmarch or drag them out of the classroom ... that seems to me a recipe for escalation. Even if you attempt to 'guide' or steer them out, you are in dodgy territory. Regulations might talk about 'reasonable force' but it is a grey area ... who is going to decide what's reasonable ... what if some other kids' description of what you did or views on what is reasonable differ from yours ... what if there is no other adult in the room as a witness?
>
> (Second year of teaching)

> At our school, the protocol on this is clear; you always try to get another adult present in such circumstances unless there is an urgent safety issue.
>
> (Mentor)

> In this school, refusal is very common. When they have had their warnings, they come to the last one and often refuse to go out. You are then in the hands of the school system. I've learned that you can often deal with it later. If they don't go out, that's their problem, they know that they will be in trouble later because of this and I notice that they often go quiet because they know that they will be in trouble and they have gone too far. I used to spend a lot of time and emotional energy trying to get them to go out, now I just get on with the lesson and move on. There's no 'show' for them all to enjoy, you try and just get on with the learning, not let them have the show they are looking for.
>
> (NQT in a difficult school)

They don't always go out quietly, sometimes they do refuse ... and I'm one of the senior team who go round the school picking kids up and sorting out things like this ... taking them down to the remove room. One kid in my lesson last week just point blank refused to leave the room. So I just said he'd have to do a half hour detention and moved on. It wasn't a perfect solution but it allowed me to move on to something else ... to carry on with the lesson – but you have to make sure that you follow it up – the kid does the detention.

(Head of sixth form)

Even in difficult schools, physical restraint issues were felt to be unusual situations, not day-to-day occurrences, but there was a clear view that using force to control pupils was an absolute last resort:

In our school, there is very little need for physical contact and restraint issues ... I've been in classrooms now for two years some of which was spent in difficult schools and it's never happened ... it's never come to that.

(Second year of teaching)

Physical contact? Do it as little as possible, but the dictum during my training to not touch the children at all isn't realistic. You do sometimes have to break up fights and I have been advised that the next time I do it, I should say to the child 'I am holding your arms because you are putting your safety and the safety of others at risk'. Last time I broke up a fight one of the parents complained, but the HOY [Head of Year] gave her short shrift; I'd expect most schools would support you as long as it was clearly necessary to touch the child.

(Second year of teaching)

In the PGCE year or when I started here I would not have gone near a pupil, not have even thought of it. Now I am established, it's less of an issue, not a big deal but I'm still careful. I might just touch the back of someone's bag and point them in the right direction or signpost them to move in a particular direction, hold my arm out to shepherd them somewhere ... relaxed and low key. It's a judgement issue that comes with knowing the kids you are working with and being comfortable with them.

(Second year of teaching)

Avoid it at all costs ... no, at almost all costs. With all rules there's always an exception. Don't give people a rule and say it's unbreakable. The world of teaching is too complex for that but ... It should be absolutely a last resort, there's usually a way round it. Unless, there's a safety issue ... if a pupil is endangering the safety and well-being of other pupils.

(Teacher educator)

I have done it (been in physical contact with pupils) and have usually regretted it afterwards. It's about being professional, and once you get into that territory, it jeopardises that. You take it into territory where they are more at home than you are, into their world. You need always to be in control of yourself. Once you are in

physical contact with pupils of one sort or another, you are in dangerous and unpredictable waters. Having said that, if pupil safety is involved, you have to step in.

(Teacher educator)

How do teachers cope when they are not in full control of the classroom?

Both the interview responses and the questionnaire surveys (Haydn, 2002) suggested
that many teachers have to teach classes where they do not feel in completely
relaxed and assured control and are not working at levels 9 and 10 of the scale (see
Chapter 1). Many teachers acknowledged that they sometimes had groups where they
did not enjoy their teaching. How did teachers respond to that situation? A variety
of suggestions emerged (see Box 4.8).

Some of the coping strategies were as much philosophical as practical. One strand
of this was remembering that (usually), lots of teachers are finding it difficult to get
to level 10:

> I'd had a bad day and my mentor advised me to just have a walk round the school
> during a lesson when I wasn't teaching. I saw other teachers having a tough time
> and it made me feel a lot better.
>
> (Trainee)

> We do have issues with behaviour. We've got some lovely, lovely kids, but also, a
> small minority who are really difficult. I've had to develop a thicker skin, to realise
> that it's not just me, it's not personal. You see other, more experienced teachers
> having trouble and it makes you feel better.
>
> (NQT at a school 'with serious weaknesses')

> You worry about it and if you are sensible, you talk about the issues, the pupils
> who are doing particular things to give you a hard time, and this usually helps to
> get things in proportion. It might not provide a magic answer but you realise that
> it's not that big deal, it's not beyond the parameters of what's happening to other
> teachers.
>
> (Teacher educator)

One advanced skills teacher talked of how important it was to try to not take it
personally when pupils were aggressive and rude, and how difficult it was to do this:

> It is incredibly hard not to take it personally, not to think that their awful behav-
> iour should in some way have been prevented or minimised by you. I still take it
> personally after all these years, even as I tell younger teachers that they mustn't
> take it personally. It is crucial for your psychological well being at this school but
> that doesn't make it easy to do.

'Keeping things in proportion' was also suggested as a strategy for coping with
unsatisfactory pupil behaviour and deficits on the 10-point scale: remembering that
level 10 is not a natural state of affairs, and that lots of pupils with problems are
prone to misbehave and 'try it on'. In going into the world of classrooms, you are,

Box 4.8 Coping strategies

Change the format of the lesson

'I change the order of things. Do my "fun" starters at the end of the lesson instead of the beginning as a reward for being cooperative . . . being reasonable.' (NQT)

'With the worst groups I've stopped "classic" teaching in the sense of having some sort of exposition, oral introduction to the lesson. I don't talk at the start. When they come in, the activity will be on their desks and I will tell them to do it straight away. Even with really tough groups, some of them will just get on with it, or will slump, heads down. This narrows down the number of kids you have to sort out. Then you work on them, by name, trying to cajole them, settle them down. And I try to have something planned as a reward for the end of the lesson . . . we'll finish with a video if . . .' (NQT)

'I used to resort to a series of worksheets, doable tasks, fill in the missing words, things to keep them occupied. Now I'm more experienced I would probably do it differently, but then that was the only way I could get through the day.' (Seven years in teaching)

'If it's Thursday or Friday period 6, I have to make radical changes to my planning. There's a real difference in terms of what I can do with them and my planning has to take account of that. You just develop a better understanding of what school is like from their point of view. A lot of them have had enough, they don't want to be in your lesson they want to go home, they are looking forward to messing about with their friends and socialising. You've got to bust a gut to make it either really structured and purposeful, or try really hard to have something that might interest them, grab their attention, at least try and plan a bit of fun or interest into the lesson, even if that means going a bit all over the place in terms of content.' (NQT)

(Several teachers mentioned using short extracts of a 'watchable' video as a means of getting through the lesson with difficult groups.) (See also, Chapter 3.)

'Keep going'

'I've learned that you have to take some things with a pinch of salt. With some groups you have to let some things go, just pick up on big things.' (NQT in tough school)

'With some groups I just plough on, just keep going unless there is a major atrocity. Sometimes they subside a bit when they realise that I'm not rising to it, that I'm just carrying on with the lesson, and they just put their heads down, slump over the desk. I know the theory is that they get worse and worse until they find out what your limit is but this doesn't seem the norm.' (NQT in tough school)

I still ignore some things, you can't pick everything up, but this one thing – not talking when you're talking – that's a key one. But if you start "Where's your tie 'boy?", "Put that gum in the bin now", "You, stop banging that ruler", "Stop swinging on your chair", "Turn round now" . . . it's about priorities, the art of the possible, one step at a time.' (Third year of teaching)

'I learned to battle through. You have to let some things go ... sometimes even some of the ground rules you've been trying to establish ... because it's one of those days and you just do the best you can. You've got to keep going, don't stop, focus on the kids who are learning and complying even if there are not many of them.' (Mentor)

'Keep calm'

'It is important not to start getting narky with all of them just because you are under pressure. You've got to stay polite, calm and reasonable, even if you don't feel like that inside. You need the patience of a saint some days and you've got to be fairly thick-skinned ... you mustn't take it personally.' (NQT)

'The biggest thing was just learning to keep calm under pressure. Don't let them wind you up. I learned it almost by accident when I went in one morning feeling really tired and not very well. I didn't give up, I didn't just let them do whatever, but I perhaps came across as a bit more relaxed and they didn't seem up for it as much.' (Second year of teaching)

'I know you're not supposed to do it but I would sometimes pop out for a minute ... not far and with an excuse ... but it sometimes just gave me chance to compose myself, to calm down, to gather my resources for another round.' (Third year of teaching in a tough school)

'I remember the Bill Rogers thing about dealing with the things you can control, not the things that you can't control. I try really hard to keep calm, even when provoked, I try hard not to let it get to me. You can make a mental effort not to get angry or upset or exasperated and that has helped me.' (NQT in a tough school) in a sense, leaving the adult world with its developed and generally accepted conventions of appropriate behaviour and going into an environment where many of the inhabitants have not yet understood and internalised these conventions, and part of the teacher's job is to help them to get there:

> It's not a nice feeling not being fully in control of a lesson but you've got to keep things in perspective. Not giving up, not stopping trying but being philosophical about things not being perfect. Not thinking that life will never be the same because 8R were not fully under your control.
>
> (Teacher educator)

> Some of them (teachers) seemed to have the ability to shrug things off . . . to think after a bad lesson, a rough ride . . . tomorrow's another day, to learn to be resilient. Not to give up, to stop trying, but not to just brood about it in a sort of negative, passive way.
>
> (Teaching assistant)

> Some teachers were just so professional . . . always calm, polite and composed, even when they were under pressure. Some of them also seemed able to put incidents behind them once they were over . . . to walk away from it and just move on to the next class.
>
> (Teaching assistant)

It might be helpful to think in terms of a sort of 'Richter Scale' of pupil atrocity to try and keep things in perspective:

> I think of the atrocities that happen in the world . . . 9/11, beheadings, terrorism, muggings – or even the stuff that happens in this school, and in the great scale of things the fact that one small child with problems doesn't want to do the work doesn't seem such a big deal. I've still got to try and do my best to sort out the best possible way forward but it doesn't seem quite so desperate.
>
> (NQT working in a difficult school)

Teachers' views of the characteristics of colleagues who were good at managing learning in the classroom

Pupil behaviour and classroom climate are influenced by factors other than teachers' 'organisational' skills in managing learning within the classroom. Much depends on the planning that has gone into the lesson (see Chapter 3), on the skill with which teachers interact with pupils (Chapter 5) and teachers' assiduousness in following up incidents after the lesson. However, teachers did have opinions about the 'within-class' skills that were likely to be conducive to good pupil behaviour. The six most frequently referred to qualities are described below.

Getting started with the learning: not letting anything stop the learning

The DfES (2004: 7.3) has pointed out that learning 'can often be derailed by administrative and organisational tasks' (a degree of irony here). One mentor spoke despairingly of a trainee who would often spend several minutes giving the books out, or spelling out rules, dealing with administrative matters, clearing up missing homeworks, talking to pupils who arrived late. Experienced teachers had a range of strategies for dealing with pupils who were late, or who arrived without equipment, but the underlying principle behind action was to not let these matters take up a second more learning time than was essential: to get them started on learning as quickly as possible and sort out possible reprisals later, perhaps at the end of the lesson. It was felt that some trainees and NQTs allowed pupils to 'stop the learning', and drift into a situation where the teacher was 'telling off' someone, but where there was nothing much for the other pupils to do, so that they too drifted into 'messing about'. One teacher suggested that it would be an interesting experiment for teachers to time how long it took them to get all the pupils in a class either listening and attentive, or working:

> We give them something the second they come in. You've got to try and get the learning going as soon as possible, to get them engaged and interested. Don't give them time to think about messing about because they are bored and nothing is happening. So sometimes we are waiting at the door as they come in and give out a post-it note or sheet or something that they have to do. Or something on the board which they can all get going with.
>
> (Advanced skills teacher)

> I try to set a purposeful tone to the lesson from the moment the kids walk in. When the students come in, the starter is already up on the board, so the majority of students settle down straight away and get on with it; then I can concentrate on picking off any naughties – people who won't sit down, don't have a pen, refuse to take their coat off etc., and I try to get this done as briskly as I possibly can.
>
> (Second year of teaching)

> The kids can tell straight away ... that some teachers mean business. The control comes from the first few seconds of the lesson, right from the start, the way they come into the room. With some teachers, within a few seconds of them coming into the room, the pupils are learning, the lesson has started. With others, ten minutes have gone by and there is no learning going on, the lesson hasn't really started, it's still chaos, lots of kids aren't sure what they are supposed to be doing and some ... an increasing number, are starting to mess around ... there are some pupils who in spite of all this are quiet and well behaved, who are just resigned to the fact that here is yet another lesson where some kids will spoil the lesson, where it will all go pear shaped, where they will not get to learn ... they quietly and philosophically just watch or doodle in their exercise books.
>
> (Teaching assistant)

Rogers (2002) points out that getting the pupils prepared for learning can start even before the start of the lesson by 'corridor calming', to remind pupils of the transition from 'social time' to 'learning community' time, and several experienced teachers described how they met pupils as they came into the room, just to settle things down.

Clear instructions

Fontana (1994) argues that this is an aspect of managing learning in classrooms that is undervalued. In the pupil survey (see Chapter 5) many pupils' main complaint about being in classrooms was that they simply did not understand what was going on and what they were supposed to be doing. Many of the teachers interviewed also regarded instruction as an underrated skill, and one that was perhaps 'taken for granted' by some trainees, who might assume that pupils would be as quick to take things on board as adults:

> The teachers who are good at this are calm, purposeful, organised, know what they are doing. If it gets a bit chaotic, they are prepared. Instructions are very clear. The pupils know exactly what they are supposed to do ... they cannot plausibly say that they don't know what to do because it is so clear. When pupils are not sure what it is they have to do, that's when things start to get iffy.
>
> (Teaching assistant)

> On first placement, a lot of trainees are not clear in giving instructions to pupils about the tasks to be done, and don't realise the need to patiently repeat those instructions so that the pupils know what they are being asked to do. It's a real art, giving really clear instructions and patiently, calmly reinforcing them.
>
> (Teacher educator)

One teacher had the idea of 'the core'; meaning the absolute minimum that pupils needed to do, clearly spelled out:

> I ask myself, 'Do they know what the core is ... the absolute minimum that they have got to do if they are to leave the lesson without consequences?'. I have the list for the core on the board so I can point to it at any time in the lesson. The core must be absolutely manageable for any pupil. So that there is no excuse for not doing it if it gets referred upwards ... they will not have a leg to stand on if they have to explain it to a deputy or year head. 'You must do at least 15 lines ...' and I will point to the line that they have got to get to avoid consequences.
>
> (Third year in teaching)

Cowley (2003) also makes the point that repetition and modelling are vitally important tools for controlling pupil behaviour. Sometimes there is no substitute for showing pupils what you want them to do, going through it with them, giving them the first example, worked through. And pupils often do need to be told what to do more than once; they won't all get it first time round.

'Clear warning, then do what you said you would do' (head of department)

Several teachers used the metaphor of 'the yellow caution card', to stress the importance of giving pupils a clear warning before imposing a sanction. Having given a clear signal that if a pupil does not desist, the teacher will do something reasonable, plausible and specific, it was felt to be important that teachers should be as consistent as possible in doing what they said they would do. Vagueness, 'bluster' and false last chances ('I won't tell you again', repeated several times) were not thought to be helpful. I can remember walking past a class in the school where I used to teach to hear a teacher saying to the class, 'If you throw one more thing at me . . .', and being met by a volley of missiles (mainly paper) reminiscent of the battle scene in the Olivier version of Henry V. More words were spoken but no action was taken. Decisiveness, polite, calm firmness, consistency, and being 'eminently reasonable' were mentioned as desirable characteristics:

> A punishment should never come as a surprise to a pupil. It should be apparent to them and to everyone in the room that it is coming. They shouldn't be able to say, 'Well, that came out of the blue, I'd no idea the teacher was going to do that.'
>
> (Teacher educator)

> It quickly becomes apparent to pupils whether or not a teacher is actually going to do something if they mess about . . . whether there will be any consequences. Pupils quickly work it out . . . 'he's not actually going to do anything . . . he's just going to keep telling us off' . . . then some of them start exploring exactly how far they can go . . . because that's what some kids are like.
>
> (Teacher educator)

> If teachers just keep telling them off . . . nagging them, continually sending out negative signals, betraying exasperation and impotence . . . or jumping up and down, getting narky, speaking in a loud 'teacher' voice . . . it's actually worse than doing nothing. Just ignoring it and getting on with the lesson, trying to work round the fact that some kids aren't behaving well would be better . . . not ideal but at least it wouldn't make things worse.
>
> (Teacher educator)

> A couple of weeks ago I was doing a roleplay and they were messing around so I stopped it and went back to working from the text books. After that . . . after I had done what I said I would do . . . they would stop when I threatened to stop a 'fun' activity. They realised that if I said I was going to do something, I would do it.
>
> (NQT)

> The kids actually said to me . . . 'go on sir, you keep saying you are going to kick X out if he farts again but you just warn him again and again. You never do it do you?' I felt I couldn't be seen to then respond to that but it made me realise that I had just been going on about it without doing anything. This was obvious to the whole class. You would think this would be obvious, that you would know you were doing it, but I didn't.
>
> (NQT)

> If I learned one thing from the lecture on class management it was to follow things up between the end of one lesson and the start of the next . . . If a pupil has been going out of their way to mess you around and give you trouble, do whatever you can to show that you can inconvenience them, and that you have a lot of resources at your disposal . . . taking breaks and dinnertimes, the school system, form and year teachers, heads of department. And when this works it makes you feel more confident about sorting out other pupils, other classes.
>
> (NQT)

The worst of all worlds is to consistently rebuke the whole class as a body, without singling out individuals who have behaved badly, and to not take any action against those individuals but continue with group denigration. Brophy and Evertson (1976) argued that this creates a 'negative ripple effect' with classes, and leads even the more compliant pupils to siding with disruptive elements.

'Calibration' and choice

Teachers spoke of the skill with which some colleagues carefully 'graded' their responses to pupil transgressions, and went through a series of carefully considered steps, of gradually increasing seriousness, from the most polite and friendly of requests, to calmly but firmly sending a pupil out of the room. They did not 'close-off' options by using a high-level sanction too precipitately, thus leaving themselves less room for manoeuvre later, and leaving a smaller range of intelligent 'choices' for pupils:

> It is possible to intelligently anticipate the sorts of thing that might occur and to make contingency plans ... at least think through what your options are in terms of steps ... friendly, polite but firm request to stop doing whatever it is ... clear warning of minor, low-level, eminently reasonable consequences if they don't comply, a sort of yellow caution card ... whether there might be a stage where you invoke the school system or colleagues in the department, form teacher ... year head. Some trainees are better than others at this sort of anticipation and contingency planning. Some go from nothing to thermo-nuclear in one step.
>
> (Teacher educator)

> You've got to point them towards the right choice ... 'Do A and you will get in less trouble than if you do B ... you won't be inconvenienced ... you won't get hassled as much ... think about it ... is it worth it?'
>
> (Three years in teaching)

> They like group work so you can offer that as a reward if they do a written task or behave reasonably during QUAD [question, answer and discussion] work. You can use the text books as a warning. 'If you are ok ... group work, if not ...'
>
> (NQT)

Olsen and Cooper (2001) make the point that it is important to have a clear hierarchy of sanctions in dealing with pupil transgressions, and to deploy them consistently over time. Vacillation, indecisiveness and inconsistency can antagonise pupils further. One teacher made the point that with some teachers, pupils have got a pretty good idea what will happen to them when they do something wrong before the teacher has said anything about it.

Looking at the pupils and noticing what they are doing, how they are feeling

This, again, might sound like stating the obvious, but several mentors felt that some trainees were more alert and aware to what was going on in the classroom than others, and better at 'reading signals' from the class – about whether they had stopped listening, had switched off, were getting restless, needed a change of activity, an attribute Wragg (1984) termed 'withitness', and which might be regarded as a combination of observation, alertness and sensitivity. Managing up to 30 individuals is a complicated business, and there are sometimes judgement calls to be made over things such as positioning within the class, and the balance between helping individuals and maintaining surveillance of the class as a whole:

> Some of them don't really look at the kids they are teaching, or not in a way where they are receiving signals ... it's not just about eye-contact ... it's about having antennae ... to notice when they are starting to go off task, or are getting a bit too noisy ... or large numbers are not listening to what you are talking about.
>
> (Experienced teacher)

> Good trainees are generally alert to what is going on ... they might not be able to stop things but at least they see what's happening, they are not always turning their back on where the trouble is coming from.
>
> (Teacher educator)

> Don't start helping individuals until everyone knows what they are doing ... until they have settled down. Repeat the instructions to the group as a whole until they are all doing the activity, *then* start moving round the class and interacting with individuals.
>
> (Teacher educator)

> Just things like sensing that towards the end of lessons, you sometimes have to step back and keep an eye on them all, and not get too drawn in to working with particular groups or individuals.
>
> (Mentor)

Perseverance

Together with being 'quick to learn', this was the quality that was mentioned most frequently by teachers to explain why some trainees and NQTs became more successful than others in managing their classrooms:

> As much as anything it's about persistence and consistency. It took a while with some classes but now things don't usually go below around level 7. It's about developing a shared understanding of the parameters of what's acceptable.
>
> (NQT)

> I teach in what some might call a 'bogstandard' comprehensive school ... we get some kids who are just a delight to teach and some who can be quite difficult but who you can get through to if you work hard at it and do the right things consistently.
>
> (NQT)

> I did have to battle with some classes when I came here ... with kids who had been here at this school before me ... who are you, new person, who do you

think you are? A bit of it is about determination and perseverance. Not giving up. 'You are not going to win, we will have a good lesson.' It's a sort of sense of will that eventually gets through to them. You gradually get more of them on your side.

(NQT)

Obviously they [trainees] are going to have to work with some classes that are difficult ... that are tricky even for experienced teachers. The test here is whether they are resilient, whether they keep trying in the face of consistent failure and disappointment over a series of several lessons rather than being passive, not trying anything, not even asking about what they might do. They are not judged on what levels they get to, they are judged on whether things are going in the right direction and whether they kept trying.

(Head of department)

I spent most weekends of my NQT year obsessing about a year 8 class that tortured me every Friday period five and every Monday period one. I was annoyed with myself at the time for letting them ruin my weekends, but the hours I spent reading and planning and thinking about how to deal with the little beggars paid off in the end. I teach the same class this year and most of them have chosen history for GCSE.

(Second year of teaching)

Several mentors and heads of department felt that it was helpful to survival in the classroom if the trainee or NQT could differentiate between the things that they could do something about, and the factors that were beyond their control. It was a question of finding the right point on the continuum between giving up because the situation is hopeless, 'these kids are impossible to teach', 'this school is a zoo', and pointless and counter-productive self-flagellation because you can't make things perfect. Teachers have to be pragmatists. It's about having a sophisticated understanding and good judgement of 'the art of the possible': asking the question, 'what is the best I can do for this group of pupils given the circumstances, and the factors which are beyond my ability to change?' and answering it intelligently. This is illustrated in the following extract, from an experienced and successful head of department, working in a challenging school:

It's the art of the possible ... sometimes there isn't an easy answer. It's a matter of damage limitation. Your job is to do the best you can in the circumstances ... to battle away and get as many pupils as possible to learn in spite of everything. It's partly about determination to keep going ... to get across to them that we are here to learn, that learning is important.

(Four years in teaching in a tough school)

Teacher testimony suggests that with some teaching groups, it takes time, patience and, perhaps, an element of remorselessness to get to the higher levels on the 10-point scale. No 'quick fixes' or easy solutions were apparent. There was certainly an element of 'training' or behaviourism in establishing basic ground rules for behaviour and an ethos of 'we are here to learn' in the classroom. But they also spoke of massive benefits in return for the hard work invested in this endeavour, in terms of the quality of teachers' working lives, the degree to which they could relax and enjoy their teaching. Many were also keen to stress that once ground rules and patterns of working have become established, and relationships with pupils put on a stable basis of mutual respect, life gets a lot easier, and less time and effort are required in terms of how much time following up and 'sorting out' of pupils is necessary. Pupils sometimes become 'unthinkingly quiet' when the teacher talks or wants to start work, because they have just got used to the teacher's way of doing things, and it is this 'unthinking' good behaviour that is perhaps one of the hallmarks of really getting to 'level 10' with a class.

It's important to remember, it's not a battle. It's a campaign, in that the result is decided over a period of time, a series of lessons, not within one lesson or a few days. And it's a strange sort of campaign, in that the struggle is partly to persuade 'the enemy' that you are really on the same side (see Chapter 5).

SUMMARY

• It can be helpful to think about what control is for and how much control you need to be in relaxed and assured control of the classroom.

• Decision making in this area is often about finding the right point on a range of continuums rather than 'right or wrong' judgements.

• There are commonly encountered problems related to pupil behaviour where teachers need to experiment with a range of approaches to see what works best in particular contexts.

• Teachers often have to make hard decisions about whether to keep difficult pupils in the classroom or to send them out of the class and these decisions are, to some extent, influenced by school 'norms' and cultures.

• There are sometimes occasions where there is nothing you can do to get a pupil or pupils to behave perfectly within the course of the lesson, and you have to think about what to do when you are not in complete control of the lesson.

• Experienced teachers have a view about the characteristics of colleagues who are accomplished at managing pupil behaviour.

• Making significant progress in improving the working atmosphere in classrooms with particular teaching groups was generally thought to be a gradual and sustained process rather than something that could be achieved within the space of one or two lessons.

5 Understanding pupils

I'm afraid this is not what most pupils understand by the word education. They understand it as being made to go to a place called school, and there being made to learn something that they don't much want to learn under the threat that bad things will be done to them if they don't. Needless to say, most people don't much like this game and stop playing as soon as they can.

(Holt, 1984: 34)

I am of the fervent belief that if there is a secret to teaching well, it is this: you must like the children you teach and be able to show them you do. It is the key to a vocation.

('Secondary Teacher of the Year', Philip Beadle, *The Guardian*, 28 March 2006)

Understanding pupils' reactions to being in classrooms

When asked to describe the characteristics of trainees and NQTs who were more successful at managing pupil learning, many teachers talked about their ability to 'get on with' the pupils. This was felt to derive in part from their skills of inter- action with pupils, but also, the degree to which they developed an understanding of the pupils they were teaching, in terms of their attitude to being in the class- room, learning a school subject, and to the enterprise of education in general. In the words of one teaching assistant, 'just understanding what makes them tick helps you gauge your interactions with pupils'. Olsen (1997) makes the point that it is helpful to have an understanding of common pupil 'gambits', in the sense of the moves pupils sometimes make, the games that they play, in order to establish some form of positional advantage over their territory, and to test out the strength of what some of them see as 'the opposition'. Wragg (1993a) argues the case for trainees devoting some time to close observation of individual pupils, particularly those who appear to have some problems with behaviour, in order to develop a keener under- standing of their motivation and responses to particular classroom events. He also makes the point that pupils have a clear and consistent view of the teachers they regard as good or incompetent:

> Surveys over a long period of time, since the 1930s, show that in general, pupils expect teachers to be slightly strict, rather than very strict or permissive . . . they

Box 5.1 'Some pupil misbehaviour stems from the fact that pupils are bored and not interested in learning what is presented to them in classrooms'

expect fair use of rewards and punishments . . . they prefer teachers whose lessons are interesting, who see them as individuals, who can explain things clearly and who have a sense of humour but who do not engage in sarcasm.

(Wragg, 1993b: 22)

As Schostak (1991) and Elliott (1998) have pointed out, the decision to disengage from schooling on the part of pupils may well be a rational one, rather than a manifestation of 'deviant' behaviour. Many pupils do not enjoy school, do not want to learn the subjects prescribed by the National Curriculum and do not 'see the point' of many of the things they are asked to do in classrooms. Some pupil misbehaviour stems from the fact that pupils are bored and not interested in learning what is presented to them in classrooms.

As adolescents, they also have not always acquired the social skills and conventions of behaviour that are appropriate for group situations. Some trainees were felt to be quicker than others to grasp that it is in the nature of things that pupils will sometimes 'mess about' in classrooms: 'This isn't a tough school but even here, most kids will mess about given the chance' (NQT). Moreover, it seems that a normal reaction to the presence of a new teacher, is for pupils to test out what norms of behaviour the new teacher is likely to tolerate. There can also be resentment of 'intruders', and it is especially difficult for trainees who are stepping into the shoes of well-respected and popular teachers, or who are patently not from the local area. Several NQTs commented on a 'we were here first' mentality among some classes:

It's a small rural comprehensive and I'd come from a tough inner-city school. They all grew up together in the small village, I'm an outsider, they really resent my presence ... 'What are you doing in our school?' It reminds me of that scene in *Deliverance* – 'Duelling Banjos', a lot of them were really foul.

(NQT)

Most of them know that you are new to the school, and they are testing you out every few seconds to see what they can or can't do.

(NQT)

With Year 9, I'm new and they're not and that makes a big difference to their attitude.

(NQT)

Not writing off pupils as 'evil', 'unteachable' or 'thick' was thought to be an important first indicator of whether trainees and NQTs were likely to be able to develop good working relations with their teaching groups. In the words of one teacher educator:

One of the things that is fundamental if they are to succeed with pupils on a human level is that they have respect for young people and a realistic understanding of them – not misunderstanding adolescent misbehaviour as anything other than it is ... realising that it's not personal, it's not an extreme attack if someone flounces, sulks or pulls a face, it's what adolescents do. They've got to have the intelligence and good judgement to distinguish between those incidents and behaviours that are directly designed to undermine their overall control of the class and those that aren't. Not making a big deal of something that doesn't merit it.

Several teachers stressed that it was important to delineate between genuinely difficult pupils who were severely troubled, and what were sometimes termed 'harmless' pupils who might be 'daft as brushes and willing to join in with the fun', but who were not fundamentally determined to destroy the lesson:

Of course, there are a few spiteful kids who don't care about spoiling it for the rest. You've got to be firm and persistent with them and be prepared to use the full weight of the school's support systems. But most of them aren't like that even at our place. They just don't realise that they are not behaving sometimes ... that tapping and talking and walking round are a nuisance ... they do some things without thinking, because they're used to doing it. You have to train them not to do these things, gradually, over a period of time.

(Third year of teaching)

The other idea which it was thought helpful for new teachers to be aware of was that teachers can change pupils' attitudes to learning. Although there are many pupils who have a limited commitment to learning, a lot of them are 'biddable' to the idea of learning. Rogers (2002) estimates that even in quite challenging schools, there will be between 60 and 70 per cent of pupils who are willing to work with 'a confident, relaxed, respectful and non-aggressive teacher', although much would depend on the skill with which they were 'lured' into learning. This was borne out in several of the interviews with teachers working in challenging circumstances:

We have lots of classes where there are some kids who will mess about if they can, and others who are quite keen to learn, or at least they're open to the idea of learning.

(NQT)

You look at your register, for a tough group, and realise that there are quite a lot of really nice kids in there, it's just that this fact sometimes gets lost in the chaotic atmosphere, and you only think about the difficult ones, you forget that some kids just get on with it or talk to their neighbour if there is stuff going on ... You very rarely get a class where they all join in the troublemaking.

(Third year of teaching)

Trainees are prone to give whole-class punishments in a way which is really unfair. It is very unusual for every pupil in the class to be misbehaving. They must focus on the pupils who are the real troublemakers and try and sort them out or limit the damage they do to the lesson. They should not give blanket punishments which do not discriminate. You just alienate the whole class, including those who would have quite liked to learn something but couldn't because the teacher couldn't control the class.

(Mentor)

We sometimes run a quick check about how they are feeling when they come in to the room. Quick show of fingers out of five to show how ok they feel, how energetic and motivated for work they feel. It sounds daft but it sends a message to them that we do care about them, about how they feel. And we might make at least a show of making allowance for how they are ... have a quick good fun activity, something light hearted to get them into it.

(Advanced skills teacher in a challenging school)

In terms of working with pupils within the classroom, one of the skills thought to be helpful was the speed and accuracy with which teachers could work out which pupils were likely to be a real challenge to their authority, which would go 'whichever way the wind was blowing' (that is, would be likely to join in if there was some disruption to the lesson), and which were 'solid citizens' who would get on quietly with their work, even in the course of significant disruption of the lesson.

Another view expressed was that pupils did not, on the whole, bear grudges: their grievances were more to do with having to be in a classroom, having to learn something they weren't interested in, rather than personal hatred of the teacher (which is not to say that teachers did not sometimes take misbehaviour arising out of this personally):

The other thing is that for all their faults, most of these kids don't bear grudges, they soon forget. They have other things in their lives, you are not that important a bit of their lives.

(Teacher educator)

After one lesson I ran out and burst into tears and I had the same class in the afternoon to face. It was almost like a fresh start in the afternoon. The kids here don't remember ... this sort of thing happens a lot at this school. Sometimes you can build things up in your head before a lesson and then you find that it's not that bad ... it's back to fairly low-level stuff.

(Second year of teaching)

Give them a chance not to be difficult. One of the biggest things I have learnt since my PGCE is that kids change from lesson to lesson or even from hour to hour. When you are training, a mauling at the hands of a difficult child seems momentous to you; you convince yourself that the child is out to get you and you wonder how you will ever overcome the humiliation. The child may well see it differently; some of these characters have several such confrontations every day, and the chances are that s/he will have forgotten it by the next lesson.

(Second year of teaching)

One further point about pupils in classrooms: overwhelmingly teachers regarded the vast majority of pupils as rational in their behaviour. They might be volatile, truculent, immature, manipulative and incredibly accomplished in the art of winding up adults, but in the last resort, they would usually make rational choices when offered ways out, or when given options. They were felt to be intelligent in terms of 'who they tried it on with'. For this reason, consistency was felt to be a valuable asset for teachers trying to establish themselves with new classes:

One of the teachers uses the school system to the letter, every time. First offence, name on board, just a warning, second incident, name underlined, which means that they miss their break, third time, they have to do after-school detention. The kids are not daft ... After their name goes up, the vast majority of them keep their heads down because they know what will happen. Every time the same procedure. They know where they stand.

(Teaching assistant)

Understanding that pupils differ

Many of my trainees are surprised when they arrive at placements in small, rural schools, thinking that behaviour will necessarily be less problematic than in larger, city schools, and finding that this is not necessarily the case. There is some evidence to suggest that the difference in classroom climate in inner-city and rural classrooms is less than is popularly represented in the media (see Chapter 7).

Several NQTs explained that it had taken them some time to get used to working with pupils from different demographic backgrounds. Two examples are given below:

We don't have huge behaviour problems but a lot of the kids I teach are not academically motivated. On teaching placement I had a lot of city kids, some of whom were very keen to get to university and some of whom were disaffected and disruptive. So I have different problems here. At X school, I could just give them the notes and they would take them down, keen to get on. Here I have to think how to get them to want to take the notes down, to get them to want to do well.

(NQT)

Their parents don't have a tradition of going into higher education, education isn't a big deal. They are difficult in a different way to the city kids. Sullen, obstinate, wanting to be left alone, for you not to interfere with their life in any way. Passive resistance. I found it difficult in a different way to the 'in your face' city kids. You had to find a different way round it. You had to sort of lure them subtly into being interested in a low-key understated way. They would be suspicious of too much enthusiasm, someone trying too hard, trying to convert them.

(NQT)

There were also felt to be differences between older and younger pupils, in terms of what sort of teacher 'personality' was more likely to appeal to them:

What works with pupils depends on how old they are. Younger pupils are more seduced by presence, performance skills, sense of humour ... having a bit of fun. Older pupils can often be turned off by 'show-offs' and place more value on good subject knowledge, being good at explaining things and well-prepared lessons.

(Head of department)

Corrie (2002: 1–2) also notes the importance of understanding that some pupils, particularly those displaced from war zones 'would prefer the ground to swallow them up rather than attract the teacher's or peers' attention'. One of the skills that teachers need to develop is sensitivity in gauging both the extent and speed of efforts to initiate contact with particular pupils.

Attention was also drawn to the different types of pupil who might pose problems in the classroom, and for new teachers to work out appropriate strategies for dealing with them. A study by Gutteridge (2002) showed that there was no clear consensus among teachers about which pupils were disaffected from learning, and some pupils who had been identified as disaffected by their teachers denied that this was the case when subsequently interviewed about their supposed disaffection. Mellor (1997) provides guidance on the handling of attention-seeking pupils and Oakley (2002) gives interesting insights into 'RHINOs' (pupils who are 'really here in name only'), who tend to drift through school quietly underachieving and doing as little as possible to get by without getting noticed. Several teachers pointed to the existence of a number of pupils who enjoyed confrontation with teachers, and who would attempt to 'wind up' teachers so that they could enjoy the sight of them being angry:

The best way of getting some kids out of the classroom is to order them not to leave their seat, to stay in the room. It then becomes a badge of honour to disobey you. With one or two kids, telling them they have to leave the room is the surest way to keep them in. They won't budge and enjoy the drama that then unfolds.

(NQT)

Shouting, getting mad, just doesn't work, they are used to it, some of them love it, it turns them on, they are looking for an argument, it's the best bit of their day. Just being quiet, firm and patient and being prepared to just repeat what you have asked them to do ... nine times out of ten at our place it diffuses things. They will often throw a strop but eventually ... in the absence of the reward of some sort of public showdown, will get on with it or at least subside ... keep quiet.

(NQT in a difficult school)

Although what pupils were like varied both between and within schools, the over-arching challenge for the teacher was getting them all to want to learn. The next section of the chapter provides pupils' views on the teacher characteristics which they believed were likely to get them to want to learn.

Pupils' views on what makes them want to learn

The last few years have seen a dramatic increase in the amount of literature giving pupil perspectives of classrooms and schools (see, for instance, Munn *et al.*, 1990; Lang, 1993; Barber, 1994; Nieto, 1994; Ruddock *et al.*, 1996; Flutter and Ruddock, 2004). Pupils are clearly very experienced when it comes to teachers, and by the time they have gone through secondary school will have been taught by a wide range of teachers.

The survey described below was undertaken by six teachers and two researchers[1] working in five schools in Norfolk as part of the NASC (Norwich Area Schools Consortium) project (Elliott *et al.*, 2001, see also http://www.uea.ac.uk/care/nasc/ NASC_home.htm). The main aim of the survey was to gain greater insight into the factors that influenced pupils' attitude to learning. The questionnaire was completed by 708 pupils across the five schools. Although it was possible to disaggregate the data to look for age, gender ability and school effects, it was clear that there were some factors that *all* pupils felt had a strong influence on their attitude to learning, irrespective of gender, age or ability. (The full results of the survey are available online at http://www.uea.ac.uk/~m242/nasc/cross/cman/quest.htm.)

In our initial discussions, our combined experience as teachers led us to a sort of hunch that what the teacher was like as an individual would be an important part of pupils' attitudes towards learning, and that it was not just a matter of school subject, or how that related to pupils' career aspirations. Another proposition was that pupils' attitude to learning a subject/being in a classroom was not just related to the technical or pedagogical competence of the teacher, or even their professional qualities, but that it related in part to what the teacher was like as a person, what we termed 'reasonable human being' qualities, which might, we thought, impact on the relationship between the pupils and the teacher, which, in turn, would influence their attitude to learning and the degree of their engagement with learning.

We therefore 'brainstormed' a list of 'teacher characteristics', which were a mixture of: technical/pedagogical capability, (e.g. 'Explains things well', 'Controls the class well'), professional qualities (e.g. 'Marks and returns your work promptly', 'Always seems well prepared'), and personal characteristics, which might also be defined as a teacher's 'style' of teaching (e.g. 'Is friendly', 'Says hello or nods to you outside the lesson'). The pupils were asked to indicate whether they thought each factor was 'Very important', 'Quite important', 'Not very important', or 'Doesn't matter'.

In terms of teacher characteristics likely to reduce disaffection and engagement, pedagogical and 'reasonable human being' qualities tended to score higher frequencies than professional ones, although there was some overlap.

The four top frequencies overall were good subject knowledge, the ability to explain things well, 'being friendly' and 'talks normally'. Within the professional cluster of factors, 'dresses smartly', 'sets regular homework' and 'makes you work hard' had the lowest frequencies, 'prompt marking and returning of work', 'punctuality to lessons', and 'not being absent', the highest.

In the 'pedagogy' cluster, 'variety' and 'ability to use computers' scored lowest, 'ability to explain' and 'good subject knowledge' the highest. In the 'personal characteristics' of the teacher cluster, 'being strict' and 'acknowledging pupils in the corridor' gave the lowest frequencies, with 'friendly', 'talks normally', 'sense of humour' and 'polite' scoring highest. Pupils preferred teachers who were friendly rather than formal, relaxed rather than strict, but ability to control the class was viewed as most important overall.

Although there were 'school effects' and 'subject effects', analysis of the responses to the questionnaire as a whole indicated that 'teacher effect' was by far the strongest influence on pupils' attitudes to learning. When asked to identify factors that inclined them to make an effort to learn in the classroom, teacher characteristics were most commonly cited across all five schools involved in the survey, and were far more prevalent than, for instance, references to the employment or career path utility of particular school subjects. (Religious Education was an exception to this pattern. For subject dimensions of pupil disaffection, see http://www.uea.ac.uk/~m242/nasc/cross/cman/leasteffort.htm).

Box 5.2 gives the frequencies from the question on teacher characteristics relating to aspects of their 'professional' persona as teachers. These responses suggest that a

---

Box 5.2 Professional characteristics of teachers which pupils felt had a positive influence on their attitude to learning

Teacher characteristic	% of pupils regarding this characteristic as 'very important' in having a positive influence on their attitude to learning
Marks and returns your work promptly	50.0
Is nearly always on time for lessons	45.7
Doesn't set too much homework	39.0
Always seems well prepared	37.0
Is very rarely absent from the lesson	32.6
Uses the school rewards system quite a lot	26.1
Is formal in their approach to pupils	19.6
Dresses smartly	15.2
Makes you work hard	13.0
Sets homework regularly	6.5

Box 5.3 Pedagogical characteristics (teaching skills?) of teachers that pupils feel have a positive influence on their attitude to learning

Teacher characteristic	% of pupils regarding this characteristic as 'very important' in having a positive influence on their attitude to learning
Knows their subject really well	78.3
Explains things well	76.1
Makes it interesting	67.4
Is good at stopping other pupils from spoiling the lesson	65.2
Doesn't set too much written work	65.0
Has good ideas for lesson activities	54.0
Sets homeworks which are enjoyable to do	50.0
Makes helpful comments on your work	50.0
Is good at controlling the class	47.8
Makes topics seem relevant	41.3
Sets work which is quite difficult but which you can do, or at least have a go at	37.0
Uses the video and television well	34.0
Uses group work and discussion quite often	31.0
Makes the topic seem important	30.0
Uses computers sometimes	23.9
Uses lots of different teaching methods	21.7

lot of pupils consider it important that teachers mark and return their work promptly, and that teachers should try to arrive promptly to lessons and not be absent too often. It raises interesting questions about homework; do teachers need to think about the quality and forms of homework that they set? Might some homeworks do more harm than good? It is important not to misconstrue the findings; 15 per cent of pupils think it is very important that teachers dress smartly, it doesn't mean that the other 85 per cent of pupils prefer teachers who do not dress smartly. Nor should the results be taken at face value. A small sample of 708 pupils across five schools may not be typical of national patterns. However, the results might get teachers to reflect on aspects of their professional persona, and explore what is important to the pupils that they teach.

Box 5.3 gives the pupils' views on the comparative importance of 'pedagogic' qualities, or what might be termed 'teaching skills'. Again, it is important that teachers do not accept the figures above as 'truths'; the same survey done today, or in different

Box 5.4 Personal characteristics of teachers that pupils feel have a positive influence on their attitude to learning (the teacher as 'reasonable human being'?)

Teacher characteristic	% of pupils regarding this characteristic as 'very important' in having a positive influence on their attitude to learning
Talks to you 'normally'	63.0
Is friendly	63.0
Is enthusiastic about their subject	54.3
Has a sense of humour	52.2
Lets pupils talk as they work	50.0
Uses praise and encouragement	45.7
Lets pupils sit where they want	45.5
Talks to pupils politely	45.4
Is relaxed in their approach to pupils	45.3
Is strict	34.8
Says hello or nods to you outside the lesson	21.7
Sometimes talks about things in general	17.4

schools may well elicit significantly different outcomes. I suspect that skilful use of new technology may well have a higher place today than the lowly place it was accorded here. But the outcomes may lead teachers to reflect on their practice in helpful ways. Is it possible that we have been spending too much time on group work skills and not enough on skilful exposition? What are our strengths and weaknesses in the areas outlined above; are there aspects of teaching to which we have not given sufficient thought? In terms of teacher development, the important thing is that teachers reflect on the wide range of professional, pedagogical and personal qualities that have a bearing on pupils' attitude to learning in their classrooms.

Box 5.4 gives the pupils views on the comparative importance of a range of 'personality' type teacher characteristics. The responses corroborate the findings of Munn *et al.* (1990), that a complex combination of factors influence pupils' disposition towards learning.

The most common factors that 'put pupils off' being in the classroom or learning a subject were (in order of frequency), other pupils disrupting the lesson (over 200 responses), too much written work, teachers talking too much, and not being able to sit where they wanted to in a lesson. All these factors elicited well over 100 responses. Being bored, not being able to see the purpose of learning and 'not understanding what is going on' were also common responses.

In response to a question that asked them to identify factors that made them feel positive about being in a classroom, teacher characteristics, as with other questions, emerged as most influential, with (perhaps unsurprisingly) a composite image emerging of a friendly, polite and approachable teacher, with good skills of exposition and the ability to control classes. Many pupils mentioned being able to sit next to friends and being allowed to talk during the lesson as being important to them. 'Doing things' and being able to 'discuss issues in class' were also cited as positive aspects of classroom life.

Although not all pupils identified a lesson which they thought was particularly good or enjoyable, and some pupils stated, without apparent rancour, that they could

---

Box 5.5 Several pupil comments suggested that teachers talking for too long was a cause of disengagement from learning

'He's just not my sort of teacher. He's like a Duracell battery, he just goes on and on.'

'When the teacher keeps on talking and talking.'

'Teacher continuously talking. '

'Teacher talks too much'.

'The teacher talking for the whole lesson.'

'not remember any lesson like that', those who did respond to this question often gave interesting and illuminating responses. 'Special occasion' lessons figured prominently, as for example: 'English, when a poet came in'. So also did lessons where pupils had learned to do something that they had previously regarded as beyond their capabilities. Lessons where talk and discussion were a major part of the lesson also featured prominently. A selection of some pupil responses to this question is given in Box 5.6.

The last question asked the pupils if there was any other comment that they would like to make about teachers, lessons, and 'how you are taught in school in general'.

Box 5.6 One good lesson?

(Pupils were asked if they could think of one lesson which they thought was particularly/ memorably good – 'interested you, made you want to learn more, helped you to understand or do something which you couldn't do before')

'My P.E. lesson where I learnt how to give a good serve in badminton.'

'Maths, where I found out that algebra isn't as hard as it looks.'

'A maths lesson: the teacher explained something rather abstract, simply and with much clarity.'

'Geography: because we had class discussions and it was fun and we were allowed to talk.'

'French. The teacher made it interesting and he put it out in such a clear and understanding way.'

'I enjoyed a history lesson when we had to act out Roman scenes.'

'It was an English lesson: a speaking and listening exercise. It was good because the whole class was involved in a debate with good arguments put forward by everyone.'

'I believe discussions or debates in English or R.S. are extremely worthwhile: they enable you to voice your opinion as well as listen to others. You feel less intimidated when speaking out.'

'Drama – the teacher was very enthusiastic and some people in the group were quite shy, but by the end they were all joining in and weren't as shy. We played different games as a group and got to know each other.'

'P.E. – I learnt how to do something in gym that I was afraid to do. This made me feel more optimistic about things, and interested in other gym work.'

'Maths – because I wasn't so good at algebra and I am not too bad now.'

(The full dataset from this question is available online at http://www.uea.ac.uk/ ~m242/nasc/cross/cman/onegoodlesson.htm).

Again, not all pupils responded to this question, and a few responded at the level of invective, but there were some pupils who were unreservedly enthusiastic about their school experience, writing comments such as: 'It's brilliant', 'I'm taught well and enjoy most lessons' and 'The school is good, the teachers are nice'. There were also some comments that expressed concern about the quality of life, personal welfare and state of mind of their teachers, for example: 'Teachers should relax more', 'Teachers should loosen up a bit', 'Teachers shouldn't get so stressed' and 'Teachers are good at getting you through ABCs but after that they seem to think that if you don't do well they will die.'

Although there were 'school effects' and 'subject effects', analysis of the responses to the questionnaire as a whole indicated that 'teacher effect' was by far the strongest influence on pupils' attitudes to learning. When asked to identify factors that inclined them to make an effort to learn in the classroom, teacher characteristics were most commonly cited across all five schools involved in the survey, and were far more prevalent than, for instance, references to the employment or career path utility of particular school subjects.

There were some tensions in terms of pupil preferences compared to some of the teachers' preferred ways of working in classrooms (see Chapter 4). It was clearly important to many pupils to be able to sit with their friends and sit where they wanted, and there was widespread resentment when this was not allowed. Many pupils also resented the imposition of school uniform and what they saw as 'petty conformism' rules (see Box 5.7). Also, pupils did not generally like 'strict' teachers, but one of the most common complaints was about teachers who could not control the class, and where pupils were spoiling the lesson, supporting Davies' assertion (1998), that the majority of pupils would like more severe sanctions to be applied to disruptive pupils. Box 5.8 gives some of the pupil comments relating to disruption. There were over 200 overall.

Overall the pupils' responses echoed the sentiments of experienced teachers in the sense that they were also aware of two agendas pertinent to classroom climate and 'the right to learn': that teachers should try to make the work interesting, and that they should be able to stop pupils spoiling the lesson for others. There was also evidence of pupils valuing what we had termed 'reasonable human being' qualities.

Teachers' views on 'getting on' with pupils

As detailed in Chapter 3, most teachers believed that the 'bottom line' in establishing good working relations with pupils was the quality of the learning experience that the teacher provided for pupils over a period of time. It was felt to be about 'how good the lessons are', and interactions with pupils were felt to be secondary to this. However, they also believed that how the teacher interacted with pupils was an important contributory factor to classroom climate.

Many of the comments of teachers about teacher–pupil relations corroborated the views expressed by pupils, although many pupils did not like the use of seating plans, and a smaller number had reservations about the imposition of uniform and dress codes. In the following five areas, there was a significant measure of common ground between the views of teachers and pupils about teacher attributes that were likely to lead to good working relations with pupils.

Box 5.7 Other responses to the 'Any other comment?' question

'Some teachers hate you and are horrid to you – that makes you hate and rebel against them even more.'

'Some teachers cannot control their class. If you say one thing wrong they go mad ... then we see their weak points.'

'In the extreme, the school resembles a fascist state where everyone must look the same (uniform) and individuality (such as differences in uniform, hairstyle) is shouted down.'

'I think the school should find out how good a teacher is at teaching, not just knowing the subject before they employ them. Lots of teachers are really clever, but just can't explain it or teach.'

'There are far too many unimportant rules: no bright hair colours, no piercings, one ring – unimportant – change the rules!! Sorry but they have absolutely no effect on my work.'

'Never ever call a pupil stupid like Mrs XXX does. No one ever volunteers to answer a question because if you get it wrong she'll yell at you in front of everyone. This is the worst thing to do if you are a teacher. Please tell her not to do this ever again because everyone hates it, and her, and science.'

'I think a teacher who looks like they are having fun teaching you is better than a teacher who's only doing it because it's their job.'

'Some teachers don't teach you much, but make you work from books.'

'School is okay, but some of the teachers are really strict and they make you sit in alphabetical order.'

'There needs to be more talking – group discussions to get people comfortable with expressing what they think, and people know they are interested.'

'I think a good teacher is someone who relates to the class, is fun, humorous, and knows what he/she is doing, and is also strict.'

'In some of the lessons, some of the teachers cannot keep a class under control, so it is harder to work.'

'I feel this is a good school in general, but is sometimes spoiled by bad behaviour on the part of some students.'

'I get worried when one of my teachers doesn't seem to know their subject well or have to spend most of their time controlling the class. There are several of these that I have lessons with.'

Box 5.8 What most puts you off being in a classroom/learning a school subject? (Comments relating to disruption)

'When the teacher lets the pupils get out of hand.'

'In a group who mess around and the teacher can't control them.'

'When teachers can't control the lesson.'

'If the teacher takes too much time trying to keep the class quiet.'

'Getting stuff throwed at me.'

'When everyone is talking and you can't hear the teacher talking.'

'A teacher that commands no respect from his/her pupils.'

Tone and manner in talking to pupils

Although there are obviously some occasions when teachers might need to raise their voices in order to make themselves heard and move to a situation where they can talk 'normally', there was an almost universal consensus that anger, scorn and shouting were not helpful ways forward and were generally counter-productive. 'Losing your temper' (or even pretending to lose your temper) was thought to be inadvisable:

> If you are a teacher, you can't say 'the red mist came over me ... I didn't know what I was doing ...' How well will that stand up? You read about things like that in the papers ... good teacher, awful pupil, and in a moment, the teacher's career is jeopardised, the pupil has won. They have nothing much to lose, they love it, they've got you in trouble. Think about it.
>
> (Teacher educator)

> There are some trainees ... and teachers ... who go in there and wind them up ... who can generate a riot out of passive and dispirited kids who were just slumped quietly over their desks.
>
> (Teacher educator)

> You might intimidate some pupils by shouting and getting angry but there are significant numbers of pupils who enjoy the sight of the teacher jumping up and down and getting exasperated. It is probably more interesting than the worksheet or whatever it was that they were doing.
>
> (Mentor)

> It was as if he had just come from watching *The Professionals* or *The Sweeney* on TV. He thought he could face down the kids by being really up-front aggressive, right in their face, eyeball to eyeball. This might work with some kids, some of them will back down and be intimidated by such an approach but it's a very high-risk strategy. There are some kids in most schools who would rise to this and react in kind, storm out, knock chairs over, tell them to F. off or worse. A strutting macho approach is like a red rag to a bull with some of our pupils.
>
> (Head of department)

> If people go in with an aggressive 'I'm not going to stand any nonsense from you lot ...', our kids are very 'in your face' ... there are lots of them who will take the teacher up on this ... it gets them stirred up.
>
> (Experienced teacher)

> Some trainees try talking to them in sergeant major mode, exploding, 'You will do this ...', 'I'm not having that'. It's exactly not the way to talk to our kids, it's like a red rag to a bull, it winds them up, they will make a conscious attempt to behave badly.
>
> (Head of department)

> I did learn that shouting isn't very effective.
>
> (Teaching assistant)

Sean Neill, co-author of *Body language for competent teachers* (Neill and Caswell, 1993) argues that effective teachers are likely to be both more relaxed, and more decisive during confrontations with pupils:

> They are less likely to shout, and they use non-verbal techniques to defuse situations. Their manner is confident and relaxed. Often they stand in a casual pose, leaning against a desk or with their hands in their pockets. They don't pace up and down like caged beasts, fumble or rub their faces, indulge in anxious self-grooming or hide behind piles of books – all unconscious actions correctly interpreted by pupils as a sign of weakness, uncertainty or downright terror.
>
> (Quoted in Newnham, 2000: 17)

Two qualities stood out in teachers' views about talking to pupils effectively. Many echoed Neill's emphasis on the importance of being calm and relaxed in manner and tone. Two examples are given below:

> You quickly realise that it's no use just shouting and bawling at them. The ones who seemed good at it to me seemed to be calm quiet and relaxed, even when under pressure, when there seemed to be a lot of noise and aggro. I noticed that sometimes they took a bit of time ... or bided their time and had a think about the situation before taking action. The really good ones would go up to problem pupils and just whisper something quietly in their ear and the pupils would subside. I don't know what they said, what the magic words were.
>
> (Teaching assistant)

> She's great, talks to them in a normal, confident manner, very natural, uses the usual range of techniques for getting them settled – has obviously read Bill Rogers, particularly good at counting down.... 54321 ... in a confident and relaxed manner, and even our year 9s fall in with the routine. There's definitely an element of behaviourism in the way they get conditioned to respond if people are calm, firm and consistent and make it really clear to the kid what the procedures and norms are.
>
> (Head of department, describing a strong trainee)

Cangelosi (2000) makes the point that tone is as important as volume in talking to pupils. This extended to the intonation that teachers should adopt when imposing sanctions on pupils; that it should be low-key and understated rather than loud and declamatory, with phrases such as 'Right ... that's it!', or 'I've had enough of this, just get out!' (shouted):

> One piece of advice: 'Say things as a polite statement not a question or request ... the 'as if ...' intonation, low-key, relaxed, 'just straighten that chair up, thanks'. When I started I wouldn't have dreamed of talking like that, it wouldn't have sounded polite but I've learned that tone ... intonation matter.
>
> (Second year of teaching)

> There is less chance of refusal if they have been asked to do something in an eminently reasonable and polite way which gives them no chance to take offence, and if it doesn't seem big deal. Sometimes teachers don't make enough use of very

small sanctions, which serve the purpose of getting the pupil to accept the teacher's authority or risk seeming ridiculous and 'out of order' for refusing to do something that is such a small thing. So, 'Can I just see you for a minute at the end please Alan', said as a statement rather than a question, and moving on quickly with the lesson, leaving the matter as accepted, is better than, 'Right, you boy, see me at the end!'

(Mentor)

I saw a trainee handle a pupil who was trying hard to force a confrontation very skilfully by just staying calm and unflustered, not rising to her provocations. After a clear, firm warning, he eventually sent her out to the remove room and just walked away from the consequent invective and noise by moving to help some other pupils, ignoring her and getting on with the lesson. In the end she just despaired of getting the drama she wanted and mooched off.

(Teacher educator)

You have to come across as a reasonable person ... fair, consistent, using sanctions more in sorrow than in anger, to try and keep the other pupils tacitly on your side, thinking that it was the pupil's own fault that he got into trouble. Reasonableness in the face of difficult pupil behaviour can be helpful ... disarming even. Interpersonal skills as well ... the way you talk to them. The skill with which you present alternative possibilities to them, and the tone of your voice.

(Teacher educator)

Several mentors mentioned a tendency of trainees to talk more loudly than necessary when their control of a class was uncertain, rather than getting the pupils quiet and then talking to the class in a quiet and natural manner, as against a 'big', mannered 'teacher voice'.

Another 'strand' of being relaxed was just having a calm, confident demeanour generally; not being too pompous and formal, taking yourself too seriously, or entering the room as if you were expecting trouble. Rogers (2000) talks of some teachers adopting a demeanour of what he terms 'manic vigilance', as if they are firmly expecting pupil 'ambushes' at any moment, rather than radiating a calm assurance that it is going to be a good lesson, everyone will be fine:

One of the best pieces of advice I had in my PGCE year was from a teacher who said, 'Don't walk into the classroom as if you are apologising for your presence, don't sneak in, show confidence, walk in with a relaxed assurance even if you don't feel it ... as if you really believe it's your classroom, you're at home here'.

(Second year of teaching)

Often students who are really quiet and quite shy at the university are fantastic with the kids when they get out into school. It's not about being big, having a loud voice, an extrovert manner. A sense of humour is very useful if it comes to you naturally but you don't have to be a stand-up comedian. Sometimes it's just being relaxed enough to see the lighter side of things, to keep things in perspective, to smile when you've made a mistake or done something daft. Not to be too concerned with your dignity, your ego.

(Teacher educator)

Yes, I try to make the lessons interesting where I can, to have at least something that might interest them but some of it is down to your interactions with the pupils. Being able to have a bit of fun with them ... sometimes it's just the way you talk to them ... you get to the stage where you can be a bit daft with them. If you make an embarrassing mistake it's important that you can laugh at yourself in an unselfconscious way. At the end of one of my very first lessons, one of the kids pointed out that my flies had been open through the lesson. The only thing you could do was try and laugh about it ... to pass it off in an unselfconscious and relaxed way and carry on.'

(Third year of teaching)

In terms of talking effectively to pupils, a second quality was mentioned, to be used in conjunction with being relaxed. It was felt that some teachers had the ability to say things in a way that was quiet, calm and relaxed but which came across to the pupils as 'meaning business':

It's not about volume but tone ... a quiet purposeful sense that you mean it ... it will happen.

(Teacher educator)

There's a second phase to the calmness thing ... it has to be combined with a sense of firmness ... will. They need to make it clear that in addition to being calm, patient, not flapping ... that you are displeased with an aspect of their behaviour and that if it doesn't stop ... if they are not careful ... something unpleasant or inconvenient will happen to them. There are fewer of my trainees who combine both of these qualities. Sometimes they are strong in one or the other. Both bits are essential.

(Teacher educator)

The best of them have what I call 'the killer instinct', by which I mean an absolute clarity about what they expect of kids that is couched in terms that the kids absolutely understand. They spell it out, they apply the basic policies and conventions for behaviour and follow things up remorselessly ... whatever it takes. This sense of will gets across to kids. They often can 'let kids off' at the end of the day when the incident has been considered, explored and investigated, but it will be on their terms.

(Head teacher)

Improving classroom talk and active learning

Two of the most common grievances expressed by pupils were that they found teacher exposition boring or incomprehensible, and that lessons were dominated by written tasks. Neither of these lesson activities lend themselves to interaction between teacher and pupils, and several teachers acknowledged that too often, the pupils' role in the lesson was fairly passive, with very little opportunity to talk and discuss the lesson content with other pupils (see also Arnot *et al.*, 2004). Lawlor (1989: 67) argues that this is of no import:

Why should greater emphasis be put on pupils discussing amongst themselves and with the teacher (as opposed to more formal questions-and-answers)? It is not clear. There is no reason to imagining that pupils learn from talking. Indeed, they may not want to talk. They may have nothing to say.

Much depends, of course, on the quality of the teacher's skills of exposition. It is possible that the continuing 'shoehorning' of more and more 'competences' into requirements for initial training have reduced the time spent on developing trainees' skills of exposition and questioning, and yet these are clearly crucial areas, given that there are few lessons where the teacher will not talk to pupils for some part of the lesson. One of the things that can influence pupils' engagement in lessons is the degree to which the teacher can get the pupils interested, and enable them to learn, just by talking to them and explaining things to them. With some teachers, 'telling a story', explaining something skilfully, or leading a lively discussion can be one of the highlights of the lesson for pupils. With others, it can lead to a dreary interlude where pupils either don't understand or where they stop listening because they are bored.

Although many pupils expressed positive views about lessons that involved discussion, debate and argument, these activities require high-level teacher expertise, and teachers felt that some trainees and NQTs struggled to manage such activities, and tended to retreat to less challenging ones. The link between effective teacher talk and positive pupil behaviour is made explicit in the Standards and Effectiveness Unit's resources, *Classroom talk for learning and management* (DfEE, 2001), which contain a range of useful suggestions for improving the quality of classroom talk.

But part of a teacher's skills of exposition lie in knowing when to stop talking, because the pupils have stopped listening:

> Sometimes trainees find it hard to 'read' a class as they are talking and fail to notice that they have had enough, they have turned off, they need a change of activity.
>
> (Mentor)

> Above all, I never talk for too long ... and in my school with most groups that means 8–10 minutes max ... It's important to read the kids' body language; it's easy to get carried away by your own eloquence and not notice that half your top set is drooping with boredom. Asking lots of questions and having some nice images on the whiteboard can increase their attention span to about 15 minutes, but after that it really is time that they did something; otherwise, they'll become restive.
>
> (Second year of teaching)

Several teachers felt that with trainees and NQTs in particular, concern over classroom control led to an excessive reliance on written work, and written work whose primary purpose was to control the class, rather than to get pupils to learn. Experienced teachers tended to believe that getting pupils involved in some form of 'active' learning (which did not include copying work and low-level writing tasks) was one of the best ways of improving relations between teacher and pupils. Initiative and resourcefulness in developing an 'archive' of teaching approaches that would provide an escape from an ascetic diet of worksheets and text book work was felt to be one of the characteristics of more successful trainees and NQTs (see Chapter 3).

Box 5.9 How good are the teacher's skills of exposition and questioning?

a I'm fairly confident about this aspect of my teaching; when talking to my teaching groups, I think I can generally interest them and hold their attention, whatever the topic. QUAD activities are usually lively and stimulating.

b I'm OK; I feel relaxed and confident in talking to my teaching groups, and talk quite fluently and effectively to them most of the time. I think I explain things quite well. Sometimes they are interested in what I say, and they enjoy the bit of the lesson where I am talking to them. I can think on my feet fairly well and feel comfortable with QUAD activities with most groups.

c Reasonable, but it's an aspect of my teaching that I will need to work on. Sometimes I suspect that they do not find my exposition helpful or interesting, and I don't really enjoy this bit of the lesson. I find QUAD activities quite difficult and sometimes they don't really take off.

d Definitely a weakness; I am aware that pupils are frequently bored and restless when I try to talk to them at any length, even on topics where my subject knowledge is quite good. I don't feel confident or relaxed when doing QUAD activities with them.

e I'm so bad at this that I avoid doing it as much as possible, I talk for about 10 seconds and then set them some written work or a group work task.

Establishing boundaries and being consistent

By some way the pupils' biggest single grievance, and one that was apparent in all five of the schools surveyed was teachers who were unable to stop some pupils messing about in the lesson. Pupils had a clear preference for teachers who were able to control the classroom, preferably in a relaxed, understated and 'non-strict' way.

This was not seen as a contradiction by mentors and experienced teachers. It was not thought to be a question of 'nice cop or nasty cop'. It was thought possible for teachers to be 'quite strict but in a subtle and relaxed style' (experienced mentor). Although it was thought to be important not to be either too austere or too 'chummy' in manner, the idea of a simple continuum that just considered 'degree of warmth' was felt to be unhelpful. It is, perhaps, more helpful to consider teacher attributes in their interactions with pupils on two axes, with the desirable position in the quadrant being in the top left-hand corner; polite, approachable, friendly, but quite firm and consistent in enforcing ground rules and school policy.

In terms of trainee and NQT misjudgements in this area, the following suggestions were offered by mentors in focus group interviews (see also pages 73–4):

- 'Too confrontational or conversely afraid to confront pupils when necessary – not getting the balance right.'
- 'Packing away too early in the lesson, or even letting them out before the bell – a recipe for trouble.'

- 'Threatening punishments which are implausible.'
- 'Not giving kids a clear warning before they impose sanctions.'
- 'Not being consistent – it's as important for teachers as it is for referees.'
- 'Arriving late for the lesson.'
- 'Saying they will do something and then not doing it.'
- 'Dithering – think carefully but then be decisive.'
- 'Shouting too much.'
- 'Not developing standard ways of doing things that kids can get used to.'
- 'Not using the official school systems.'
- 'Not marking and returning books promptly.'
- 'Being over-familiar, trying to be "matey" with pupils. The kids loathe and despise this.'
- 'Not getting to know the kids' names. It makes it so much easier when you do this.'

Skilful use of rewards and sanctions

In his work on assertive discipline, Canter claimed that 'the single most important attribute we've found that distinguishes successful classroom managers from less successful ones is that they praise their students frequently' (Canter, 1992: 63). Over the past decade schools have generally become more alert to the importance of responding to positive as well as negative aspects of pupils' behaviour. Rogers (1990), Cowley (2001) and others argue the importance of 'catching them being good' and praising them for it. McNamara (1999) makes the point that some teachers and some schools are more alert than others to the possibilities of noting and responding positively to good behaviour by pupils. Some year heads commented on the reluctance of some trainees and NQTs to use praise and reward systems, whether in the form of merit marks, commendations, letters to parents or more tangible rewards such as cinema/football tickets, MacDonald's vouchers and trips outside the classroom:

> Of course merit marks don't work for all our kids, but they do for some of them. Although it doesn't take a moment to award a merit mark or whatever, some teachers just don't find the time to get round to it. And yet often it can oil the wheels of getting kids to enthusiastically do something, settle quickly or whatever. It's as if they can't quite be bothered or don't think about it. It's just one of the things that can help a bit in terms of your overall relations with your teaching group.
>
> (Year head)

> Sometimes just a word of praise . . . a casual comment . . . nothing big deal, just to show that you have noticed that they have made an effort, even if it's just a quick word as you are returning their exercise books, it doesn't even have to be a reward or recorded.
>
> (Year head)

But several teachers argued that it was not a matter of the 'volume' of praise or rewards that was dished out, but the discernment and skill that was used in praising and rewarding pupils. Some felt that trainees sometimes used praise in a way that rendered it almost meaningless to pupils:

There is a tendency to overuse words like 'brilliant' and 'fantastic'; some kids are told they are brilliant just because they have managed to sit down in their seat successfully. The pupils are not daft, they know when they are being patronised, they know when praise is sincere.

(Mentor)

There was also a view that trainees were prone to give 'group praise' fairly indiscriminately, in a way that reduced its effectiveness:

Often at the end of the lesson, they will tell the whole group that they have been terrific and thank them for working so well. This would be ok if this was actually the case, but when it is patently not so, the few kids who have just got on with it and been ok are not thrilled to bits to have been accorded this 'batch' accolade.

(Head of department)

Some of them use praise like chucking manure on a field.

(Mentor)

This strikes a chord with several other studies on the use of praise and rewards. Parsons (quoted in Dickson, 1993: 135) makes the point that criticism that is constructive and conveyed sincerely can be more effective in motivating children to learn than 'throwaway' and vacuous use of praise:

A well chosen criticism can convey as much positive information as praise; abundant or indiscriminate praise can be meaningless; insincere praise which does not convey the teacher's expectations for the student can have detrimental effects on many students.

One mentor gave an example of this in recounting an incident where a pupil responded to a floridly excessive assessment of his written work by pencilling 'Piss off Sir' after the tribute to his work.

Persaud (2004) also mentions the potentially toxic effects of praise 'overdose':

'Praise, like penicillin, must not be administered haphazardly. There are rules and cautions that govern the handling of potent medicines – rules about timing and dosage, cautions about possible allergic reactions. There are similar regulations about the administration of emotional medicine.' So wrote a psychologist giving advice to parents in the 1960s.

For starters, there is clear evidence that excessive praise for tasks the child sees as easy is demotivating; he or she infers that the adult has a low opinion of his or her ability. There is also evidence that children may devote less time to pursuing tasks if praise is withdrawn. They are driven to perform to obtain praise rather than for the intrinsic joy of the task itself.

Elkins (2002) found that experienced teachers were often able to motivate students and manage their behaviour without the use of a formal system of rewards and penalties. Signals, both positive and negative, were often little more than nods of approbation, or questioning glances. He also noted that 'very little praise was directed to the class as a whole: praise was used with discrimination and was directed towards individuals' (Elkins, 2001: 5.7).

Shreeve and Boddington (2002: 44) found that consistency of approach, with all members of staff using the same 'currency' with rewards and sanctions was a factor in pupils regarding school systems as 'fair and purposeful', and that systems that concentrated on positive reinforcement, 'a high level of use by teachers of rewards and praise and a low level use of penalties' were thought to be most effective by pupils. In schools in the sample where the system was used inconsistently by teachers, pupils saw it as unfair and ineffective and teachers ceased to value it as well.

What mentors wanted more than anything of trainees was that they should remember the 'positive' side of the equation in their relations with pupils – the potential of praise, discerningly applied. Also, that they should be consistent in their application of sanctions, carry out threats after a clear warning, and work within the parameters of school and departmental systems and the custom and practice of what most teachers tended to do.

One head teacher made the point that it was helpful if there were ways and means of reducing or putting aside sanctions that had accumulated. Suggestions included remission for aspects of positive behaviour, or a specified time without further transgressions:

> If at all possible, there must be a way back for the pupil ... a way of getting back on track, back to rewards and things being positive. If there isn't any possibility of some constructive way forward, some of our kids will just say F. off then, I can't be bothered to try to behave.

One other point emerged about the use of sanctions, which related to trainees and NQTs developing an intelligent understanding of the extent of their power in particular situations; grasping when they were in a strong position, and when this was not the case, and adjusting their responses accordingly. In particular, this related to the use of privacy; that in some situations, it was better to sort the issue out later, rather than in front of the whole class, when pupils might be reluctant to lose face. This ties in with Rogers' idea (1997), that consequences can be deferred: what matters is the certainty of consequences, not just their immediacy. Also, the fact that the teachers' position vis-à-vis pupils is usually strengthened after the bell goes when there is a chance to detain pupils and have them discussing matters 'in their time', rather than during the lesson. Thus, it is easier to sort things out at the end of a lesson immediately preceding break or dinner time, rather than one where pupils have to move straight on to someone else's lesson. It is also generally easier to get pupils quiet and attentive if, after the bell has gone, it is made clear that they can go as soon as they have listened quietly to whatever it is the teacher has to say. In the extract below, a teacher educator recalls 'getting it wrong' in his decision making:

> You've got to weigh up how much power you've got in any particular situation. I remember once going past a group of kids messing about outside the gym ... the teacher hadn't turned up and they were just messing about. I brusquely told them

to line up in twos and be quiet. Within two seconds they had worked out that I was from the lower school and didn't know any of them from Adam ... no names, not even what form they were. So they didn't fall into line ... they perhaps understandably ... given the sort of kids they were ... took advantage of their temporary position of superior power and gave me a hard time. I had to walk on without having got them to behave as I wanted. If I had been 'lighter touch' – said something like, 'Can you do me a favour.... Sorry you're left hanging about.... I've got to get to a class but I'll call into the office and get someone to come down ... can you just chat to each other until someone comes down ... thanks', and moved swiftly on, I would have got a much better result.

Four other factors emerged as being considered important in using sanctions intelligently:

- 'calibration' – using the measures available in proportion to the offence and in the right order;
- giving a clear warning before imposing sanctions;
- being consistent in approach;
- following things up.

Get to know the pupils

This would appear to be rather stating the obvious but mentors felt that this was an area where some trainees and NQTs were much more accomplished than others. It was acknowledged that depth of previous experience of working with young people gave some trainees an advantage in terms of their ability to be natural and unself-conscious in tone with pupils in the initial stages of their teaching, but mentors also believed that skilful interaction with pupils was something that could be cultivated:

> Even just at the level of getting to know their names ... this makes things so much easier ... instead of having to point, or say 'you over there in the corner'. And yet some of them teach for weeks without getting anywhere on this.
>
> (Head of department)

> The pupils are often genuinely quite impressed when someone gets to know their names really quickly. I can remember one teacher offering to give pupils 10p if he didn't know their name in the second week he taught them.
>
> (Teacher educator)

> I hadn't realised what a big thing it was not to know the pupils' names, what a psychological barrier it was to getting on with them, how insulting it was to them to be called 'you', or pointed at, or just referred to by the class name ... 'Right 7R' ... Since then I've worked really hard to get to know their names as soon as possible, either through photos on record cards or name cards on desks. It can really impress them if you go in and pick up their names within the first couple of lessons.
>
> (Second year in teaching)

Some of them hang back when observing lessons in the early stages of placement, they are practically pressed against the wall, they look awkward, spare parts. Others drift into low-key and casual conversations with pupils without it being intrusive or clumsy. It is possible to try too hard and intervene in a counter-productive way. It's not how much they do, it's how skilfully they do it.

(Mentor)

One head of department stressed the importance of sensing when not to intervene:

You get better at learning when to leave some kids alone for a while. They come in and you can see them glowering ... seething about something ... obviously in a mood. You can just keep a quiet eye on them to monitor how things are going, leave them alone and ten minutes later ... if the lesson is ok and there's something that is interesting or 'not too bad', if most of the other kids are getting into it ... they'll gradually thaw out a bit and settle down.

(Advanced skills teacher)

Skilful 'teacher talk' to individual pupils was felt to be particularly important in establishing good working relations with more difficult pupils, this included demonstrating to pupils that teachers had a concern for them in general terms, not just in terms of their progress in a school subject:

Obviously, some colleagues are more accomplished than others at dealing with difficult pupils. Some are incredibly resourceful and talented at getting round pupils who are abrasive and volatile ... at establishing some sort of working and personal relationship with them. Some just don't know how to talk to them ... their tone and manner is all wrong. They seem to be permanently stuck in 'telling off' mode.

(Year head)

Most of them respond to someone who is genuinely doing their best. Going the extra mile ... it's obvious that you've at least tried to get hold of something that might interest them ... bits of incidental banter, acknowledging them in the corridor, just a nod, a slight smile. Getting to know them, building up an affinity with different types of kids ... the quiet shy ones, the feckless ones, the ones who hate lessons but are into sport or music.

(Third year of teaching)

I used to make a big effort to talk to them at some point in the lesson. In an informal, relaxed 'no big deal' sort of way ... incidental comment, just chat, 'Things ok David?' and then keep on strolling casually round the room to talk to other pupils and groups.

(Teacher educator)

I try and find or create some opportunity to say something that isn't telling them off or telling them that they can't do something.

(Head of department)

There was one really difficult girl who is horrible to all her teachers, and I noticed that she had her art folder with her. I asked her if I could have a look at it, and looked through it quite carefully, trying really hard to make appropriate and interested comments. It made a real difference in how she was ... for a couple of weeks ... But you've got to realise that they don't all want this sort of attention, you've got to play it by ear.

(Trainee)

Some teachers suggested that there might even be a sort of 'sympathy vote', whereby at least some pupils would not be too vile if it was thought that the new teacher was at least trying their best, was a nice person and was not constantly carping on about how bad the class was:

Just getting to know them ... there was one girl who when I first walked in used to get up on a desk and throw all the text books around the room. I've just tried to keep polite and firm and now she is usually ok. We talk as she comes into the room ... casual banter ... and say hello in the corridor ... and now she leaves me alone, I'm not saying she is perfect or cured, reformed, but she leaves me alone, not because I have any hold over her or have scared her into submission, but because I have got to know her and she now thinks I am 'ok'.

(NQT)

There are so many kids here who can be absolute nightmares in the classroom, and then as you get to know them, in the corridor can be really nice ... as long as you are not inflicting your subject on them within the confines of the classroom, they are ok. It's all about getting to know them, and then so many of them turn out to be nice kids.

(NQT in a challenging school)

As you know this is a difficult school but he has fitted in really well ... he has been great. He just gets on with it, does his best, he's a really nice person and even though he has a rough ride with some classes, this gets through to a lot of the kids. He does things outside the classroom, he gets hold of lots of bits and pieces to try and make the lessons interesting. They can see that he is making the effort. This makes no difference with some of our pupils ... they can be hard as nails ... but he doesn't antagonise the others by getting angry with all of them ... by shouting and blustering.

(Advanced skills teacher talking about an NQT)

I've read a lot of books about classroom management and talked to a lot of teachers, but in the end what's really improved my classroom management is experience – and confidence. I now have the confidence to be myself with the kids and use all the resources of my personality (sense of humour, energy etc.) to build relationships with them. Class management is so much easier if every child in the room knows that you are pleased to have them there, and that you know something about them and what their strengths are.

(Second year of teaching)

Two other points of consensus emerged relating to interaction with pupils. The first was the importance of not betraying dislike of pupils. It was acknowledged that some pupils are easier to like than others, but it was also felt that pupils should never have a sense that a teacher 'liked' some of them more than others. Pupil feedback also suggested that pupils had a keen sense of the importance of even-handedness in dealing with pupils:

> You must make it clear that there are no grudges ... that they don't come in the classroom as marked men. I have a sign in the classroom saying that it's a fresh start, they know that what happened last lesson is history. Of course in my own mind I am keeping an eye out for some pupils but they mustn't know that.
>
> (Five years in teaching)

> It's difficult but vital not to bear a grudge and to act as if each lesson was a new start, greeting them as if you are pleased to see them. I have a very challenging tutor group and the teachers who have lost the kids' goodwill completely are those who give a dog a bad name and hang him; there is nothing so demotivating for a child to arrive at a lesson in a good mood, intending to do some work for once, and be immediately shouted at for their behaviour in previous lessons.
>
> (Second year in teaching)

> The pupils can tell which teachers care about them and which ones don't, and they can tell when teachers don't like some pupils. You might not take to some pupils ... find them as enjoyable to teach as others ... but you can't let that show. You've got to pay scrupulous attention to your position in the classroom, eye contact, body language, time spent on incidental conversation. The kids pick up vibes very quickly.'
>
> (Experienced teacher)

One head suggested that one of the characteristics of teachers who were good at establishing good working relationships with their teaching groups was that they had what might be termed a 'statue of liberty' approach to pupils, and genuinely did like (almost) all the pupils:

> By far the most important one of all is does the teacher like the students, and I mean all of them, is there a general liking for even the ones who can be difficult, the eccentric ones, because that comes across to the class straight away. They can feel loved or they can feel disliked and their response will be very much linked to that.

The other area of consensus related to the importance of patience: understanding that it took time to build positive relationships with pupils, and that trying to force the issue, to rush in and try too hard, to be intrusive, would not work. If pupils thought that this was from page whatever of the 'How to succeed in teaching' handbook, they would not 'buy it':

One of the bottom lines is that you've got to take an interest in them, to show you care about them. This takes time.

(Teacher educator)

There are judgement issues about not trying too hard . . . rushing at it . . . being intrusive and phoney. Sometimes you need to sense when to leave them alone but in the longer term you try to establish some sort of contact or relationship with them even if it's just acknowledging their existence . . . try just nodding to them in the corridor . . . very low key . . . just to acknowledge that you know them. If it does more harm than good, don't carry on doing it.

(Teacher educator)

Not everyone's got the facility to talk to pupils in a really natural and unaffected way. Most trainees have to work on it over a period of time. It's about relationships with the pupils and the groups . . . it takes time . . . you can't do it in one lesson and in a sense you can't rush it. If you are seen to be trying too hard it could even be counter-productive.

(Teacher educator)

The ones who were really good with their classes seemed to have been able to build up a way of being casual and detached, but in a friendly, vaguely interested sort of way.

(Teaching assistant)

Other suggestions for cultivating positive working relations with pupils

The importance of modelling the behaviour you want from pupils

Kids have a keen eye for hypocrisy; people not practising what they preach. If you forget to say please and thank you, if you are inconsiderate and rude, or disparaging in your comments to pupils, you will get it back in spades.

(Year head)

If you apologise sincerely when you have made a mistake, got something wrong, it makes a big difference to how pupils rate you, compared to people who find it very difficult to admit that they have made a mistake.

(Year head)

Working with pupils outside the classroom

I went on a school trip and got to talk to pupils that I didn't really know at all. It was a real eye-opener. My relations with the kids when we got back to school were transformed. They treated me like a different human being . . . or rather, as a human being rather than as a teaching operative.

(Second year of teaching)

I took the year 9s for football, and after that they left me alone. They were on my side, 'Leave him alone, he's ok'.

(Second year of teaching)

(I once offered optional 'early' lessons immediately before pupils' external examinations and was surprised by the number of pupils who turned up, and by the change in their attitudes to me as a teacher after this offer).

Use privacy and colleague support whenever possible

In my department we had an office near to the teaching rooms so it was great for getting that bit of privacy away from the other pupils in the class, and if there was someone else, a colleague in the room, it shifted the power balance in your favour, they were aware that you now had a grown-up witness and had to be careful. And they were not in front of their friends so the bravado, the defiance was gone.

(Second in department)

Involving parents

The NASC survey of pupils' views on effective sanctions revealed that pupils viewed a phone call or letter to parents as the most effective sanction available to teachers ('Sanctions and rewards', *Times Educational Supplement*, 25 November 2005). This was easier for NQTs than trainees, but several teachers stressed that in some cases, it was one of the few really powerful deterrents available to teachers, one that could genuinely frighten some pupils:

Building relationships with pupils' parents . . . some groups were very difficult early on but then I tried contacting parents and trying to work with them . . . if they were made aware of things it could have a great impact. Ok, there were some kids who rarely saw their parents . . . it didn't work with all of them . . . but it worked with a lot of them.

(Six years in teaching)

I learned after about a term that phoning parents was a very powerful deterrent. I did it with probably the most difficult pupil I teach. He was acting tough . . . 'I don't care . . . phone them'. I did ring and got him . . . said they weren't in but he sounded really nervous. I said I would ring again tomorrow, which I did. He had been lying, they had been in, and his mother was appalled both at what he had called me and the lying, and was very supportive. That stopped the problem with him. It took a bit of time but it was worth it.

(NQT)

A succession of research reports have stressed the beneficial influence of effective communication with parents (see, for example, Mortimore *et al.*, 1988; Lund, 1996; Porter, 2001). One question that NQTs might ask themselves is to what extent they make optimum use of parental involvement in their efforts to improve classroom climate and pupil behaviour.

Audio or videotaping lessons

Some trainees seem to have difficulty seeing what's going on in the room, or under-standing what's going on. Videoing can help, we ask our trainees to try and video some of their teaching and they often say that they find it helpful ... it sometimes points things out very clearly.

(Teacher educator)

Audio or videotaping things seems to make it more concrete for them ... of course they sometimes feel uncomfortable and nervous about it but most of them get something out of it ... it's so much more vivid than just reading things that have been written on a piece of paper ... they see it for themselves, you don't need to say anything ... the penny drops. We advise them to do it at some point in the placement ... some get round to it, others put it off ... make excuses. I would say that on balance, the ones who get stuck in and do it are the ones who do well.

(Teacher educator)

It's particularly good for things like making them aware of what the pupils are doing when they are talking ... the level of noise ... the number of kids listening ... or rather not listening. They can also reflect on how effective their exposition is ... often a chastening experience but a powerful learning experience for them. It stops them blithely continuing to do things that aren't working well.

(Teacher educator)

Don't give whole-class or 'blanket' punishments

This is so obviously unfair. Unless it is about retrieving something that has been stolen, it is hard to defend. Pick on the ones who have done something wrong. Differentiation applies to sanctions as well as planning. It is not that difficult to grade your sanctions according to how badly pupils have behaved. For instance, you can detain some pupils for longer than others.

(Head of department)

This writing on the board, 'Three minutes' ... for everyone in the class, whether they were talking or not. It's the same principle as the Nazis used during the French Resistance.

(Mentor)

You've got to be very careful not to stereotype by gender. One of our biggest problems at the moment isn't boys but really hard girls, working in gangs. But you should never generalise by gender. It's very rarely all the boys or all the girls, so you shouldn't say, 'Right all the boys stay behind', and yet I've seen it happen, and some really well-behaved, quiet pupils get treated as if they are miscreants.

(Head teacher)

As with other aspects of teaching, teachers believed that the ability to get on well with pupils, to talk to them in a skilful and appropriate manner, and to develop good working relations with teaching groups, were skills that could be developed –

as long as the teacher was open-minded in approach, prepared to experiment. Progress was felt to be more difficult where teachers stuck to their preconceptions, their established way of doing things and found it difficult to change their approach. In the words of Miller (2001: 104): 'It's difficult to change the way you see the world. We take on a certain view when we are young then spend the rest of our lives collecting the evidence.' It is, of course, difficult to change how you are as a person, but mentors felt that some trainees were more open-minded and adaptable than others:

> Some of them have little idea how to talk to our kids when they arrive and have a very artificial way of addressing them, referring to them as 'ladies and gentlemen', or talking to them in a stiff, formal manner in a way which makes the kids look at each other, eyebrows raised ... It's how quickly they learn that matters, whether they are quick at picking things up and learning from others. Some of them make fantastic progress over the course of the placement, others don't change.
>
> (Mentor)

> On the whole it probably is best if they come in with the ability to talk to pupils in a natural and appropriate manner, but the danger is that if they are 'a natural' with the kids, they are not always as good at developing their skills further ... there has been no major trauma to get them to question their practice and get them to experiment with, for instance, talking really quietly to classes, experimenting with different ways of talking to the class, to add a bit of variety and interest to their interactions with pupils.
>
> (Mentor)

If there is an overarching message about establishing good working relations with pupils, it is that at least part of it is linked to having 'reasonable human being' qualities. The pupil survey confirmed our hunch that pupils' response to teachers is influenced as much by what they are like as people as their pedagogical and professional attributes. If you are selfish, hypocritical and unpleasant to other human beings, you may still be able to flourish in some jobs, but not as a teacher. In the words of one respondent in the pupil survey: 'I like lessons and do well in lessons where the teacher is nice so there should be a teacher training course which teaches teachers to be nice.'

These sentiments were echoed by a head of year working in a difficult school:

> With the sort of kids we get at this school, you can't force them to learn. The only way you get anywhere with them in the long term is if you learn to get on with them, to build up a reasonable working relationship with them. Often, this is far from a perfect modus vivendi, but it is generally more productive than declaring war on them.

SUMMARY

*   It is important to understand and take into account that some pupils find learning difficult and do not have a deep commitment to learning the subject that you are trying to teach.

- There is a body of research evidence that sheds some light on factors that can impact positively on pupils' attitude to learning.

- Pupils' perceptions of teachers who incline them to want to learn are influenced by a range of factors, including professional, pedagogical and 'personal' characteristics.

- Teaching is not just a matter of technical competence. What the teacher is like as a person, as a human being, has an important bearing on pupils' attitudes to being in the classroom and having to learn a school subject.

Note

1   Those involved in the project were Bob Burns, Dominic Boddington, Wynne Feather, Terry Haydn, Lesley Howell, Dave Jones, Debbie Rolfe and Barbara Zamorski.

6 Working in schools

> I was at a school where you did quite commonly get some of the lower levels on the scale. It came to a point when I realised that you can't separate how you manage your classes from the way the school operates as a whole ... the institution, the culture ... you don't operate in a vacuum ... it's the art of the possible and you've got to adjust intelligently to the situation. It was helpful to come to that realisation.
>
> (Experienced teacher)

In Chapter 4, teachers mentioned three 'key criteria' in particular for being in reasonable control of a class: (a) pupils not talking while the teacher was talking; (b) the teacher feeling confident in undertaking any form of activity with pupils; (c) pupils not being able to impede the learning of others.

It was clear that the degree of difficulty in achieving these three desirable conditions for teaching would vary enormously between schools. There were schools where it was felt that getting the pupils to be quiet ought to be within the compass of any competent teacher within a few weeks to a term of experience, and others where it would be a real achievement for a new teacher. Similarly, there were schools where an established teacher would generally feel able to undertake most forms of lesson activity, and others where it was acknowledged that even the most experienced teachers had to modify their teaching approaches in order to maintain control, often in a way that limited learning opportunities for pupils.

Teacher testimony suggested that the biggest variable, in terms of the overall classroom climate prevailing in a school, was the pupil population, with the caveat that even in schools that had large numbers of disaffected pupils, good teachers could usually make a difference (see Chapter 7 for further development of this point).

Other factors felt to have a bearing on classroom climate included the degree to which teachers worked collaboratively to support each other, the effectiveness of school systems, and the degree of support that classroom teachers received from senior members of staff. With all these factors, teachers suggested the need for new teachers and trainees to work out the ways things worked within a particular school, and adapt their practice accordingly. This corresponds to Klemp's idea of the development of 'situational understanding' as being an important component of professional effectiveness (Klemp, 1977).

Respondents were also at pains to stress the importance of adjusting to working within particular school cultures. Given the requirement to have experience of working in at least two schools to achieve QTS (DfES/TTA, 2002), most trainees are aware of the fact that schools can be very different to work in. Lawton (1997) makes the point that there are very different types of school in terms of school 'culture', varying from 'formal' (high pressure to achieve, weak social cohesion between staff and students), 'welfarist' (relaxed, informal, friendly), 'hothouse' (all under pressure to participate, high expectations for work and personal development), and 'survivalist' (social control and cohesion weak, social relations poor, teachers striving for basic control). There was some evidence to suggest that this led to a degree of paradox in terms of which schools were easiest to work in for new teachers. Some schools that were 'at the sharp end' had well-developed mechanisms for protecting the well-being of staff and strong staff solidarity, others had more negative features of a 'survivalist' culture, as the following two extracts illustrate:

> Yes, control is an issue even in this school.... And there are times when there is a bit of a 'mob' atmosphere in some lessons ... it goes beyond what might be termed 'low-level' disruption. Overall this school is much less challenging than one of the ones I did my teaching practice in, but that school was used to dealing with disruptive pupils, the system was geared up for it, there were good mechanisms in place. I actually felt much happier in my dealings over control and discipline in that school and felt that I handled things better there. This school is only just learning to do this.
>
> (Third year of teaching in a school high in the league tables)

> At my previous school there was a message on the staff room door ... Do not knock unless it is absolutely urgent ... it was a sort of ... you've had your hour of a lesson, now leave us alone in our bunker before we have to do another mission. It didn't send out very good messages.
>
> (Third year of teaching)

It is helpful for new teachers to develop an understanding of school cultures, partly because they should ideally be able to cope in a variety of contexts, and partly because it may give them an understanding of the sort of school in which they will be able to enjoy their work.

Working with colleagues

'Everybody knows'

Several teachers mentioned the importance of being honest and open about problems of control, partly because it was not a phenomenon that it is possible to conceal, and partly because it opened up avenues for professional dialogue with other colleagues who might have useful experience to share, and advice to give. This might vary from practical advice on what steps to take in particular contexts, re-assurance that the pupil or group were difficult with lots of teachers, or just general 'cheering up' and moral support, reminding them that it takes time to get classes 'sorted out':

It's one of those things that all the teachers ... and the senior management team in the school have a view on, an opinion about, even though it's not written down anywhere, and often not talked about explicitly in the staffroom or in departmental groups ... it's more of a sub-conscious awareness, a discreet mental note ... how good colleagues are at managing classes and pupils ... where they are in the scale ... from 'As good as it gets in this place' to 'God, they have a terrible time don't they, how can they bear to keep coming in every day to face that?

(Head of department)

I don't want colleagues to suffer in silence and put up with more than they should. You need teachers to be honest if they are having difficulties with pupils. It's no use pretending because in the end, things get out anyway if there are problems. There are very few classrooms without windows.

(Head of department)

One real low point was when they were throwing books across the room over my head with me as piggy in the middle. I was so demoralised that I went to see the deputy head about it and told him I was just about at the end of my tether. He was great ... he let me get it out of my system, he was sympathetic and supportive and he just listened to me and let me pour it all out. Sometimes telling people about it can help you to get it out of your system. Most teachers are good colleagues, they will respond by telling you about their battles and mistakes. It's not a good idea to bottle it all up or pretend that things are ok.

(Head of department)

At first, in your first year, you can feel you are a bit on your own but I soon learned that I could mention things to the deputy head, I could tell the form teacher or the year head and the whole apparatus of the school system could lean on ... put pressure on a pupil who was going out of his way to mess me about. I learned to use the school system and colleagues more intelligently. Year heads and form teachers are great for knowing whether or not threatening to tell a kid's parents about things will work or not.

(Third year in teaching)

If I had to give one piece of advice to a new teacher about class management it would be to talk to people ... the old lags who have been doing it for years, the newbies who are having as much trouble as you. The only people I've seen fail are the ones who lock themselves in their classrooms, get mauled lesson after lesson and don't talk to anybody because they don't want to be seen as weak.

(Second year in teaching)

Practical and moral colleague support

In the same way that groups of pupils acting together can sometimes make life difficult for teachers, it was felt that teachers could also collaborate effectively to find ways of discouraging pupils from misbehaving. In some cases this was purely at a level of 'moral support', in others it extended to practical strategies for trying to ensure that a teacher did not get isolated with a particularly difficult group of pupils.

Bill Rogers' work is often seen in terms of providing advice for teachers working within their own classrooms, but a substantial part of his writing relates to the ways in which colleagues can support each other by working collaboratively (Rogers, 1995, 2002).

One example of this is where a department established a general guideline that if a colleague felt that the working atmosphere with a particular group was slipping below level 5 or if there were major 'issues' with particular individuals, pupils at the root of the problems would be sent to work with a departmental colleague who had an 'A' level (or similar) teaching group, according to a prearranged timetable. This was considered to be a lesser evil than allowing some lessons to degenerate to the lowest levels on the scale, where little or no education could take place. This also had the incidental advantages of acting as an effective deterrent to disruption – pupils did not like not being with their friends and sitting with older pupils who regarded them with a degree of condescension and curiosity. It also sent the message to pupils that they were confronting the department, or the staff as a whole, rather than crossing individual, isolated members of staff. The system also meant that all members of the department could support colleagues who were under pressure from difficult classes, all members of the department were 'givers' and 'receivers' over a period of time. Several heads of department acknowledged that there was some form of departmental arrangement for being flexible with pupil groupings:

> We try to manage things in house, within the department with everybody contributing and helping each other. People in the department have different talents. X is good with the younger kids, he's got a nice paternal manner, I'm ok with the older kids because I've been here for a while so I knew them when they were little year 7s, sometimes people have just got a way with particular pupils because they like art, or they are a good form teacher, or they are in the football team.
>
> (Head of department)

> We exchange kids across the department so that if someone has got a group with several difficult pupils we can pre-arrange for them to be sent to someone who's not under pressure elsewhere in the department if they raise their heads over the parapet. I want these moves to be made rather than have some kids wrecking a perfectly good lesson.
>
> (Head of department)

In other cases it was simply a question of 'keeping an eye out', having someone hovering to provide support (and act as a witness) if there was a likely trouble spot, or an outbreak of noise that might signal an incident. In some cases it was a question of a department working closely together, talking about problem pupils and groups and coordinating 'counter-measures', in others it was just whatever colleagues happened to be in the vicinity:

> In our department if there is an issue with a pupil, a teacher next door or across the corridor, the head of department or whoever will be there keeping an eye ... You feel confident because it feels like the department's territory.
>
> (NQT)

If there's an upset, an issue, my head of department pops over, hovers support-ively, he's there for me, helping me to cope in my NQT year is clearly a high-profile item on his job description. I know that if there is any trouble, if anything blows up, the support will be there. That's incredibly important if you are new in a school. But all the staff are like that, there's an English teacher who teaches next to me keeps an eye out, and if there is any noise he nips out on the corridor just checking things are ok. The head of KS3 also has an office on the corridor, and that's an extra port of call, a useful extra space.

(NQT in a challenging school)

There's one guy on our corridor . . . not in my subject . . . who just always keeps an eye out . . . who is just 'about' when there's noise, an incident. Just another adult being there to witness things makes kids more careful, and you don't feel on your own. It's low-key, understated support, it doesn't make you feel a failure. It's sensitively done.

(Third year of teaching in a tough school)

At the end of my second lesson with a year 9 group, I was in tears afterwards. They were really horrible. But I got a lot of support from the department. The second in department, my mentor, would be about at the start of the lesson, pottering about or doing the lesson as a team-teach, or hovering nearby, popping in and out to pick up books . . . 'How are we getting on?' . . . he was almost making it like a double act. He managed to do it in a way that didn't undermine my authority. They knew what was going on, but they also knew that we were all acting together, on the same side, and that if they went too far, the others would support me and do what was necessary to sort them out.

(NQT)

In some cases collaborative action extended to a form of departmental or staff mafia, where if a pupil was messing around one colleague, he or she would be given a hard time by other teachers. There are clearly difficult tensions here, about pupils coming into the room with a clean slate, not bearing grudges, taking each incident at face value and so on, but it was felt that in some circumstances only concerted action by a group of colleagues would be strong enough to discourage some pupils from attempting to disrupt lessons, or that, at least, they would 'get the message' more quickly if it came from a group of teachers, and make it clear that they could not isolate a teacher from colleague support:

The department is great, both in terms of giving me good advice and giving direct support when it's needed. So if a kid has been messing me about, they both take this on and we all try and make sure that between us we discourage the kid from going out of his way to mess us around.

(NQT in a tough school)

If a kid is messing one of us about, he will get it from all of us. We will all go out of our way to inconvenience him and make it clear that we can do things to discourage them from spoiling the lesson. But it's just as important that as soon as they stop, you make it clear that it's all over, the incident is closed and you treat them in a polite and friendly way.

(NQT)

The idea that teachers can work collaboratively to improve classroom climate and change 'the balance of power' between teachers and disruptive pupils sounds so obvious as to be hardly worth stating, but it was clear from the testimony of teachers in their first three years of teaching that some of them felt that support could have been stronger, and that not all departments offered the same degree of colleague support to new teachers. In some cases, problems with 'the grown ups' had proved more corrosive of morale than working with difficult pupils:

> Yes, I've had some difficulties and problems with particular pupils and classes. Things that have really got me down. Real low points ... I think most NQTs probably experience these troughs. But my worst moments haven't been with the pupils, it's when you have problems with the people you work with. If you have good colleagues who are helpful, supportive, nice. . . . It's worth more than having easy classes.
>
> (NQT)

Heads of department and year heads also made the point that some teachers were better than others in terms of being 'givers' or 'takers' in class management issues. It was felt that some teachers were more prepared than others to invest time and effort to work on problems of pupil behaviour, to support collegial systems and to support others. This might be reflected in attitudes to break duty, being prepared to chase up pupils for personal detentions before using school systems, or simply offering support for others. In the following extract, an experienced teacher talks of the response of a colleague when asked to keep an eye on his class so that he could attend to a minor emergency nearby:

> He looked at me mystified, you could see things going round in his brain and settling finally into simply not understanding in what way keeping an eye out for someone else's class would in any way, shape or form help him in his career, help him to get on.
>
> (Head of department)

Several heads also made the point that some teachers tended to be quick to pass responsibility and blame for pupil misbehaviour upwards, rather than fully exploring individual and collegial avenues for dealing with problems. Some also felt that some departments were more proactive than others in playing a full part in the struggles to cope with disaffected and disruptive pupils.

From a teacher's perspective, several teachers made the point that departmental and school systems for preventing and containing disruptive behaviour were often heavily dependent on strong support from senior colleagues if they were to be effective:

> Things have been much better since we got a good learning support system, somewhere for them to go when they need to calm down. It's not billed as a punishment cell or sin bin, it's not a big deal as long as they go straight away, but it does depend on strong support from SMT. They must know that if they don't just go quietly, then it gets serious and something will happen ... it might be parents in, it might be losing breaks and dinnertimes.
>
> (Four years in teaching at a difficult school)

As in so many areas of teaching, these issues raise difficult questions about the point at which teachers ask for help, and make the decision whether to handle something on their own or use the school or departmental system. Heads of department and year heads liked to feel that individual teachers would be open, keep them abreast of situations, ask for advice about such decisions, and be prepared to put in time and effort generally in chasing things up and trying to sort out problems arising in their lessons. NQTs' decisions were influenced not just by their relations with their head of department, but by how difficult the overall school situation was, as the following extract demonstrates:

> I'm lucky, the kids just don't mess with my head of department. If I say 'I'm going to send you to Mr X', they are genuinely scared, not in a physical sense but they start being more compliant, trying to get out of it. I try to use this sparingly . . . I've only done it a few times, I prefer to sort it out by myself if I can but I don't think he minds as long as I just do it occasionally. He wants to be helpful and supportive, and he wants me to let him know if there is a pupil misbehaving in one of the lessons in his subject. At this place that is feasible, but I'm aware that in some of the schools I've been in, the scale of pupil misbehaviour would make this very difficult.
>
> (NQT)

One further aspect of working with colleagues is perhaps worthy of note, and that is the enormous difference that general colleague 'solidarity' and mutual support can make to teacher morale when working in difficult schools. The following extracts are from interviews with NQTs working in tough schools:

> I've really enjoyed it in a sick and twisted, bizarre way. Not all the time . . . sometimes it's awful, really bad moments, bad days, a few bad weeks. But the staff are brilliant, get on really well. Just things like having a game of football together at the end of the week. There was a leaving do the other day and nearly everyone went and had a great time. There is a sense of togetherness, of solidarity. I was really worried when I took this job . . . it's a much tougher school than the ones I did in my training year, but I've enjoyed it a lot more in spite of not being in control of my classes. I would not have believed that it could be enjoyable to work like this.

> I couldn't enjoy it . . . I couldn't have survived, if my colleagues weren't so helpful and supportive, my head of department is fantastic. Everybody helps each other, we're all in the same boat . . . the kids don't make much allowance for the fact that you might have been working here for years, they are difficult with just about everybody. This means that we all have to help each other. This gives a fantastic feeling of solidarity.

Consistency of approach and general professionalism

Teachers and teaching assistants felt that consistency of approach was in teachers' own interests, not just in the interests of the senior managers, 'the system' the school as a whole. It related to 'quality of life' issues, such as how easily the pupils would routinely respond to teacher requests, staff morale and an absence of inter-staff bad feeling and grousing:

> You have to fit in with how different teachers teach ... it's their classroom not yours ... but it does make you realise how much difference it would make if they all did the same thing and it's slightly irritating when you see them not doing what is supposed to be 'school rules'. The pupils are very quick to pick up on this. You see the same kids acting very differently depending on who the teacher is ... of course, it depends on who they're with as well ... which mates they are hanging out with in a particular lesson ... whether there is a 'critical mass' of potential followers, whether there's 'an audience'.
>
> (Teaching assistant)

> Cliché, but 'singing from the same hymn sheet' ... if everyone picks up on some-thing, it makes a difference. If some staff can't be bothered, or try to court popularity with the pupils by not bothering about uniform, spitting, ties, swearing or whatever ... it doesn't make it any easier for the rest of us. The kids are incredibly quick to exploit these gaps, these weak areas.
>
> (Three years in teaching)

> I have problems with some teachers who are reluctant to pick pupils up on uniform. They think it will make them popular ... 'I'm not bothered about all that crap ... I'm like you', but it doesn't work with the pupils ... they are seen as weak, the kids aren't daft, and it doesn't make the job any easier for the rest of us.
>
> (Head teacher)

> Sometimes there is a problem with new teachers who don't like sticking to this ... sometimes they feel that they've got a 'special line' to pupils ... a special way ... but it sometimes undermines what other colleagues are trying to achieve. We get it most with less experienced teachers and perhaps amongst teachers who exhibit a degree of immaturity which often manifests itself in being too familiar with the pupils.
>
> (Head teacher)

One head teacher also stressed the importance of 'lateral responsibility' (Fullan, 1993), pointing to the fallacy of the media portrayal of a cosy conspiracy of professionals colluding in negligent practice:

> A peer group of professional colleagues does not welcome into its ranks incom-petent teachers. Colleagues have very low tolerance levels for such teachers, and on the very rare occasions when such teachers appear, they (the staff) demand that action is taken.

This was particularly apparent in the feedback relating to teachers who were being prone to frequent absence, disparagingly termed 'the two days a fortnight merchants' (teachers who frequently had days off) by one respondent.

The head teacher's perspective

A sample size of 12 interviews is clearly not large enough to draw wide-ranging and authoritative conclusions on head teachers' views on classroom climate and pupil behaviour, but some of the following extracts will hopefully illustrate at least some of the difficulties and tensions involved in this area for head teachers.

As Smith (1993: 16) points out, heads *in practice* carry ultimate responsibility for the school's progress and the pupils' safety and well-being 'and are thus often placed in an unenviable position . . . They must of course uphold the law of the land and expect their teaching colleagues to do the same'. They often have very difficult decisions to make in the area of balancing standards of attainment for the overall pupil body, with principles of educational inclusion, and as Chapter 2 attempted to outline, there are often very difficult tensions in this area. One of the things that appeared to irk heads was the oversimplification of issues in this area. In the words of one head: 'The frustrating thing is when parents, governors, the LEA, officials, less successful colleagues take a simplistic view of things and suggest that it is all fairly straightforward matter, that you can have simple rules in this area.' Another head admitted that: 'We share the same tensions faced by class teachers, on the one hand trying to be consistent and fair, and on the other, try to make some allowances for pupils with problems,' with the caveat that, 'obviously we often have to make the bottom line decisions over difficult cases.' All the heads I spoke to acknowledged the unfairness of the present system. In the words of one head:

> One of the advantages of our position is that we are heavily oversubscribed as a school and the pupils are aware of that . . . I can say to them that they don't have to come here, they could go elsewhere. Some of them are under the impression that I would kick them out at the drop of a hat and I don't disabuse them of that. At my last school I couldn't use that; we were undersubscribed and having to practically pull pupils off the streets.

Box 6.1 describes some of the dilemmas that heads mentioned in this area.

'The beast in the cupboard'

One of the things that heads most wanted from colleagues was an appreciation of the complexity of decision making in this area; an understanding that there were no easy solutions and that everybody had to work to do their best in what were often difficult circumstances. A head of department had argued that what some teachers wanted from heads was to be 'the beast in the cupboard', by which he meant that the head should be someone whose name could be mentioned to pupils in a way that would evince fear and cringing remorse from pupils. Several of the heads I talked to understood the phrase and, perhaps understandably, felt that some teachers had unrealistic expectations about the degree of 'shock and awe' that head teachers might be expected to induce in pupils:

> Some of them are looking for a heroic rescuer . . . someone who will make it all go away, someone to kick the year heads into zero tolerance of students instead of realising that we are all in it together. What you aim at is absolute and tireless

Box 6.1 Head teachers' dilemmas

'Different constituencies or interested parties want different things in this area; you are under pressure from the LEA not to exclude unless it's desperate, you have good teachers coming to see you to say that they think the kid ought to go, you know many parents would want a lot lower bar on exclusion. One question worth asking is how you would feel if your kid was in the same classes at that pupil, but that can't be the only question you would ask.'

'Heads have to make really difficult decisions over whether and how to exclude pupils from lessons or even from the school. This idea that we exclude kids at the drop of a hat ... if anything it's the other way. I feel that in one case I got it wrong ... persevered too much trying to keep a pupil in and lost a really good member of staff as a result. They went somewhere else where they felt they could enjoy their teaching more.'

'There is a massive tension at the heart of the job; the pressure to raise standards and the fact that you went into it to help all pupils, not just the ones who are good at learning. A lot of teachers want to be 'Statue of Liberty' type teachers, but there are really tough decisions to be made about doing your best for all of them.'

'I understand heads resorting to encouraging some pupils to stay out of school. We've just explored all paths ... personal support plans, partial timetable, isolation, everything, and still ended up excluding two pupils after taking up enormous amounts of time and school resource.'

'You want to be fair to all teachers and all pupils, but you also feel you should support your staff through thick and thin, acknowledging that everybody makes mistakes sometimes, but as in many schools there are personnel issues.... I know there are certain staff ... small minority ... who are not really good enough ... or who are no longer doing the job well. These difficult issues can't be ducked by senior staff and governors, but you can't deal with them overnight ... it can take months or even a year or two years to resolve such problems.

'You've got to work with your staff and you can't run a school without their support, but you can't just exclude pupils because the staff, or some of them, want to. You obviously have to take account of their views but they mustn't feel that they can bounce you into decisions'

'So often you are dealing not with right and wrong decisions but 'lesser evil' decisions. There are times if it's best if kids go out of the lesson, I wouldn't say we are relaxed about that, it would be the wrong word, but it would be a lesser evil. It can be quite scary for teachers to feel that there's no safety valve to stop things getting out of hand, getting worse.'

'It's difficult ... some ADHD kids have really bad days when the medication isn't working, where even the lead practitioners in the school can't reason with them. But it's not a permanent state of affairs ... it's a really bad day and you are making decisions about whether they stay in the local community for their education.'

Box 6.2 **The beast in the cupboard**

'A head of department had argued that what some teachers wanted from heads was to be "the beast in the cupboard", by which he meant that the head should be someone whose name could be mentioned to pupils in a way that would evince fear and cringing remorse from pupils.'

support as long as they realise that it is part of their job to teach these kids and to do the best they possibly can for them, not to wash their hands of them as soon as they are not passively compliant.

Occasionally we've had to call police in to deal with incidents with pupils from other schools and it's interesting to see the low-level non-confrontational approach that the police take ... often taking quite a bit of stick and turning a blind ear to quite a lot of things, which is a tactic which our teachers have to learn because it is no use them being hawkish or shrill in the way they perhaps could have been just seven or eight years ago, because that's not the way public servants are allowed to behave these days.

Consistency of approach

Even in the area of consistency of approach, issues were not unproblematic. On the one hand, heads were at pains to stress the importance of whole-school approaches to the management of pupil behaviour:

> Everyone must uphold the policy for behaviour which must operate consistently throughout the school. The system mustn't depend on situational idiosyncrasies ... it mustn't be solely reliant on the talent of individuals to manage their classes ... judgements and sanctions mustn't be personal. The aim is to have a framework of support and guidance and the kids must know and understand the system. This way, the vast majority of the kids comply with the system ... with the expectations of their behaviour. This leaves a small core of kids who challenge the system, the policy, and we have to have alternative strategies for doing our best for them without letting them spoil the learning of others. This is where you might have to take them out of some classrooms.

> What I want more than anything is that they [teachers] all do the same thing, in the sense that we have a behaviour policy and that everyone tries to support it and use it so that the kids know where they stand and there is a clear sense of 'boundaries' which runs across the school, that everyone understands. This includes support staff, dinner ladies, everybody.

However, several heads also explained that absolute consistency was sometimes difficult to achieve in practice:

> There's a tension between setting consistent clear rules which one would want to uphold, and the sort of grey areas that exist in the sort of difficulties of living as families. So, for example, school uniform ... I want everyone to wear the same basic school uniform ... tie, blue top and so on ... The fact is, that if a family is splitting or in trouble, in crisis, it is possible that a pupil will come in not in uniform. So there's an area where humanity has to be there, allowing for special cases, at the same time as attempting to demonstrate that we're attempting to hold a clear consistent line and that's a real tension.

> It is difficult to get everyone to do the same thing. Teachers are well educated, they can think for themselves, they are often very creative people, they are not robots, operatives. Some policies, it's difficult to get complete agreement, sometimes you have to review a policy because you are not making it stick, it's not working. A few years ago the school was awash with chewing gum, so we decided to bring in a policy ... it was thought to be a good idea at a staff meeting ... of school detention for anyone caught chewing. At the end of a term only 17 kids had been put in detention for chewing. Seventeen staff out of 60-odd had acted on the policy. It wasn't working so we dropped it.

Zero tolerance?

From time to time, media reports on education throw up reports of schools achieving spectacular success by adopting a policy of 'zero tolerance' of poor pupil behaviour

('Not so mad hatters now', *TES*, 5 December 2003, 'Leader defends the fifth sanction', *TES*, 13 May 2005, 'How iron rules and iron discipline helped turn a school
around', *The Observer*, 10 July 2005). The idea of excluding pupils from classrooms
and schools perhaps sounds quite seductive from the perspective of someone first
going to work in the classroom, but most of the heads I spoke to had reservations
about zero tolerance approaches:

> Politicians use this phrase zero tolerance ... Moronic phrase ... Politicians would
> never want zero tolerance applied to them ... nor would our staff, nor would our
> parents ... and nor would those teachers who say they want zero tolerance in the
> classroom. They wouldn't want the head or the governing body to deal with them
> with zero tolerance. It's an unchristian phrase. An awful phrase.

> It's a phrase I loathe and despise, legally, morally, philosophically. It sends a false
> message about a fundamentally complex problem and about teachers' obligations
> towards their pupils. The community sends its children here. This is the only
> secondary school for miles around. You can't lightly exile a very young person from
> their community.

> The school has a responsibility for every pupil that it takes on roll to give the best
> education possible for every pupil who is on roll. You have got to do your best
> for all of them. You can't just kick out all the ones who are not perfect pupils and
> claim that you are running a good school. You're actually evading the challenge of
> being a good school.

> You can't have zero tolerance, we'd be putting out about half the kids who come
> here.

> We don't have the sanctions to support zero tolerance.

> I have had to exclude some pupils, but it should be a last resort, when you've tried
> everything else.

> A friend got her son into a 'good' comprehensive school and said to me [head of
> a school in special measures], 'there's no bullying there, if there is any bullying, they
> get excluded'. And I thought, yes, they get sent to a school like ours. They have
> to go to a school somewhere ... it's not a fair contest.

One head outlined the complexities of decision making in this area with reference to a particular case and stressed that many of the decisions over exclusion were
far from straightforward:

> I've got a kid eight weeks away from his GCSE exams and a parent wants him
> excluded because of a fight with their son. There are some difficult decisions to
> make; it's not black and white, clear cut. Sometimes a pupil with a record of diffi-
> cult behaviour is not clearly and obviously to blame for an incident ... it might
> have been an incident with a pupil who has an even worse disciplinary record.
> Can I deal with it by some form of internal exclusion ... what if there's another

incident ...? Do I think about what is the right thing to do ethically and morally ... about what the staff think? About what particular middle class parents think ... about what it will look like in the papers if there is another, more serious incident ... do I just look to protect my own position rather than what's best for a disadvantaged pupil who has been making good progress overall in difficult circumstances? Zero tolerance ... the only people who advocate it are people who know nothing about working in ordinary schools.

Heads explained that they worked hard to achieve zero, or very low, tolerance of pupils being able to spoil the learning of others, but some admitted that this ideal was difficult to achieve in practice for some schools, and that if every teacher resorted to sending pupils out of the room for any transgression, school systems would be stretched or overwhelmed. The resource implications of remove systems, 'on-call', staff patrols, 'minding' of pupils by senior members of staff were considerable:

You have to try and find some way of giving them some form of education, within the bounds of what's possible. This doesn't mean that you can tolerate bad behaviour that disturbs lessons for other pupils.

You can try and have zero tolerance of pupils seriously interfering with the learning of others ... try and make it non-negotiable that they forfeit the right to stay in the room ... but you can't get zero tolerance per se ... you can't just wash your hands of them and even the first form of zero tolerance is difficult to achieve in practice.

It is the art of the possible ... you've got to try and provide the best curriculum possible in the circumstances. Whatever it takes within the constraints of available resources. It might be providing a teaching assistant, withdrawing them from some lessons where no good is coming out of them for being in the lesson. You have to try and put together a package of something that will suit that child and all teachers have to be involved in that and committed to it.

We do have increasing numbers of pupils with significant behaviour problems, the learning support unit which deals with pupils who are disturbing classrooms has been helpful but it is stretched to its limit and is expensive to staff. It has been helpful to have pupils coming back in from exclusion on partial timetables, just going to the lessons where they get on with the teacher, or where they don't get into as much trouble. This might sound like appeasement, or rewarding bad behaviour but it's about the art of the possible, schools have got to be pragmatic and you do have to be flexible and try out all sorts of things.

Like most heads, I have some colleagues who are better than others at handling pupils who don't want to learn, who don't want to be there.

One head stressed the importance of teachers not according difficult pupils 'victim' or 'heroic' status through their actions or through the use of school systems. For some pupils, being disruptive might be the one area that marked them out for attention and status:

The idea that you can turn schools into boot camps that will reform pupils is naïve. If you attempt to brutalise pupils they will become more brutal. The removal room here used to be very unpleasant, cold, horrible, bleak. Now it is warm, there are ICT facilities and pupils can work, and most of them do. They still want to get back with their friends and to normal life, but the experience does not push them into a 'convict' mentality. Spending time in the remove room is not seen by the other pupils as a heroic or intelligent move. It's important that when teachers take action to impose sanctions on pupils, it isn't done in such a way as to confer status on disruption and bad behaviour.

Head teacher perceptions of the characteristics of teachers who were good at managing pupil behaviour

The interviews with heads revealed that there were some differences in the ways in which exclusion policies operated (see Chapter 7), but there was a consensus that pupil intake, school systems and whole-school policies were not the only determinants of classroom climate. All the heads interviewed felt that they were reliant on having resourceful, accomplished teachers who could deal with at least some of the problems posed by disaffected pupils on their own initiative. In the words of one head: 'In a school like ours, it is helpful . . . no, probably essential, to have a critical mass of teachers who are good with pupils.'

When asked to try to identify the characteristics of teachers who were 'good with pupils', many of the responses focused on personal qualities rather than 'technical' competence. 'Some sort of enthusiasm for the subject that is in some way magnetic . . . gets across to pupils' was mentioned by one head, together with 'an inner toughness in there as well. Because you could love the kids, be really fanatical about your subject, but not have that toughness to withstand the odd phrase or comment that can upset.' But there were perhaps surprisingly few references to 'performance skills' or 'charisma'. Nor was expertise defined in terms of teachers having mastered a broad range of specific teacher 'competences' (DfES/TTA, 2002). It was acknowledged that there were different ways of being 'good with pupils', but many of the qualities described were not related particularly to teaching skills, but to general understanding, 'empathy', and inter-personal skills. Box 6.3 gives details of heads' responses.

As with teachers' views in this area, another strand that emerged was the ability to learn from experience and to develop skills of interaction with pupils to higher levels, sometimes, to be able to change themselves, how they were as people to at least some degree:

It's possible to be very clever in some ways and a bit dim in others. Some of them don't appear to be able to grasp that some of the kids don't want to be in the room, don't want to learn the subject. They are reluctant or slow to take these considerations on board when they are planning their teaching approaches.

One of the challenges for teachers is to say . . . 'Right, I am having major problems . . . why?' and to be able to do something about it, to rectify personal weaknesses.

I've seen teachers who've been at it for over 30 years and they are still in level 3 territory. They just blame it on the kids all the time and don't change how they are.

Box 6.3 Head teacher comments on the characteristics of teachers who were good at managing pupil behaviour

'A lot of teachers come into the profession having been good at school, good at learning, loving their subject. The best ones have an understanding that some pupils have got none of those things. They can somehow empathise with that even though it's alien to their experience.'

'A lot of the ones who are good at it are a funny mix of being perfectionist in some ways and easy going in others. Perfectionist in that they want to do their best for the kids, have high expectations, want to get good results, but easy going in that they just get on with it. It's never perfect in schools, there are never quite enough resources, things are too thinly spread, you have to work with the kids you've got not the ones you'd like. They are copers ... they don't just moan when things aren't perfect.'

'As well as setting clear boundaries for the pupils, they are aware that when some pupils cross those boundaries, it's not necessarily their fault, or the fault of management, but that some pupils are very troubled and have genuine problems with some aspects of life in classrooms. There are different 'types' of teacher, in terms of their beliefs about pupils and about school systems, but both 'traditional' and 'liberal' teachers have this in common – they see part of their job as to use their professional skills and the resources of the school system and colleagues to help these pupils and to stop them spoiling the learning of others. It's an incredibly difficult skill, even at a school like ours, which is not 'at the sharp end' and many of my colleagues are very accomplished at it.'

'More than anything, they just develop an ability to talk to pupils, collectively and individually, in a natural and appropriate way, to get through to them, whether in the classroom or out in the playground.'

'The ability to connect with the children. To empathise. To understand what it's like for them. Yes, you know your subject and care about it and them, and can communicate that to them.'

'They are good not just in a technical way ... seating plans, know their names ... it's how you are with them. Work on your relationships with pupils ... give up some of your spare time to work with them outside the classroom, it's a very powerful tool.'

'It's to do with how people are. I can't think of anyone who's good with pupils who is not also good in terms of their relations with colleagues.'

'I watch her lessons and she just comes across as a normal human being. They operate within the normal ranges of human behaviour, not overpowering, shaky, miserable or sulky, just natural.'

'If they sense you are not bothered about them, you've had it. They can sense that very quickly.'

'I've got some where it's about calm, steely determination and others where it's meticulous planning and preparation. There are different ways of being good with pupils.'

Although in a sense you've got to be yourself, to be natural ... perhaps you can't go in just as yourself in the sense of saying, 'This is how I am, I'm not going to change' ... you can refine, experiment, adjust and work on your teaching persona.

Personal characteristics also featured prominently in heads' views on teachers who really struggled to get on with pupils. Although official regulations for gaining QTS stipulate that trainees must become proficient in every single strand of the Standards in order to be passed, several heads suggested that teachers might have some technical weaknesses in their teaching but still establish very positive working relationships with their teaching groups. However, basic personality traits were more fundamental barriers to getting on with pupils:

If you don't genuinely like kids it's difficult. I have one or two colleagues who treat pupils like something smelly they've just trodden in. It's something trainees need to think about. If you don't get some sort of buzz ... some sort of intrinsic pleasure out of working with young people at least some of the time ... don't go into it. Do something else with your life.

When she has difficulty with the children, she is very blaming of them, and blaming of my senior colleagues.

I have one colleague ... I'd hate to be taught by her. She's an absolute misery. I don't like talking to her. She is in many ways highly intelligent but just absolutely miserable and negative about just about everything.

I can think of a teacher at our place who has horrendous problems with some of our kids. She doesn't shout at them, she spits at them ... she pulls a face when she's told them off. It's clear that she hates them. She never chills out. She doesn't have any fun in the lessons, the lessons are boring.

The ones who have apocalyptic outbursts and send kids out saying they will never ever teach them again. Or who storm out in a temper.

Heads had different approaches over the handling of exclusions. Some had eliminated exclusion as a policy and kept pupils in some sort of contact with the school almost whatever the offence, others saw exclusion as a necessary evil. There were also different views about sending pupils out of the classroom. Some saw it as a pragmatic 'safety valve', others preferred supervision in an exclusion room rather than pupils sent out onto corridors. One head saw sending pupils out as very much a last resort:

I don't like pupils being removed from the classroom. It means they are not learning and that things have broken down. You can also get a little group together who can say 'we are special' in a particular sort of way and they have to live up or down to that. I would rather teachers used punishments, used the school system, came and talked about it with me or the year head.

These variations mean that it is important for trainees and NQTs to find out what school and departmental approaches are in these areas. It is about adjusting intelligently to whatever situation you find yourself in.

Heads were also keen to emphasise the complexity of issues relating to behaviour management. Some wryly recalled previous 'solutions' to problems of pupils' behaviour, such as 'Assertive Discipline' (see for example, 'Teaching creed seen as wonder cure for unruly schools', *The Observer*, 28 March 1993):

> We are talking about complex human behaviour ... there are a huge number of variables. Those who see simple solutions to complex issues are being unhelpful.

> The Secretary of State's recent comments just show that they don't really understand the complexity of the problem ... there are rarely simple solutions, all sorts of factors and variables influence the working atmosphere in classrooms and the extent to which teachers can be comfortable and relaxed in their classrooms. And even though I think things are not too bad here, we never get it completely right, you sometimes err on one side of the line or another when you are trying to balance keeping kids in the classroom and not letting some pupils spoil the learning of others.... You think you've made progress and then things change and you get slightly new challenges to the system.

Several heads emphasised that the institutional nature of schooling, the constraints of the curriculum, the nature of testing arrangements and limits on resources made it difficult for some pupils to have a positive experience of schooling. Some acknowledged that they worked in schools where even their best teachers would still encounter difficulties with pupils. But they all believed that the ability to establish good working relations with pupils was fundamental to teacher effectiveness, and that it was one of the attributes at the forefront of their thinking when appointing staff. They also believed that just as individual teachers made a difference to the degree of pupil engagement in learning, teachers working collaboratively could make a significant difference to pupils' willingness to commit to the general project of 'education'.

SUMMARY

- There is a massive difference between the degree of challenge involved in working in different schools in the UK in terms of classroom climate and pupil behaviour. New teachers need to take these differences into account when reflecting on their progress in this area.

- Most teachers have 'a view' about the extent to which colleagues are able to cope with difficult teaching groups. Refusal to acknowledge or talk about problems with pupil behaviour is not generally thought to be an effective way forward. Experienced teachers felt that new teachers who were able to have an honest and open professional dialogue about behaviour issues were more likely to make progress in this area.

- The skill with which teachers were able to collaborate effectively with colleagues in the area of pupil behaviour was felt to be an important determinant of success and progress in managing pupil behaviour.

- It is important to understand the perspectives of head teachers and year heads, and the difficulties and constraints of decision making in this area when making decisions about the management of pupil behaviour. 'Zero tolerance' of poor pupil behaviour was not generally thought to be an easy or straightforward option.

- Schools have a range of approaches and strategies relating to decisions about sending pupils out of the classroom and excluding pupils from school. Teachers need to be flexible and adaptable in working in a range of school contexts.

7 Telling the truth about the working atmosphere in the classroom

> Ms Kelly was met by laughter when she argued that behaviour was generally improving. But there was applause when she said 'It only takes a few pupils engaged in low level disruption to make life a misery for pupils and teachers. That means that we have to do something about it.'
>
> (*The Guardian*, 14 April 2006)
>
> Things are, I think, getting better.
>
> (Kelvin Hopkins MP, Westminster Education Forum Seminar on Pupil behaviour and school discipline, 7 December 2005)
>
> Most of my job is people control. It'd be nice if it was teaching Art, just teaching Art, but it isn't.
>
> (Quoted in Goodson and Hargreaves, 1996: 63)
>
> My school . . . taught me to work, to read and to think. It gave me great friendships. It filled me entirely and utterly for nearly the space of seven years. Outside the cottage, I had nothing but my school, but having the school, I had everything.
>
> (Barker, E., quoted in Mortimore, 1995: 33)

How prevalent is the problem of deficits in the working atmosphere in the classroom?

Nearly all the teachers and heads who were interviewed acknowledged that the working atmosphere in classrooms was an important educational issue, and that it was a cause of educational underachievement and inequality of educational opportunity. It was also felt to be an important influence on the quality of teachers' working lives. Teacher testimony also revealed that it had a significant influence on learning objectives and teaching methods in many schools.

There are differing views of the scale and prevalence of deficits in classroom climate. It is difficult to ascertain precisely how severe the problem is in particular schools, and in how many schools pupil behaviour is a major problem. As Perks (2005: 10) argues: 'The trouble is, bad behaviour is one subject teachers don't discuss freely in public. The reason is simple. Every teacher has painful memories of the time it went wrong for them.' Moreover, given 'the market' in schools, it is difficult for schools to be completely open about the extent to which behaviour might be a problem. Neither does the process of Ofsted inspection guarantee that the issue of pupil behaviour will be discussed with complete frankness, and that arrangements during the course of the inspection will be completely representative of normal arrangements for dealing with difficult pupils (see, for example, Taylor, 1994).

Politicians from the governing party, perhaps unsurprisingly, have suggested that 'things are improving' (see opening quotations), and media reporting of recent Ofsted findings in the area of pupil behaviour suggest that problems of classroom climate are limited to a small minority of schools, with behaviour being reported as 'good or better in 90% of schools' ('Behaviour: are you winning?', *Times Educational Supplement*, 4 March 2005: 8).

However, other sources have been less sanguine about the issue of pupil behaviour (see, for instance, Davies, 2000; Galton and MacBeath, 2004), and have suggested that deficits in classroom climate are more widespread. A study of secondary schools conducted at Keele University claimed that 92 per cent of pupils in their GCSE year suffered from disruption to their learning through pupil behaviour ('Teenagers respect for teachers plummets', *Times Educational Supplement*, 5 April).

The issue of behaviour in state secondary schools is sometimes presented as primarily an 'inner-city' issue (see for example, Moser, 1994). When I moved to work in East Anglia, having worked in Manchester and London, I made the mistake of assuming that classrooms in small schools in semi-rural or coastal areas would be significantly quieter, gentler places than the inner-city schools I had worked in. Although such schools may not have such high concentrations of 'pupils with problems' (DfEE, 1993), it soon became apparent to me that the difference was not as stark as I expected, and that there are few schools that do not have some pupils who find learning difficult, or who do not want to learn. This is borne out by recent inspection findings. Although Ofsted (2005a,b) reported that behaviour was satisfactory or better in a majority of secondary schools, David Bell, then Head of Ofsted, added the caveat that no schools were free from low-level disruption caused by a minority of pupils:

> All schools to a greater or lesser extent, even if they are otherwise orderly or successful, have to deal with a number of pupils who cause disruption. You can have relatively small numbers of pupils having quite a substantial and disproportionate effect on the others.
>
> (Quoted in *The Times*, 3 February, 2005)

This echoes earlier findings from a survey of over 10,000 pupils in the Midlands. Barber (1994) found that 25 per cent of pupils acknowledged behaving badly, sometimes or often, and 33 per cent said that they encountered disruption on a daily basis. Barber warned that a disruptive minority of 10 to 15 per cent of pupils was seriously undermining the quality of education for as many as half of all secondary school pupils.

Evidence presented to the House of Commons Select Committee on 'Performance in city schools', suggested that the absence of a reasonable climate for learning was, in itself, a cause of pupil disaffection. MPs visiting an inner-city school were told by one pupil, 'You have to be pretty dedicated to learn in this place' (House of Commons Select Committee for Education, 1995).

An earlier survey that I conducted suggested that classroom climate was variable in large numbers of schools, with 51 out of 53 trainees reporting that they experienced or observed lessons that were under level 7 on the 10-point scale (see Chapter 1) in the course of their school placements. Their estimation of the 'average' level prevailing in schools was 6.5 in an inner-city context, and 7.0 in a 'mixed' initial teacher education partnership (Haydn, 2002). A follow-up survey in 2002–4 again suggested that most trainees would observe and experience widely differing levels of control in the schools they were working in. On the positive side, 93 out of 100 responses indicated that trainees had worked in schools where at least some class-rooms were 'operating' at levels 9 and 10 on the 10-point scale, and many of them were working in schools where most lessons were at the top three levels on the scale. Also, only 18 respondents reported having seen or experienced the bottom three levels on the scale. However, 38 responses stated that levels had *on occasions* gone down to levels 4 and 5 on the scale. The overall pattern of responses suggested that there were wide variations between schools, with some schools where behaviour was not a massive problem, and others where deficits in classroom climate were the norm rather than the exception.

Interview responses confirmed that classroom climate and pupil behaviour were *to at least some extent* a problem in nearly all schools. None of the heads I spoke to believed that behaviour was not a problem in their school, in the sense that pupil attainment was never limited by classroom climate. Several of them also indicated that at meetings with fellow heads, behaviour was generally acknowledged to be an issue that affected most or all schools:

> I would be surprised if there were any schools where pupil behaviour did not have *any* impact on pupil attainment.

> Every timetabled lesson of every day there will be some lessons in the school where pupil behaviour will affect teaching and learning outcomes.

> We all talk about this [pupil behaviour] ... the issue for us is certainly a powerful one. I would conclude quite confidently that if it is a problem for us, a compre-hensive school with an intake that if anything is skewed upwards, it is likely to be a problem for most other schools.

> It's a really big problem ... and we're not a school in desperate straights ... we don't have an exceptionally large number of difficult pupils ... we are rural, in the 50s for 5 A–Cs at GCSE and could be in the 60s ... but discipline is a big issue for us. I'm an experienced teacher and I find it difficult to get the working atmos-phere as it should be with some groups. We have some pupils now that, if I'm being honest, we are at a loss to know what to do with, in terms of keeping them in school, which we try hard to do, and yet not let them spoil the learning of others.
>
> (Assistant head)

It is always difficult to measure whether discipline in schools is improving or deteriorating over a period of time (Charlton and David, 1993), and Galloway (1987: 29) has suggested that talk of increasing numbers of difficult pupils is a perennial part of 'educational folklore'. However, there was very little in the interview responses to support politicians' claims that things were getting better in the area of classroom climate, or John Patten's claim that poor pupil behaviour affects 'a small number of pupils in a small number of schools' (Patten, 1994). Although not all the heads and teachers I spoke to said that things were getting worse, no one suggested that managing learning in classrooms was getting easier.

Variations between schools

It is important to stress that there were some schools where both heads and teachers felt that pupil behaviour was not a major problem, and that deficits in classroom climate were occasional and minor. Several respondents felt that levels of behaviour never dipped below level 7 on the scale. Some NQTs reported that even within the course of their induction year, discipline problems had almost evaporated with all or most of their classes:

> This school is a bit of a litmus test in terms of controlling pupils. I reckon any teacher who is reasonably ok at working with pupils and using the school system intelligently won't have too much trouble once they have settled in and got their reputation established.

> I'm very happy here and don't have any classes where I don't look forward to teaching them.

> I'm aware that it's not a particularly rough school ... there are a couple of classes where you have to just give some thought to how you are going to manage the class ... but with most of them, you can pretty much go in and do whatever you want and just get on with it.

But such responses were in a minority. More commonly, teachers in their first years of teaching had a mixture of classes; some of which were comfortably under their control, others which still required careful handling.

One of the most striking aspects of feedback was the number of teachers who had obtained posts in popular, oversubscribed schools, but nonetheless admitted to having to battle to control some of their classes. One head of year made the point that even in a school that was far from being at 'the sharp end', balancing the interests of all pupils was an issue that required difficult decisions on an almost daily basis:

> This is not a school in desperate circumstances, we are heavily oversubscribed, parents are desperate to get their kids into the school. But within a few days of becoming a year head I had been obliged to make several quite difficult decisions about what to do with pupils who were spoiling the lesson for other pupils by behaving badly ... deliberately trying to undermine the teacher ... quite blatantly breaking the basic rules of behaviour.

Teachers frequently expressed frustration as not being able to stop some pupils spoiling the learning of others and admitted that they had some classes that they did not enjoy teaching:

> Even here there are classes where I can't do what I would like to do with classes. There are times when I have to get the text books out and get them writing because some pupils are messing around. It's tragic really because there are lots of kids who do want to learn, it's very unfortunate. It's not just me, there are teachers who have been here for years who have to do the same things.
>
> (NQT)

> This could be a fantastic school ... the fabric of the building was terrible and now it's a pleasure to work in but so many lessons get spoiled by low-level disruption, even for experienced teachers. You feel drained by the effort of keeping on top of them and guilty because you know that there are lots of kids who just want to learn.
>
> (Experienced teacher)

> Pupil behaviour is the main problem ... not just in our school ... it was in my last school as well. When you meet colleagues from other schools and talk about things in general it's a problem that comes up all the time, probably more than was the case a few years ago.
>
> (Experienced teacher)

Recent official enquiries into discipline in schools (Elton, 1989; DfEE, 1993; Steer, 2005a) have all stressed that serious incidents of disruption in schools are rare and that the most common and pressing problem relating to classroom climate is persistent low-level disruption in classrooms. The interviews with teachers suggest that this position may have been overstated, and that there may be quite a number of schools where disruption frequently goes beyond anything that might be construed as 'low-level'. Many experienced and successful teachers, including assistant heads and advanced skills teachers talked of working at some of the lower levels on the scale with some of their teaching groups, having to deal with serious incidents quite frequently, having to deal with children whose behaviour was quite extreme, and being under pressure not to exclude pupils whose behaviour was clearly interfering with the learning of other pupils. A small selection of such comments is given below:

> We had three fights in the corridor outside my room this week ... one kid had broken ribs. Trying to carry on teaching your 'A' level group and sort all that out ...
>
> (Fifth year of teaching)

> The impact he's had on other kids is phenomenal. Within ten seconds of going into X's classroom, he'd thrown a chair at someone and kicked a cupboard in.
>
> (Head of department)

> I remember a colleague saying that if such and such a kid was in, he would rather keep his son off school for the day.
>
> (Head of department)

For most of the week we had a pupil join the school from the unit at X school. He just completely disrupted every lesson he went in. It wasn't doing him any favours and it was ruining the education of lots of other pupils.

(NQT)

We have some kids who pretty much do as they like. They just go to the lessons they enjoy, where they're with their mates and drift off for parts of the day. If you send them out they will just wander off, I dread to think what they get up to. We do get cheesed off about what these kids have to do to get excluded.

(NQT)

The whole issue of the minority undermining the education of the majority is crucially important to parents and teachers but schools ... or rather some schools ... are being forced to take pupils that they are just not equipped to cope with.

(Head teacher)

Well I'm an AST ... I'm not saying that that means that I'm superman but it's reasonable to say that there are some who struggle even more than I do and I go down to about level 4 with some groups.

(Advanced skills teacher)

I am very experienced and am accepted generally by the staff as someone who is good at dealing with the kids but even I am finding it incredibly difficult to cope with the large numbers of pupils who are really serious cases, who are off the scale in terms of their behaviour. No one can do anything with them. It is impossible to stop them interfering with the learning of other pupils, but it appears to be just as impossible to get them alternative provision.

(Advanced skills teacher)

It is a condition of life in this school that you have to face serious disruption on a daily basis, pupils screaming obscenities, refusing to comply with requests to stop appalling behaviour, threatening, spitting, swearing. Staff have to learn how to cope with it and just do their best in the circumstances. You can't teach in the normal sense of the word, and you feel wretched for the poor kids who would like to learn but can't, you know you are letting them down.

(Assistant head)

The head is great, he leads from the front, he takes difficult classes, he is always about in the school, but he can't stop the really difficult kids running riot. He tries his best to get kids excluded, but it's a real struggle, there is a lot of pressure to keep them in.

(Head of department)

There are just too many really difficult ones; the system is overwhelmed. The poor head is at his wits' end trying to get yet another senior member of staff to 'mind' a kid and keep him isolated from normal classes; yesterday there were at least six, and there just aren't enough senior staff to just drop everything with pupils and 'mind' one pupil for the whole day.

(Advanced skills teacher)

> We are under pressure from the LEA to keep pupils in, there is sometimes a clear hint that if the number of exclusions rises, this might trigger an Ofsted inspection.
>
> (Head of department)

> It's not just calling out, speaking out of turn or when the teacher is talking ... One child came into the room and bit someone ... in a matter of fact sort of way I sometimes have to look under the desk to see if a pupil might be lurking there at the end of a lesson.
>
> (Head of department)

Teacher responses suggested that there were massive variations in the degree of challenge that trainees and NQTs would face when they started teaching in schools, and large numbers of schools where pupil behaviour was an issue that would have a major influence on teachers' planning for learning in the classroom. There were also major differences in schools' policies on excluding pupils, arrangements for 'internal exclusion', and sending pupils out of the classroom (see Chapter 6).

What are the implications of these findings for beginning teachers and how should they react to these inconsistencies and variations? First, the reality is that if you are a teacher starting to teach in British secondary schools, you will probably have to deal with some pupils who do not want to learn, and who may try to disrupt the lesson and interfere with the learning of others. The severity and scale of this problem, and the numbers of potentially disruptive pupils will vary between schools, but it is part of being a teacher in the UK, it goes with the job, and learning to cope with these pupils is an important part of being or becoming a good teacher.

Second, trainee teachers need to have good self-awareness of their strengths and weaknesses in this area, and of their 'tolerance' and resilience levels. Teacher educators often talk of 'good-fit' placements, where the school suits the particular profile of the trainee, even though both might have some flaws. There is always a danger that trainees might be tempted to accept a teaching post because of commuting, or similar convenience considerations, rather than one that suits their particular abilities. Trainees need to have a sense of what they will be able to cope with in their NQT year and whether or not they are well suited to working 'at the sharp end'. This came through in the responses of head teachers as well as less experienced teachers:

> We have a broad spread here, lots of bright well motivated kids, some less able ones, a few very difficult ones, and that's the sort of school I feel comfortable working in. I never wanted to work in the independent sector for philosophical reasons, but I know I could not work in schools which have massive numbers of disaffected and disruptive pupils so that even good teachers can't teach effectively and make the difference that they can to children's lives here.
>
> (Head teacher)

An NQT working at a school that was probably around the middle of the spectrum in terms of pupil intake reflected that they had probably judged what they could cope with reasonably well and was enjoying the NQT year:

> I suppose most people who go into teaching from a better paid job do it because they want to make a difference. A bit of me thinks I ought to have gone into a

difficult school in inner London where I used to work but I'm not sure I would be up to that. But I can see with the kids at this school ... if they think you are dedicated to doing things for them, you will get things back.

Third, trainees and NQTs need to keep in mind that pupil behaviour is often very difficult in the first weeks or even months of school experience, and often becomes less of a problem as the new teacher gets to know the pupils and gets acclimatised to the ways in which the school systems work in this area (see Chapter 6). Fourth, if you teach classes where the working atmosphere is not at levels 9 and 10, it is not necessarily your fault, and it does not mean that you are necessarily working at a school that is badly run. It might be worth reflecting on how levels in your classrooms compare to those of your peers, it might be that you work in a school that has more than its share of difficult pupils. Finally, trainees have to understand that they just have to do their best to adjust to the challenges of working in a particular school, to make the best of whatever school context they find themselves in, to learn to be flexible, adaptable and resilient. There is no way that initial teacher education providers can standardise the experiences that trainees get in schools, although it is helpful if trainees can gain experience of working in schools that are at different points on the continuum in terms of the prevailing classroom climate. It is probably not helpful for trainees to work in two schools that are at the less challenging end of the spectrum.

The positive side of working in challenging classrooms

Although many of the teachers interviewed regarded classroom climate as an important facet of their professional quality of life, and spoke of the pleasure of working with classes where control was not an issue, there was no simple correlation between how 'comfortable' the school's pupil profile was, and how much they enjoyed their jobs. Experienced teachers who were working in tough schools spoke of the 'surprising' reactions of some NQTs who were having to teach very difficult classes that were not fully under their control:

> I find it hard to believe but he says he is happier here than at X school.
>
> (Advanced skills teacher)

> She says she prefers this place to X school which is astonishing in a way.
>
> (Assistant head)

> A student who had been on placement here was offered interviews at two other schools in less challenging circumstances than ours, and said that she wanted to work here ... that she liked the kids here, she wanted to work in a challenging school.
>
> (Head teacher)

'There was no simple correlation between how 'comfortable' the school's pupil profile was, and how much teachers enjoyed their jobs.'

Teachers often spoke in very positive terms of the experience of working in difficult classrooms, for a variety of reasons. A representative selection of comments is given in Box 7.1.

Part of this was a view that it was good professional development to gain experience of working with pupils who found learning difficult and did not want to learn. It is not generally enjoyable teaching classes that are not fully under the teacher's control, but it is a very useful learning experience. It is questionable whether it is possible to learn class management skills purely at a theoretical level. Some Quaker hostels used to bear the inscription 'Behold, you have been refined in the furnace of affliction' and perhaps there is something of this in the rite of passage to becoming the sort of teacher who attains exceptionally high levels of expertise in managing classrooms. Several teachers attributed their progress in this area to their experience of working in difficult schools. As Barrow *et al.* (2001: 22) observe, 'Some people are better at conflict because they have had more practice at it.'

'Behold, you have been refined in the furnace of affliction.'

Several responses echoed Brighouse's argument (2006: 21) that teachers:

are not in teaching just for the money. They are in it, as they might privately admit, to make a difference to their pupils' life chances. They care not just about their pupils but about the adults they will become.

There was also a belief that less naturally scholarly pupils were more appreciative of the efforts of their teachers, that 'you got more back from them'. Although very few teachers believed that teaching successfully in difficult contexts was fully appreciated by society and bestowed high status and public recognition, some did claim satisfaction in doing something that many people would probably find difficult (see Box 7.1).

Although many teachers made positive comments about some aspects of working with difficult classes, several added the reservation that it was not good for even experienced teachers to work with a timetable that comprised of predominantly or exclusively difficult teaching groups over a sustained period. Heads talked of 'demoralisation' and the 'grinding down' of teachers who were constantly engaged in trying to limit and contain disruption rather than working on the more creative and rewarding processes involved in classroom teaching. Some of the teachers who believed that teaching difficult classes had enhanced their teaching skills made it clear that they did not want to spend the rest of their lives struggling to get sufficient control to be able to teach effectively, and even those who admitted to enjoying working in challenging contexts added the proviso that there needed to be very strong support from the school's management team, so that in the last resort, there were not children 'beyond control'. Enjoyment of 'getting through' to pupils and 'winning them round', had to be balanced against the frustration of not being able to teach in a more relaxed and creative way, and the guilt of knowing that some pupils were spoiling the learning of others. Given that many teachers go into teaching because helping children to learn is a fulfilling activity (Spear *et al.*, 2000; Penlington,

Box 7.1 Teachers' comments on positive aspects of working in challenging classrooms

'It makes you a better teacher'

'It was like accelerated training. I developed a much more outgoing and proactive teaching persona. You couldn't use overt authority because authority wasn't accepted so you had to change your approach, it made you develop a lot more initiative because you couldn't just rely on the system. You learned to cope with things much better, not to flap or get flustered. I got better at not looking phased by things, even if I was a bit phased inside. I developed a way of being almost unreasonably nice in terms of the tone in which I talked to pupils, which actually worked with some pupils, and which didn't make things worse.' (Teacher educator who had worked at a school in 'Special Measures')

'In some ways I didn't enjoy school X, as you know I was tempted to pack it in. It's horrible going from a school where you are pretty much in control to one where the kids are running riot right through some or most of your lessons, it's utterly demoralising at first. But it is very character building. Not just in terms of coping, resilience, but how much you learn from people who are fantastically good at working with difficult kids. You know that at the end of a placement where you have survived in a difficult school that you are a much better teacher than you would have been if you'd been at an easier school. The sense of achievement you get is worth a lot. Whether you want to work at a tough school full time for several years is another matter. Some people do, they get a kick out of it. I wouldn't want to do it for a living, but it's stood me in good stead doing it for a term.' (Third year of teaching)

'Making a difference'

'At first the main pleasure was with the easier classes but part of the pleasure now is having to battle with them and win them over. Sometimes a kid will grudgingly admit that your lessons have been ok and that can be a fantastic feeling.' (NQT)

'There is a thing about the value added in schools like this. I've got a kid in my year 10 who struggled to write sentences . . . I couldn't get anything out of him. He just used to tell me to F. . . off and that he wasn't going to do the work. And I marked his work the other day and he just might get a D, or even a C. I had a smile on my face for three days.' (Second year of teaching)

'We took a difficult pupil from another school . . . the move has been a success, and that can be good for a school's morale, most teachers do want to help pupils with problems, not just the bright and untroubled ones.' (Head teacher)

'You don't win with all the kids all the time but you can win with some of them and when they begin to take pleasure in learning and to get a kick out of being able to do something that they couldn't do before . . . you get a really good feeling about that. I'm not sure it would be the same with a school where all the kids were pretty well motivated anyway.' (Advanced skills teacher)

'Appreciation from pupils'

'It's hard work and there are sometimes days when things don't work out and it all seems like a waste of time . . . a losing battle. . . . But not all the time, it's great when you get through, make progress, things go well . . . and a lot of the kids do seem to appreciate the efforts you go to, to find something that works, that's ok. (Experienced teacher)

'The pressures are just different elsewhere . . . arrogant precocious middle-class kids who take things for granted, demanding parents who think their offspring are cleverer than they are . . . sows' ears and silk purses. I have worked at other schools and the grass isn't always greener. A lot of our kids really appreciate it when you take them on a trip or take them for football, or lay on a lesson with some good bits in it.' (Head of department)

'It's difficult, not everyone could do it'

'I have found it quite moving sometimes when they do well. You get some intense good times but you also have bad days as well. But it's never boring and you know that you are doing something that a lot of very clever people would find it hard to do.' (NQT)

'If you can get on with our kids it's a very rewarding and enjoyable job. You know that some of the people you trained with couldn't cope. Any teacher who comes to work here has a tough time for the first few weeks but once you have gained their respect, you get respect back and that gives teachers a good feeling . . . A sense of real achievement. You know that you have done something difficult and worthwhile.' (Head teacher)

2002; Cockburn and Haydn, 2004), not being able to help children to learn removes a significant part of the pleasure and purpose of the job. There were some scenarios where teachers felt that things were so bad within particular schools that even experienced and effective teachers were not able to 'make a difference' to the extent that they would like, and were leaving the profession, with a degree of regret, as in the example below:

I'm an experienced teacher, I've been at the school for a long time which makes things easier for me than many other teachers of my school and I would say there aren't that many classrooms in the school where the levels are at 9 and 10. I've found a big difference between the upper and lower school. With the sixth form, it's obviously still at level 10 and teaching is a delight, there is nothing to stand in the way of pupils learning and doing well. With years 10 and 11, I can get to levels 7 and 8, 9 if they are a good group but with my lower school classes I'm afraid the average would be between levels 5 and 7 and might go as low as level 4 with some of the more difficult sets. I really miss teaching the levels 9 and 10 classes but I've no regrets about getting away from the battles of working at the lower levels.

(Experienced head of department)

One head acknowledged that given the large numbers of difficult pupils in the school, even the most accomplished and experienced teachers had to teach 'defensively' with some of their classes:

> When you get particular groups with large numbers of difficult pupils, even good, experienced teachers are going to struggle to get complete control of the class-room ... they will have to make adjustments to how they teach.

Several senior teachers acknowledged that their situation was such that there were sometimes pupils who were not fully under the control of any adult in the building, and that the presence of such pupils was very corrosive of teacher morale:

> It's demoralising for staff to have kids like that. As long as staff think you are doing everything you can to get the problem resolved they generally do everything they can to help but it depends on the frequency of such cases. If it's a rarity, it doesn't undermine staff morale too much. Our school's a doddle compared to some inner-city schools ... it must be demoralising if every day there are some pupils who are just not under anyone's control.
>
> (Head teacher)

There was a degree of consensus that up to a certain point, deficits in classroom climate could be acceptable, could be worked with and improved over time, and not prove an insurmountable obstacle to teachers enjoying their work. However, beyond a certain point, and particularly where there was a feeling that some pupils were not fully under anyone's control, teachers felt that it was difficult to derive any real satisfaction from the job, partly because it was not possible to teach in other than a containing and defensive way, and partly because of the awareness that some pupils were not getting the education they were entitled to.

Not a fair contest?

None of the heads or teachers I interviewed believed that difficult pupils were distributed equitably across the system, and many felt that this exacerbated behaviour problems by creating a critical mass of disaffected pupil, which made it almost impossible for some schools to manage. Some heads and teachers admitted that their position of being oversubscribed gave them a big advantage in dealing with disruption:

> One big advantage of working here is that the threat of being permanently excluded from the school is a very powerful one. This school is heavily oversubscribed, it's got a good reputation – the kids know that, not just the parents. They know that if they get kicked out of here, they will have to go to X school ... in special measures, run down buildings, thought of as a dump.
>
> (Head of department)

> One of the big things we can use at this school is that we can say 'If you don't want to be here, that's ok, that can be arranged, there are 30, 40, 50 kids who want your place ... that's not what we are looking for, it's end of the line stuff,

and our exclusions are actually very low ... but it does help being in a strong position and you've got to use whatever weapons you've got.

(Head teacher)

Many heads and teachers expressed sympathy for schools that had to accept more than their share of difficult pupils, and felt that current systems for reporting school performance were in some ways unhelpful:

The suggestion that schools achieving under 25 per cent A–Cs at GCSE should be closed down was particularly unfair. So much depends on pupil intake.

(Head teacher)

You can't do this job ... going round lots of different schools ... without realising how iniquitously unfair the system is.

(Teacher educator)

The political rhetoric is still about good schools and bad schools ... this enables them to put all the blame onto heads and teachers. The reality is that it is to at least some extent about difficult schools and comparatively easy schools ... that is an indictment of the politicians who have created an unfair system.

(Head teacher)

League tables ... only telling one story. Whether it's measuring hospitals, universities or schools, they try to measure things ... they do it badly and it creates all sorts of unfairness and harmful unintended consequences.

(Head teacher of a school high in the league tables)

Naming and shaming just means huge panic, that any aspiring parents and a lot of aspiring teachers move away from the school, creates a recruitment crisis and makes the imbalance even worse, needs lots of time and money to sort out the crisis which has been created.

(Head teacher)

More than one head expressed the concern that polarisation of school intakes was likely to increase rather than recede with the creation of city academies, and that this would pose problems for collaboration between schools:

It would be an utter disaster ... a new flagship policy has to be seen to work. There is already evidence of higher exclusion rates ... difficult pupils being hived off to other schools.

What most stuck in the throats of head teachers was the inference in some recent media reporting (see for instance, *BBC 1 News*, 23 October 2005, *The Times*, 15 June 2005, *Education Guardian*, 2 May 2006) that good pupil behaviour was something that was deemed important only by independent and grammar schools and city academies, and that comprehensives were in some way not really that bothered about standards of behaviour. Heads felt that in making public pronouncements on schools, politicians often did not pay sufficient heed to the differing contexts in which schools worked:

It's not a level playing field. You get a school in special measures taking a lot of the difficult pupils in a neighbourhood being compared to an independent school . . . and being told they should learn from the independent sector when they are doing a heroic job in difficult circumstances.

Independent schools do have more control, as well as more consistent levels of parental support . . . they have ultimate power over what goes on in the school, and can get rid of any pupil who does not comply with the standards and expectations laid down. It is invidious to suggest that teachers in comprehensive schools are in some way second rate.

Teachers' comments were also resentful of what they saw as a 'blame culture' for colleagues working in difficult schools. There was a strong element of 'there but for fortune . . .' in their comments and resentment of sweeping statements from politicians about the widespread failure of state secondary schools (as an example of this see, for example, 'Kelly warns coasting schools', *The Guardian*, 5 July 2005). There was a strong feeling that the most important 'variable' in terms of school performance was pupil intake, a view echoed by Brighouse (1997), Mortimore and Whitty (1997) and (Mortimore 1999), leading figures in the school effectiveness movement. They estimated 'school effect' as accounting for 'at most' around 10 per cent of variation in pupil performance, and were critical of politicians' use of research into school effectiveness. In the words of Mortimore:

School effectiveness was immensely attractive to politicians . . . By sidelining the effect of intake, it permitted policies which focused on detail in the school and were therefore relatively cheap. And so the department for education and Ofsted were committed to hunting down failing schools and attributing their failure to the weaknesses of teachers and managers, ignoring the destructive impact of an intake which had become progressively more delinquent as the new poverty swept through the country. Whilst some schools can succeed against the odds, the possibility of them all doing so, year in year out still appears remote, given that the long-term patterning of educational inequality has been strikingly consistent throughout the history of public education in most countries. . . . We must beware of basing a national strategy for change on the efforts of outstanding individuals working in exceptional circumstances.

Part of the 'situational understanding' that Klemp (1977) sees as an important part of professional effectiveness, is for trainees and NQTs to understand that schools can make a big difference to their pupils' life chances, and need to think hard about how to improve what they do. But they also need to have an intelligent understanding of school effectiveness research. They need to get it in proportion, and understand that just because they are working in a school with below average examination results, this does not mean that they are working in a bad school, or with poor teachers. It was interesting to note that several teachers were quite supportive of the idea of extra financial incentives for teachers working in particularly difficult schools (Stubbs, 2005; Ion, 2005).

Making things better?

In the same way that teachers and heads had opinions about the factors that would enable some teachers to become more successful than others in working with pupils and managing learning in classrooms, they had views on 'school level' and 'system level' factors that might improve classroom climate and improve pupil behaviour.

Trainees and NQTs expressed a preference for working in schools where there was some system for being able to send pupils out of their classrooms, rather than being expected to contain all situations and pupil transgressions within the room. They also felt that having a 'swift and sure' school system for discouraging poor behaviour was a major boost to morale and confidence. Their views seemed to bear out Rogers' (1990) contention that it was largely about the inexorability of consequences rather than the degree to which the consequences were draconian. Sir Alan Steer, who chaired the working group into school behaviour and discipline, has also stressed the need for clarity and certainty so that everyone in the building knows 'what it is that is non-negotiable' (Steer, 2005b). Teachers also felt it was helpful if consequences were swift as well as sure:

> Here, something happens straight away when there is any sort of pupil atrocity. They are out of circulation, the other pupils are subdued because they know someone is in serious trouble and there will be consequences ... they won't be in circulation, you won't see them at break and dinnertime to talk about it. At my other school, there was a system, but it took time to process things ... you got the feeling that a few days later, someone would pick up a bit of paper and deal with it, but there were so many incidents that with the best will in the world, the senior managers just couldn't keep up with it all.
>
> (Head of department)

> It makes such a difference if the pupils know there is a system for dealing with these things, and that if they go too far, something unpleasant will happen to them, no question. If there has been a very serious incident, it is also helpful if the pupil is taken out of circulation in some way, rather than being able to tell other pupils about it.
>
> (Head of department)

Several teachers also stressed the importance of senior staff within a school 'leading from the front', and setting a good example in terms of their own interactions with pupils, and willingness to expose themselves to difficult situations:

> The head was always about ... any break, any dinnertime, he was walking round. The whole senior management team have a high profile, there is always someone senior on the corridors, keeping an eye out. There may be a question about whether this is the best use of their time as senior managers, but from the point of view of the climate of behaviour in the school and staff morale, it makes a big difference. At my previous school, we didn't see that much of the head and deputies, their offices were at one end of the building and that's where they were.
>
> (Third year in teaching)

The effect of senior staff *not* setting a good example was described by an experienced teacher who had worked at a school in 'special measures':

> You look down the corridor and notice what can only be described as chaos. Shouting, swearing – an aggressive bustle of pupils. It strikes you with a degree of trepidation that you ought to do something. You are about to say something but then you notice ... two figures beside the mob. One, a senior manager, saying nothing. Two, a senior manager, inert, turning a blind eye. So you walk on, thinking about your next lesson and run into an incident. Two pupils coming the wrong way, contrary to the new one-way system. It's not a big deal – a system you're not entirely convinced about yourself. Still – follow the school line – ask them politely to turn back. They challenge you. Observers gather. As you address one boy the other tries to walk through you. He walks into your arm and tells you that you've hit him ... and it occurs to you that the support might not be there. That the rules ultimately mean nothing because nothing will be done ... and you wonder, why bother?

White (1997) has argued that the compulsory school day should be split in half, with pupils being allowed to choose their own afternoon activities in order to make education more meaningful to all pupils and reduce disaffection and disengagement from learning. Tomlinson (2005) has also argued that educational inclusion is hampered by the increasing emphasis on examination performance, which makes it difficult for some pupils to have a positive and enjoyable experience of school:

> As long as teachers are pressed to deliver higher standards in the form of more children passing examinations and reaching targets, they will understandably be reluctant to take on the education of all children. There is little incentive for teachers to introduce new curriculum practices within mainstream schools when the emphasis is on achieving at key stages and acquiring the magic five A*–Cs at GCSE. For pupils who cannot ever achieve this, inclusive schooling is a sham.

Research by Garner into the attitudes of disaffected pupils (1999: 103) suggested that many pupils felt alienated from the educational process, and had become 'anti-school':

> The data collected suggest that the imposition of a National Curriculum, with its attendant 'academic' focus and its assessment, has had a deleterious effect on the ability of mainstream schools to offer strategic, concentrated and long-term intervention for pupils who are at risk of exclusion.

Cullingford's research (2002) revealed that even for pupils without problems, school was often a fairly miserable and angst-ridden experience. Riley and Rustique-Forrester (2002) also make the point that league tables, testing and the extension of accountability arrangements for teachers, have made it more difficult for teachers to enjoy their work, and this can have a 'knock on effect' on pupils. Several of the head teachers interviewed stressed how important it was for teachers to enjoy their work, and felt that it was as important for staff to be happy at school as it was for pupils.

In spite of these pressures, some schools have tried to create a learning culture by broadening the opportunities available to pupils beyond National Curriculum subjects, and laying on extensive extra-curricular activities which provide opportunities for a wider spectrum of pupils to achieve and to enjoy school. Several heads felt that recent initiatives to make the post-14 curriculum more flexible for less academic pupils had been helpful and many teachers emphasised the benefits of working with pupils outside the classroom, and of offering pupils more flexibility in their experience of secondary school. Perhaps not all teachers see themselves as 'social workers', but many expressed the belief that it was important to come across as being concerned about the pupils' welfare in general, and not just see them as 'National Curriculum Production Units'. Recent research by Fischman *et al.* (2005) suggested that 'deep commitment' to meeting pupils' developmental, social and emotional needs rather than concentrating purely on their academic progress had been found to have a strong beneficial impact on teacher–pupil relations and pupil progress. Many teachers were critical of current arrangements for assessment and testing, and considered this to be a major problem in terms of pupil motivation. In the words of one experienced teacher: 'By the time they get to secondary school, some of them already know that they are no good at 90 per cent of what school is now about.'

The difficulty of reconciling inclusion with 'the right to learn' for all pupils led schools into contentious areas. Some had found that excluding large numbers of pupils in the short term had led to a decline in exclusions subsequently. Homework was a difficult issue for some schools, and some had, in effect, taken homework out of the disciplinary framework and virtually made it an optional activity for pupils to do if they wanted. As one senior teacher explained:

> Take homework . . . we know it is supposed to be 'a good thing' . . . if we stopped having a compulsory homework policy and changed it so that those who want to do it can do it . . . I would imagine standards would dip over a period of time. But at the moment, the effort of trying to enforce this is proving a real burden. In one recent case, it took 11 teacher interventions and an incredible amount of staff time . . . form teachers, year heads, deputies . . . to get one piece of homework out of a particular pupil . . . a very mediocre and unsatisfactory piece of work.

Another area of disagreement was over the conditions that should prevail for pupils who had been sent out of ordinary lessons to some form of internal exclusion or 'Remove Room'. In some cases conditions were designed to be as draconian and unpleasant as possible, with isolated carrels, no talking, and no social contact with other pupils at any time of the day, in others, there had been experiments with more congenial conditions where pupils could just get on with something quietly in pleasant, relaxing and non-punitive surroundings, or a programme of outside visits to outward bound centres, football clubs, etc. As one senior teacher reported, 'Some of the staff hate the idea of rewarding bad behaviour, others think that anything is better than problem pupils spoiling the learning of others.'

There has also been strong support for the idea of schools working more closely together to handle problems of pupil behaviour. Brighouse and Whitty argue the case for collaboration between schools to reduce the temptation of schools evading the challenge of taking their share of difficult pupils:

In an age of zero tolerance and league tables, there is considerable temptation for the individual school, either directly or indirectly, to exclude pupils,
or not to admit them in the first place. Pinning the responsibility on groups of
cooperating schools seems the best way of minimising this practice.

(Brighouse, 2005)

To avoid diversity producing a hierarchy, all schools in the area need to work
together in the interests of optimum provision for all pupils, including being
willing to take a fair share of the more challenging pupils.

(Whitty, 2005)

Although the aim is that all secondary schools will be part of a group working
together to manage pupil behaviour by September 2007, there has been some 'soft-
ening' of an initial proposal that all schools should be compelled to accept a
proportion of the pupils expelled from other schools ('Top schools must be told to
take difficult pupils', *The Observer*, 26 June 2005; 'Sense and singularity', *Times
Educational Supplement*, 8 April 2005). Many of the teachers surveyed were in favour
of a more equitable distribution of difficult pupils, and several heads reported that
collaboration between schools to work for 'managed moves' of pupils who had been
excluded had improved the chances of successful outcomes for such pupils. Some
heads felt that the LEA had 'brokered' an effective points system for the equitable
distribution of excluded pupils but, overall, feedback suggested that collaboration
between schools may work better in some areas than others, and that the current
'market' in education militated against more extensive collaboration between schools.
As one head put it:

> Superficially, quite good, in reality not that well at all. The system conspires against
> it whatever the rhetoric of cooperation and federations. There has been some
> progress in terms of managed moves but there is still a game to be played where
> there are two or three schools close together or in cities. Liberal instincts come
> up against league tables and the pressures to be seen as a 'successful' school. Without
> central planning of admissions, it's never going to be a fair contest.

The importance of the working atmosphere in classrooms

Over the past 20 years, education reforms in Britain have focused primarily on
curriculum content, accountability, methods of assessment, and the provision of
'Choice and Diversity' in the educational system. As David Reynolds has noted,
'governments have pulled many levers over these last 10 to 15 years. They've pulled
the lever of school organisation, all sorts of school improvement, and the lever of
the National Curriculum' (Reynolds, 1997). One lever that has not been seriously
disturbed during this period is that of policies and regulations pertaining to classroom management and control; the balance between the rights of individual pupils,
and the authority of the school to enforce its codes of conduct and regulate pupil
behaviour. Although there is some reference to pupil behaviour in the most recent
Education White Paper, it is a comparatively minor feature, and does not radically
change the status quo.

This book is based on the proposition that the working atmosphere in the class-room has a significant bearing on the quality of teaching and learning in schools, and on levels of educational attainment. It also has a major influence on the extent to which teachers are able to enjoy their work and find it fulfilling. It is difficult not to feel that neglect of this issue stems partly from the fact that few politicians' and policymakers' children go to schools where behaviour is a major problem.

Many teachers felt that policymakers had, at best, a limited grasp of just how diffi-cult classrooms are to control. Some supported the suggestion that civil servants in the DfES should be obliged to spend some time in difficult schools as part of their training.

The issue is partly about raising levels of educational achievement, obtaining 'value for money' for educational investment, and thinking about how levels of control compare with our international competitors, but it is also about addressing a basic failure in British democracy. As Ernest Barker's quotation at the start of the chapter suggests, education can be a wonderful thing. But for many pupils and teachers in the UK, it is a flawed commodity, not as good a product as it might be because of deficits in classroom climate. This is in spite of the fact that the overwhelming majority of teachers, parents and pupils would like there to be a calm, purposeful and collaborative working atmosphere in classrooms. To what extent is there 'a right to learn' in classrooms in the UK? A British politician stated that she would 'not want to deny my children the privilege of a state education' (quoted in Haydn, 1994); but would that stretch to a state education in any state secondary school?

If nothing else, I hope that the book will persuade those concerned with the quality of educational provision in the UK that it is an important issue, and that in the words of Ruth Kelly, 'We have to do something about it.'

CONCLUSIONS

The last section of the chapter focused on some of the factors influencing classroom climate that are beyond the control of individual teachers. I would like to return briefly to some of the key points arising from the views of experienced teachers on classroom climate and pupil behaviour.

- There are factors beyond your control. If you are not operating at levels 9 and 10 on the scale, it is not necessarily your fault.

- If you are working in a school where there are substantial 'deficits' in terms of classroom climate, this does not necessarily mean that it is a bad school, and that you are working with poor teachers. There are few schools where the working atmosphere is at level 10 in all classes and there are enormous variations in the degree of challenge in this area in UK schools.

- There are no golden rules that always work; only ideas, theories, suggestions to test out against your own experience.

- It takes time to become accomplished at managing learning in classrooms; it is difficult to get to expert levels in a few months because it is a very complex and difficult art.

- The difficulties in managing learning in classrooms are particularly acute in the first weeks and months of teaching. The vast majority of trainees and NQTs find that things get much easier with time as you get to know pupils, colleagues and school systems.

- Part of becoming good at managing learning in classrooms and establishing good working relations with pupils is about investing time and effort.

- Like most things in teaching, it is partly about being a good learner and being open-minded.

- Teaching is generally a very enjoyable and fulfilling job if you are able to establish good working relations with pupils and a calm, purposeful working atmosphere in your classroom.

References

Adey, K. and Biddulph, M. (2001) 'The influence of pupil perceptions on subject choice at 14+ in geography and history', *Educational Studies*, Vol. 27, No. 4: 439–51.

Arnot, M., McIntyre, D., Pedder, D. and Reay, D. (2004) *Consultation in the classroom: developing dialogue about teaching and learning*, Cambridge, Pearson.

Barber, M. (1994) *Young people and their attitude to school, interim report of a research project at the Centre for Successful Schools*, University of Keele.

Barker, E. (1953) *Father of the man*, London, Oxford University Press.

Barrow, G., Bradshaw, E. and Newton, T. (2001) *Improving behaviour and raising self-esteem in the classroom*, London, David Fulton.

Battersby, J. (1997) Unpublished lecture on Differentiation, University of East Anglia, Norwich, 15 January.

Bennett, N. (1993) *Learning to teach*, London, Routledge.

Bernstein, B. (1970) 'Education cannot compensate for society', *New Society*, February, 387–90.

Blandford, S. (1998) *Managing discipline in schools*, London, Routledge.

Boler, M. (1999) *Feeling power: emotions and education*, New York and London, Routledge.

Brighouse, T. (1997) 'Transforming the great cities – leading schools to success against the odds', address to 3rd ICP Convention, July, Boston, MA. Available online at www.aspa.asn. au/conbrig.htm.

Brighouse, T. (2001) 'Book of the week', *Times Educational Supplement*, 30 March: 21.

Brighouse, T. (2005) 'Disadvantage', *Education Guardian*, 19 April: 6.

Brighouse, T. (2006) 'Complex motives of a modern teacher', *Times Educational Supplement*, 6 January: 21.

Brophy, J. and Evertson, C. (1976) *Learning from teaching: a developmental perspective*, Boston, MA, Allyn & Bacon.

Burden, P. (2003) *Classroom management: creating a successful learning community*, New York, John Wiley & Sons.

Calderhead, J. (1994) The reform of initial teacher education and research on learning to teach: contrasting ideas, in P. John and P. Lucas (eds) *Partnership and progress*, Sheffield, USDE Papers in Education: 59–77.

Cangelosi, J.S. (2000) *Classroom management strategies: gaining and maintaining students' cooperation*, New York, John Wiley & Sons.

Canter, L. (1992) *Assertive discipline: positive behaviour management for today's classrooms*, Santa Monica, CA, Lee Canter and Associates.

Charlton, T. and David, K. (1993) *Managing misbehaviour*, Routledge, London.

Clark, T. (2003) 'Why behaviour training for schools?' address to TTA Conference, Birmingham, 21 March.

Cockburn, A. and Haydn, T. (2004) *Recruiting and retaining teachers: understanding why teachers teach*, London, RoutledgeFalmer.

Cockburn, A., Haydn, T. and Oliver, A. (2000) 'The psychology of career choice and young people's perceptions of teaching as a career', paper presented at British Psychological Society, Institute of Education, University of London, 19 December 2000.

Corrie, L. (2002) *Investigating troublesome behaviour in the classroom*, London, Routledge.

Cowley, S. (2001) *Getting the buggers to behave*, London, Continuum.

Cowley, S. (2002) 'Nothing beats the sound of silence', *Times Educational Supplement*, 22 November: 22.

Cowley, S. (2003) *Getting the buggers to behave 2*, London, Continuum.

Csikszentmihalyi, M. (1997) *Finding flow: the psychology of engagement with everyday life*, New York, Basic Books.

Cullingford, C. (2002) *The best years of their lives? Pupils' experiences of school*, London, Kogan Page.

Davies, L. (1998) quoted in Thornton, K. 'The harshest masters of all are pupils', *Times Educational Supplement*, 24 November: 7.

Davies, N. (2000) *The school report: why Britain's schools are failing*, London, Vintage.

Desforges, C. (2004) *On teaching and learning*, Cranfield, NCSL.

Department for Education (1993) *Pupils with problems: draft circulars*, DfE, December.

Department for Education and Employment (1998a) *Survey of ICT in schools: Issue 11/98*, London, DfEE.

Department for Education and Employment (1998b) *Section 550A of the Education Act 1996: the use of force to control or restrain pupils*, London, DfEE.

Department for Education and Employment (2001) *Classroom talk for learning and management*, London, DfEE.

Department for Education and Skills (2002a) *Making good use of the plenary*, London, DfES.

Department for Education and Skills (2002b) *Survey of ICT in schools, 2002, Issue No. 7/02*, London, DfES.

Department for Education and Skills (2004) *Pedagogy and practice: teaching and learning in secondary schools*, London, DfES.

Department for Education and Skills/Teacher Training Agency (2002) *Qualifying to teach: professional standards for qualified teacher status and requirements for initial teacher training*, London, DfES/TTA.

Dickson, D. (1993) *The skill of responding positively*, London, Routledge.

Doherty, P. (2001) 'The curriculum dimensions of student disaffection: a single site case study', Ph.D. thesis, University of East Anglia.

Elkins, T. (2002) 'No hiding place': the characteristics of six good lessons, Norwich, NASC. Online at www.uea.ac.uk/edu/ddncl, 'Resources on rewards and sanctions', Section 5.7.

Elliott, J. (1988) 'Educational research and outsider-insider relations', *Qualitative Studies in Education*, Vol. 1, No. 2: 155–66.

Elliott, J. (1991) *Action research for educational change*, Buckingham, Open University Press.

Elliott, J. (1993) *Reconstructing teacher education*, London, Falmer.

Elliott, J. (1998) *The Curriculum Experiment: meeting the challenge of social change*, Buckingham, Open University Press.

Elliott, J. and Zamorski, B. (2002) Editorial, *Pedagogy, Culture and Society*, Vol. 10, No. 2: 3–8.

Elliott, J., Zamorski, B. and Shreeve, A. (2001) *Exploring the pedagogical dimensions of disaffection from learning through collaborative research. Norwich Areas Schools Consortium: final report to the Teacher Training Agency*, Norwich, CARE.

Elton Report (1989) *Discipline in schools*, London, HMSO.

Fischman, W., DiBara, J. and Gardner, H. (2005) 'Creating good education against the odds', paper presented at the ESRC seminar 'Creativity: using it wisely', University of Cambridge, April.

Fisher, P. (2000) *Thinking through history*, London, Chris Kington.

Flutter, J. and Ruddock, J. (2004) *Consulting pupils: what's in it for schools?*, London, Routledge Falmer.

Fontana, D. (1994) *Managing classroom behaviour*, Leicester, BPS.

Fullan, M. (1993) *Change forces: probing the depths of educational reform*, London, Falmer.

Galloway, D. (1987) 'Disruptive behaviour in school', *Educational and Child Psychology*, Vol. 4, No. 1: 29–34.

Galton, M. and MacBeath, J. (2004) *A life in secondary teaching: finding time for learning*, report commissioned by the National Union of Teachers, available online at www.data.teachers. org.uk/story.php?id=3084.

Garner, P. (1999) *Pupils with problems: rational fears, radical solutions*, Stoke, Trentham Books.

Goodson, I. and Hargreaves, A. (eds) (1996) *Teachers' professional lives*, Lewes, Falmer.

Gottfredson, D., Gottfredson, G. and Skroban, S. (1993) 'Managing adolescent behaviour: a multiyear, multischool study', *American Educational Research Journal*, Vol. 30, No. 1: 179–215.

Gutteridge, D. (2002) 'Identifying disaffection', *Pedagogy, Culture and Society*, Vol. 10, No. 2: 161–8.

Hallam, S. (1996) Unpublished lecture on 'Differentiation', Institute of Education, University of London, January.

Hargreaves, D. (1987) Introduction, in N. Jones (ed.) *School management and pupil behaviour*, London, Falmer Press.

Hart, D. (1996) *The Today Programme*, Radio 4, 10 July.

Haydn, T. (1994) 'Flaws in the market in education; differing performances in neighbour- hood schools. A case study of two comprehensive schools', *Education Today*, December: 3–9.

Haydn, T. (1995a) '"Send in the clowns"; the mystery of failing schools', *Education Today and Tomorrow*, Vol. 47, No. 2, Summer: 4–5.

Haydn, T. (1995b) 'Choice and diversity; theory and practice', *Forum*, Vol. 37, No. 3, Autumn: 78–80.

Haydn, T. (1997) 'Murders in the playground: the Macdonald Report reconsidered', *Westminster Studies in Education*, Vol. 20: 5–15.

Haydn, T. (2002) 'The working atmosphere in the classroom and the right to learn', *Education Today*, Vol. 52, No. 2: 3–10.

Hay McBer (2000) *Research into teacher effectiveness: a model of teacher effectiveness report by Hay McBer to the Department for Education and Employment – June 2000*, London, DfEE.

Heafford, D. (1990) 'Teachers teach but do learners learn?', in C. Winge (ed.) *Language Learning Journal*, No. 1: 86–93.

Holt, J. (1984) *How children learn*, London, Penguin.

Hutchings, M., Menter, I., Ross, A. and Thomson, D. (2002) Teacher supply and retention in London – key findings and implications from a study of six boroughs in 1998–9, Introduction, in I. Menter, M. Huchings and A. Ross (eds) *The crisis in teacher supply*, Oakhill, Trentham: 175–206.

Ion, M. (2005) 'Frontline workers who fight despair', *Times Educational Supplement*, 27 May: 21.

Klemp, G.O. (1977) *Three factors of success in the world of work: implications for curriculum in higher education*, Boston, MA, McBer & Co.

Labbett, B. (1996) *Personal principles of procedure and the expert teacher*, online at www.enquiry learning.net/ELU/Issues/Education/Ed4.html.

Lang, P. (1993) Research review: secondary students' views on school, *Children and Society*, Vol. 7, No. 3: 305–12.

Lawlor, S. (1989) Correct core, in B. Moon, P. Murphy and J. Raynor (eds) *Policies for the curriculum*, London, Hodder & Stoughton: 58–69.

Lawlor, S. (ed.) (2004) *Comparing standards: teaching the teachers. The Report of the Politeia Education Commission*, London, Politeia.

Lawton, D. (1997) 'Values and education: a curriculum for the 21st century', paper presented at Values and the Curriculum Conference, Institute of Education, University of London, 9 April.

Lee, J. (2005) 'This taskforce idea is so eighties', *Times Educational Supplement*, 27 May: 4.

Lefstein, A. (2005) 'Thinking about the technical and the personal in teaching', *Cambridge Journal of Education*, Vol. 35, No. 3: 333–56.

Loughran, J. (1996) *Developing reflective practice; learning about teaching and learning through modelling*, London, Falmer.

Lund, R. (1996) *A whole school behaviour policy*, London, Kogan Page.

Macdonald, I. (1989) *Murder in the playground: the report of the Macdonald Inquiry into racism and racial violence in Manchester Schools*, London, Longsight Press.

MacLennan, S. (1987) 'Integrating lesson planning and class management', *ELT Journal*, Vol. 41, No. 3: 193–6.

McNamara, D. (1991) 'Subject knowledge and its applications: problems and possibilities for teacher educators', *Journal for Education for Teaching*, Vol. 27, No. 2: 113–28.

McNamara, E. (1999) *Positive pupil management and motivation*, London, David Fulton.

McPhillimy, B. (1996) *Controlling your class: a teacher's guide to managing classroom behaviour*, Chichester, Wiley.

Marks, J. (1993) *Examination results, educational standards and underachievement: 1. Comprehensive schools*, London, Centre for Policy Studies.

Mellor, N. (1997) *Attention seeking: a practical solution for the classroom*, London, Lucky Duck Publishing.

Miller, A. (2001) *Oxygen*, London, Spectre.

Moore, A. (2004) *The good teacher: dominant discourses in teaching and teacher education*, London, RoutledgeFalmer.

Mortimore. P. (1999) 'Writing on the classroom wall was ignored', *The Guardian*, 14 September.

Mortimore, P. and Whitty, G. (1997) *Can school improvement overcome the effects of disadvantage?*, London, Institute of Education.

Mortimore, P., Sammons, P., Stoll, L., Lewis, D. and Ecob, R. (1988) *School matters*, London, Open Books.

Moser, C. (1994) 'Moser urges action in the inner city', *Times Educational Supplement*, 9 September.

Munn, P., Johnstone, M. and Holligan, C. (1990) 'Pupils' perceptions of effective disciplinarians', *British Educational Research Journal*, Vol. 16, No. 2: 191–8.

National Council for Educational Technology (1994) *IT works*, Coventry, NCET.

Neill, S. and Caswell, C. (1993) *Body language for competent teachers*, London, Routledge.

NFER (2000) *Who would be a teacher? A review of the factors motivating and demotivating prospective and practising teachers*, Slough, NFER.

Newnam, D. (2000) 'Make the right moves', *Times Educational Supplement*, 28 April: 17.

Nieto, S. (1994) 'Lessons from students in creating a chance to dream', *Harvard Educational Review*, Vol. 64, No. 4: 392–404.

Oakley, J. (2002) 'RHINOs: a research project about the quietly disaffected', *Pedagogy, Culture and Society*, Vol. 10, No. 2: 193–208.

Ofsted (2003) *Annual Report of Her Majesty's Chief Inspector of Schools, 2002–3*, London, Ofsted.

Ofsted (2004) *Annual Report of Her Majesty's Chief Inspector of Schools, 2003–4*, London, Ofsted.

Ofsted (2005a) *Annual Report of Her Majesty's Chief Inspector of Schools, 2004–5*, London, Ofsted.

Ofsted (2005b) *Managing challenging behaviour*, London, Ofsted.

Olsen, J. (1997) *Managing classroom gambits: working with difficult classes in schools*, Canberra, Author.

Olsen, J. and Cooper, P. (2001) *Dealing with disruptive students in the classroom*, London, TES.

Patten, J. (1994) Quoted in *The Observer*, 3 April.

Peach, H. (1988) *Your problem pupils in school*, London, New Education Press.

Penlington, G. (2002) 'Who returns to teaching?': the profile and motivation of teacher returners, in M. Johnson and J. Hallgarten (eds) *From victims of change to agents of change*, London, IPPR: 41–64.

Perks, D. (2005) 'Chaos theory', *Educational Guardian*, 3 May: 10.

Persaud, R. (2004) 'Overdose of praise can be toxic', *Times Educational Supplement*, 24 September: 15.

Pike, R. (1994) 'Standing up to a difficult audience', *Times Educational Supplement*, 2 September: 17.

Porter, L. (2001) *Behaviour in schools, theory and practice for teachers*, Buckingham, Open University Press.

Qualifications and Curriculum Authority (2006) Pupil perceptions of history at Key Stage 3, London, QCA. Available online at www.qca.org.uk/.

Reynolds, D. (1997) Quoted on *Newsnight*, BBC2, 13 May.

Reynolds, D. (1999) 'It's the classroom, stupid', *The Observer*, 28 May.

Riley, K. and Rustique-Forrester, E. (2002) *Working with disaffected students: why students lose interest in school and what we can do about it*, London, Paul Chapman Publishing.

Rogers, B. (1990) *You know the fair rule*, London, Prentice Hall.

Rogers, B. (1995) *Behaviour management: a whole school approach*, London, Paul Chapman Publishing.

Rogers, B. (1997) *Cracking the hard class*, London, Scholastic.

Rogers, B. (2000) *Classroom behaviour*, London, Paul Chapman Publishing.

Rogers, B. (2002) *Promoting positive behaviour – cracking the difficult class*, Teacher In Service Training Event, Bromley Education Services, Bromley, 11 December.

Rogers, M. (2005) Quoted in Lee, J. 'This task force idea is just so eighties', *Times Educational Supplement*, 27 May.

Ruddock, J., Chaplain, R. and Wallace, G. (1996) *School improvement: what can pupils tell us?*, London, David Fulton.

Rutter, M., Maughan, B., Mortimore *et al.* (1979) *Fifteen thousand hours: secondary school and their effects on children*, London, Open Books.

Schon, D.A. (1983) *The reflective practitioner*, New York, Basic Books.

Schostak, J. (1991) *Youth in trouble*, London, Kogan Page.

Shreeve, A. and Boddington, D. (2002) 'Students' perceptions of rewards and sanctions', *Pedagogy, Culture and Society*, Vol. 10, No. 2: 239–56.

Shulman, L. (1987) 'Knowledge and teaching: foundation of the new reform', *Harvard Educational Review*, Vol. 57, No. 1.

Smith, M. (1993) 'Who's a naughty boy then?', *Teaching Today*, Spring: 16.

Spear, M., Gould, K. and Lee, B. (2000) '*Who would be a teacher?*': a review of factors motivating and demotivating prospective and practising teachers, Slough, NFER.

Standards and Effectiveness Unit (2001) *Classroom Talk for learning and management*, London, DfEE.

Steer, A. (2005a) *The Report of the Practitioner Group on School Behaviour and Discipline*, London, DfES.

Steer, A. (2005b) Address at the Networked Learning Communities National Conference, Birmingham, 23 June.

Stenhouse, L. (1975) *An introduction to curriculum research and development*, London, Heinemann.

Stubbs, M. (2005) Lecture given at the School of Education, University of East Anglia, 15 June.

Summers, M. and Easdown, G. (1996) 'Information technology in initial teacher education: preconceptions of history and geography interns, with reflections of mentors and tutors', *Journal of Information Technology for Teacher Education*, Vol. 5, No. 2: 155–72.

Taylor, P. (1994) 'No possibilities can be excluded', *Times Educational Supplement*, 16 September.

The Teaching Student (1994) Editorial, April: 5–6.

Tomlinson, M. (2005) Quoted in J. Lee, 'This taskforce idea is just so eighties', *Times Educational Supplement*, 27 May.

Tomlinson, S. (2005) 'Inclusion', *Guardian Education*, 19 April.

Unitt, P. (1994) 'Do smile before Christmas', *Times Educational Supplement*, 28 October.

Walker, R. (2001) *Hathway Primary School: a multimedia case study*, quoted in 'Using visual evidence', paper presented at the University of East Anglia, Norwich in a conference on 'Opening up classrooms: teachers talking research', 29 September.

Wallace, B., Maker, J., Cave, D. and Chandler, S. (2004) *Thinking skills and problem solving: an inclusive approach*, London, David Fulton.

Walsh, B. (2003) 'Building learning packages: integrating virtual resources with the real world of teaching and learning', in T. Haydn and C. Counsell (eds) *History, ICT and learning*, London, Routledge: 109–33.

Watkins, C. (1995) *School behaviour*, London, Institute of Education.

Watkins, C. (2000) *Managing classroom behaviour: from research to diagnosis*, London, Institute of Education/ATL.

Watkins, C. and Wagner, P. (2000) *Improving school behaviour*, London, Paul Chapman.

Westminster Education Forum (2006) *Respect in schools: pupil behaviour and school discipline*, London, Westminster Education Forum.

White, J. (1997) *Education and the end of work*, London, Cassell.

Whitty, G. (2005) 'Comprehensives', *Education Guardian*, 19 April: 7.

Wragg, E.C. (1984) *Classroom teaching skills*, London, Croom Helm.

Wragg, E.C. (1993a) *Class management*, London, Routledge.

Wragg, E.C. (1993b) *Class management in the secondary school*, London, Routledge.

Wragg, E.C. (1997) 'Too hot to trot in the discipline dance', *Times Educational Supplement*, 19 September.

Wragg, E.C. (2005) 'Wild about respect', *Times Educational Supplement*, 16 September.

Wragg, E.C., Haynes, G., Wragg, C. and Chamberlain, R. (2000) *Failing teachers*, London, Routledge.

Zamorski, B. and Haydn, T. (2002) 'Classroom management and disaffection', *Pedagogy, Culture and Society*, Vol. 10, No. 2: 257–78

Index

Pages containing relevant illustrations are indicated in *italic* type.